1 memory
forgetting
womanartisti

i
wanted to become a construction worker
to become a carpenter
a musician and
woman writer
i
wanted to be drawing constructing carving sawing planning
writing inventing
composing making music
and
walking around standing around observing
always
every day
every day be actively doing things
daily passionately concentratedly
thinking with my hands
working as if at play
and above all
myself and
alone

i
wanted to become an artist
to become Picasso
Munch Goya Michelangelo
to make infinite columns like Brancusi
animals like Franz Marc
angels like Klee
to be an artist
unconditionally
absolutely
free
to live like a man
but but
never be a man
i
wanted to be a woman
and and and
to live like a man
work like a man
serve nobody never ever
never never never
want to become to be
a wife mother muse girlfriend female partner
never
never ever
never

i
became a woman artist
and first learn

then forget
the entire world as it presents itself

i became a woman artist
came to know everything
forgot everything
everything everything everything
the concept of art
the image of the artist
and every single principle of structuring and technique

to be a woman artist
is the great privilege
to forget everyone and everything
to invent working at art anew
i
learn by forgetting
i
work continuously
and forget continuously what I do

to begin every day from scratch
sisyphus-like
but but but
without this classic male suffering
but rather inquisitive eager for the new
newly eagerly swiftly concentratedly
rescuing my life day by day

inventing every day
so that each piece of work is of equal value
equal equal equal
at home there is nothing to be seen
my work is
away
tidied away stowed away ordered not visible

at home there are none of my own pictures hanging
whatever for
its work done
ordered away and stowed away
yet never ever
never never never
really never
never ever
thrown away and disposed of

let the smallest drawing be equally valuable as the largest extensive work!
the oil painting as the watercolour!
the film as the video!
writing as photography as carving as singing!

no selection!

whatever for
this final

ostensibly brilliant
individual work
that places the artist
god-like far away
above the everyday human being

whatever for
better and worse
in working at art everything is good
or everything bad
everything everything makes sense
if everything has no purpose
is sense-full
and free of purpose
is unusable
and free of utility
must really
always
unconditionally
be
free

routine however
is death to my working

routine!
not to be confused with skill
skill like practising on an instrument
every day
a whole life long
practising
knowledge and skill
always always practising anew
bodily intellectual spiritual rehearsing

seeing with ones eyes
thinking with ones hands
walking on ones arms and legs and feet
my brain is my body
everything is stored inside it
everything everything everything
the whole world
my entire life
a great river
whose waters are today
broad and slow
flowing towards their end

that is how i work.

miriam cahn 15.9.2013

miriam cahn
cité des arts
18 rue de l'Hôtel de Ville
cedex 04 75 180 Paris/France **Basle, 30 December 78**

Dear Mr. Morgenthaler,[1]

For some time now, I have been thinking that I would very much like to teach a course in Drawing. Starting from the situation that I am fully familiar with your vocational school and am increasingly concerned and coming to grips with the practice of drawing, I would like to construct a course that makes reference to drawing as taught at the vocational school, where drawing is essentially concerned with cubes, ellipses etc.

On account of my own experience and my gradual disengagement from this "academic" manner of drawing I would like to offer you a course that sees itself as a counter-movement to Drawing as taught in your school – as a counter-pole to this purely logical and intellectual copying and rendering of objects, people and spaces, copying in the sense of an as-precise-as-possible reproduction, and standardized inasmuch as the personality of the drawer takes second place to a so-called "objective" reproduction of what is being drawn.

I would submit that in this process the personality of the drawer misses out. If one studies the drawing products issuing from your school, one sees only minimal differences between the drawings: the personal style or touch is almost totally absent and the drawings assessed as being the "best" are those that have "apprehended" what is to be drawn in the "most correct" way, without questioning what "correct" and "apprehend" might actually mean.

I would like to offer a course that enables students to try out what things mean to them absolutely personally: what is a cube, a tube, a woman, a man, a child (a "nude" or a "figure" – what de-personalized, academic terms!) an animal, what are landscapes, spaces, movements etc. What seems important to me here is to show one's relationship to what is being drawn, to place a personal significance in every sign drawn and to take this seriously, even if it is "merely" a scrawl or scribble and not a "finished" drawing.

Now, how might such a course be structured? I start here from my own experience. First of all, I would de-rigidify and change the ROOM SPACE in which we would be working. For example, by working out, together with the students, the significance of the easels, trestles, drawing boards, standardized sheets of paper, pencils and pens etc., by experimenting with them on re-arranging and discarding this stuff, and I would try to create an empty space, where we would try to find out, yes, what do I do with myself? This leads on into the significance of the BODY and into the posture of the body in the act of drawing, where it is decisive in determining the actual style and touch. At this stage in the course I could imagine that we would do, for example, the following exercises: drawing on the floor, drawing on the wall, drawing in small groups, "blind" drawing etc., so as to reduce "brain"-control in favour of one's personal, individual movement. In this stage, I could well imagine strictly making students draw only cubes – it is astonishing how a cube becomes a personal sign if it is drawn in an unusual posture or drawn blind.

The next step would then be THE PERSONAL SIGNS. In this stage I would leave it to the students to decide what they want to depict and how. Through dialogue we would try to find out, yes, what do things mean to me and how do I represent them? Personal signs, after all, encompass all types – from those drawn exactly on smooth paper with a hard pencil to soft scribbling on large surfaces, from miniature depictions of things to unclear script-like signs. All of this cannot be judged except from the standpoint: Is this what the student WANTED? And from where might the norms come that guide him or her? For drawing is a never-ending argument between the rehearsed, standardized aesthetic conceptions and the wholly personal sign languages. Since the vocational school imparts a rigid aesthetic conception, such a "counter-course" could be only beneficial for a new debate on the subject: What is aesthetics? And it seems to me that this debate, this argument, should, after all, take place in the institutions of education, especially this one.

Actually, it is by no means clear to me where this course could be integrated: in the Preparatory Course, in the Graphic Arts Class, with the artists, the FFI,[2] the drawing instructors, the construction draftsmen, the photographers etc. Actually, it doesn't matter where. It is absolutely clear that this is an experiment and that I do not know how it will turn out and whether I can manage it. I have, however, already gained experience in working with people: I have taught drawing at secondary schools and have for a time run a painting school for children and adults. I am confident that I can work with people. Only, I cannot offer a recipe for success: it would be a matter of giving it a try.

Looking forward to your answer,

Kind Regards,

Miriam Cahn

postcard to birgit kempker

your postcards with their good + evil
mouth + hunger + a wonderful feeling reach me
just when i must travel away to teach
only 3 months
the students love the way i teach
and yet the way they look at me
i find very unpleasant
days in advance i am already panicking
hate it
will never be able to remember their names
would like never to have to look at their work
i dont care what they learn
lord, im glad i dont have to make a living with this
like some of my colleagues
whose radicalness born of loneliness has thereby
been sucked from their bones.

14.5.1994

Commission for Artists' Studios Paris
Miss Miriam Cahn
Cité Internationale des Arts
18, rue de l'Hôtel de Ville
F-75180 Paris Cedex 04 **Basle, 15 March 1979**

Dear Miss Cahn,

As the Administration of the Cité Internationale des Arts[3] has just informed us, the frais généraux must once again be brought into line with the cost of living and must be increased from ff. 520.- per month to ff. 555.- per month for a person living alone as from 1 April 1979.

Our local community will, as usual, take over around 80% of these costs and will transfer ff. 440.- per month to the Administration of the Cité Internationale des Arts as from 1 April 1979. The remaining sum to be paid by you thus amounts to ff. 115.- per month.

We kindly request you to take note of this and wish you every continuing success in Paris.

With kind regards
COMMISSION FOR ARTISTS' STUDIOS PARIS
Secretary
S. Keller

Miriam Cahn
cité des arts
Paris/France
Frau Keller, Department of Education, Basle **Paris, 6 May**

Dear Mrs Keller,

I am writing to you on account of our conversation in April concerning the situation of the Paris studio. I have also spoken with Mr Stöcklin[4] on the subject and he is also dissatisfied with the situation and has already sent you several letters on the matter. We are supposed to be paying around 20% of the "frais généraux" and both consider this to be not correct, especially after we have made a few comparisons with the situation of other artists within the cité. We have mutually decided to go on a payment strike. Mr Stöcklin will not pay for the next half year and I for the entire year.

I am not prepared to pay this sum, because there can be no talk of "artist sponsorship" if I have to pay additional costs here should I wish to stay here, or, in your formulation, "be allowed" to stay here. What you are forgetting is that I am here because of my artistic work and that when I apply for the artist's studio I am only subsequently informed that I have to contribute to the "frais généraux" and otherwise – in your words – would have to renounce the scholarship. This contribution comes to about SFr. 500.- per year per studio, a sum which seems to me absolutely affordable for the City of Basle – if it already considers itself unable to pay for the artists' stay here.

In this connection, I would like to speak in general about the City of Basle's funding for artists. In Basle, there is of course also the Art Scholarship and the Art Fund, of which the latter must be seen as indirect artist funding. Here, one must either create commissioned art, which has long been not to every artist's liking, or one is reliant on works being purchased, which means that one must take part in the Christmas Exhibition and the Art Fund Exhibition, if they have a more or less open theme. Many artists who do not work in the usual media can participate only with difficulty, since the structures of these exhibitions still derive from conceptions of art with, on the one hand, sculptors with sculptural works and, on the other hand, painters with pictures hung on walls. Thus, the only thing that remains as direct funding is the Scholarship. Its great flaw is that it is attached to the Scholarship Office and subject to its rulings. This leads to a total lack of transparency: neither can one learn publicly who receives scholarships nor be told why, and in addition the works in question are not put on exhibition. Then there is the further point that it is an unhappy mixture of competition (or art prize) and social support, i.e. in "unclear" cases tax returns are consulted – which leads to the circular reasoning that artists doing part-time jobs (or dependent on parents, wives, husbands) are assessed as people with enough "income", whereas they make their applications precisely to escape such dependence so that they can work in peace!

Moreover, for the size of a City such as Basle, SFr. 80,000.- per year is far too little, when one considers that each time some 100 artists apply, among them precisely the two Paris studio people with their claim for a minimum of SFr. 10,000.-.

That these two have to join the others and apply for a scholarship is something I consider fundamentally wrong – the City should give them funding automatically on the award of the artist's studio and not, as hitherto, that we have to pay on top.

This regulation does not stand comparison with Aarau and Germany. The City of Basle likes to describe itself in public as a city of art – the reverse is the case if one considers its direct funding of art. In the case of the Paris studio, it becomes clear that although the City was prepared to buy one studio for SFr. 80,000.- in the years of economic upswing in the 60s (the other studio was bought by the Art Society), it had only a minimal desire to bear the consequences. Real funding would mean supporting the artists financially as well over the duration of their stay in Paris, and that became too much for the City – I assume because of the attitude that this was "lost" money, i.e. financing an idea and not necessarily something that could be boasted about like a new theatre building for example.

If when putting together its budget this year to be submitted to the Finance Department, the Education Department wants to demonstrate a greater will to support art, then it needs only to consider an item of SFr. 20,000.- for the Paris studio as natural and sensible – and to demand it. Then one could talk of the City of Basle funding its artists or at least making a start in that direction.

As a comparison, I now give you a few examples that I have collected here in the cité: they may be perhaps not quite correct in detail since I have gathered them on the basis of oral information.

GERMANY:

the Paris studios are financed by the cities and the Federal states, the states changing every two years. In this case, it is North Rhine-Westphalia, Düsseldorf.

1. An artist receives 6 months in the Paris studio free of charge + 1,300 DM per month + travel expenses + one-off material costs + allowance for apartment rent paid directly by the Ministry of Culture of the state concerned.

2. Three artists get 6 months in Paris, extension possible + 700 DM per month, artist's studio free. The same goes for New

York and both are for academy students. Ministry of Culture of the state, city and private funds.

3. one artist receives a studio in New York, 6 months, studio free, 1,500 DM per month + travel costs paid by the City of Düsseldorf.

4. in addition, the City of Düsseldorf has a budget of around 10,000 DM per year for the catalogue, if one can do an exhibition. Moreover, it finances an "artotheque" with leasing possibilities for graphic works.

5. the Franco-German Youth Office, based in Bad Honnef. 4 artists receive 6 months in Paris + FFs 2,600 + travel expenses + the cost of a catalogue.

6. Duisburg: 4 artists get a 2-year scholarship, artist's studio free, 1,000 DM per month + collaboration with industry for large-scale projects.

The structures are of course different from in our country, but I want only to demonstrate that within the Düsseldorf area there are many more possibilities for an artist than with us.

AARGAU:

1. Paris: one artist gets an artist's studio, free of charge for 3–6 months. In addition, a scholarship for which it is important into which category he/she falls:

Funding category: a maximum of Fr. 10,000.-

Sabbatical year category: a maximum of Fr. 20,000.- per person

2. In addition, one can apply for work funding for a particular project.

3. Acquisitions, for which the jury partly comes into the studios. Moreover, for all these things there is no age limit.

The annual budget fluctuates in line with the overall cantonal budget, since it is simply a certain percentage of the overall budget. Artist support is in the hands of an advisory board, a specially appointed commission.

Well, that's it. Please excuse my poor typing skills and the state of my typewriter. A copy of this letter will be sent to the BASLE CULTURAL INITIATIVE,[5] of which I am a member.

COMMISSION FOR ARTISTS' STUDIOS PARIS

Basle, 12 June 1979

Dear Miss Cahn,

We answer your letter of 6 May 1979 as follows:

With our letters of 9 February 1978, we informed you of the conditions under which our Commission was able to cede you use of an artist's studio in the Cité Internationale des Arts. At the same time, we gave you a règlement général that informed you about the obligations connected with a stay in the Cité Internationale des Arts. In sending back signed copies of the application forms for a Council of Europe identity card to be submitted to the Federal Department of the Interior you declared yourself to be in agreement with the conditions stated without any reservation.

From the very outset, you were aware of the share of the general costs that have to be paid by you.

At the beginning of your stay in the Cité, you had to sign the same règlement, thus confirming that you have taken note of the contents of the regulations, are in agreement with their requirements and are prepared

to adhere to them.
Among other things, the regulations stipulate that the general monthly costs accruing are to be paid in advance at the beginning of every month.
We regularly keep the Cité Internationale des Arts informed as to which sum the City of Basle pays towards the general costs and which sum it must levy from the artists in person. It is hence a matter for the administration of the Cité Internationale des Arts to request from you payment of the sum you owe.
We will, however, inform the Cité administration concerning the refusal of payment which you have decided on and leave it to their discretion to decide whether, in the given circumstances, they choose to evict you in line with §13 of the règlement général.
Yours Faithfully,
Commission for Artists' Studios in Paris
the President: Peter Althaus[6]
the Secretary: S. Keller

Paris, 27 August 79

Gentlemen of the Commission, dear Mrs Keller,
How should I reply to you? Finally, I gave up my payment strike, since the stay here was more important to me than a power struggle which never had any chance of success. Yet I would not like to conclude without undertaking a short analysis. Our conflict, in my opinion, is one of the many small instances of how in recent years the relationship between the City of Basle and its artists functions, or rather, doesn't function.
My first letter explained in detail the reasons for my refusal to pay. The idea behind this was to stimulate a dialogue that has been going around in circles for years now – about re-thinking and re-organizing funding for artists. What I wrote there was certainly not new to you: for years you have been receiving letters concerning the Cité situation, and regarding the remaining funding in Basle a variety of attempts have been made over the past years by groups and individuals to enter into a dialogue with the Department of Education.
Now the entire further course of our little story has shown me one of the reasons for this year-long paralysis in discussions between us artists and the City. It is, as I had already supposed, an utter failure to take artists seriously on the part of the state – there can be no other explanation for your bureaucratically aggressive letter in response. A pure letter of sanction, signed by your President. What particularly annoys me now is that the same Peter Althaus wrote to me in private: "I can give the City a sympathetic interpretation of your undertaking, but I have no instruments of power at my disposal." He had the instrument of power of refusing to put his signature to such an unconscionable letter and thus to make his contribution and perhaps even to strike up discussions inside the Commission – a discussion, for example, about the relationship between artist's studio + scholarship.
In addition, gentlemen, you might ask yourselves to what extent you are actually using your competences and powers at all – my impression is that you have not taken any action for years. Yet your Commission exists to represent the interests of artists to the City authorities, to inform yourselves about what our demands are, to

check where the possibilities lie and to attempt to achieve as much as possible in the artists' interest. This little episode with the thoughtlessly signed letter of sanction now shows clearly that you are not seeking any change at all: if you act in this way here (sanctions as the only reaction to a request that we for our part have been making for years), how do you deal with our other interests? Gentlemen, this behaviour of the Commission is of no help to anyone except the Education Department, which, through this ostensibly liberal delaying tactic is spared the effort of seeking solutions with regard to artist funding, thus saving the Finance Department from having to make funds available for the same – you get the picture: savings all round at the expense of the artists. And consequently, also sparing oneself the question as to the function of art today in our City; and hence in society.
Because good funding would mean having trust in art and artists – trust that what we do, even if it calls today's society in question, in the final analysis does give something to society, the state and the City.
Given the current reality of our relationship, however, I gradually begin to ask myself whether I can give anything at all to such a blind and deaf society, to such a state and such a City, and hence have any debt to it?
Greetings, Miriam Cahn
P.S. Copies to the Initiative for Culture and Peter Burri[7]

K. (or B.) was an artist; we talked about art, the world, feelings and made love. in the morning i asked him whether he would come back. he didn't know. a few days later i met him for a meal with friends. as we were leaving, i asked him whether he'd like to come to my place. he said: always these demands, and went into his hotel. some days later i met him in the street.
– he felt pursued, he said, he didn't want to come to my place today. – i cried, he took me in his arms, i hurled my bicycle down at his feet. then he went into his hotel. a few days later we went out to eat and dance with friends. K. (or B.) accompanied me as far as the bridge and kissed me. i asked him whether he desired me at all? he didn't desire me. then why did he kiss me? – i cried and he went into his hotel.

miriam cahn
mörsbergerstr. 52
4057 basle
to Cantonal Councillor Keller **Basle, 21 March 80**

Dear Mr Keller,
On 1 April I am to appear in court. The reason for this is a charge of criminal damage to property brought by the Basle Building Authority. In Nov./Dec. last year, I executed drawings in charcoal[8] on the pillars and walls of the Northern Bypass in the vicinity of the Wiesen roundabout. This was an important piece of work for me, since I wanted to combine an extremely ephemeral material such as charcoal with an extremely hard material, concrete, built presumably to last millennia, and with a highly alienated form of construction, motorway architecture. I wanted to work with the contrast: individual drawing – anonymous construction.
Now I am being sued for this work of mine by the Building Authority. Strangely, precisely for this stretch of the motorway the Basle Art Fund is running a competition involving 7 artists, with 250,000 SFr. from the Construction Fund being available for the winning entries. Should the court's decision on 1 April not be in my favour, I will be compelled to pay the same Building Authority a high sum of money for the cleaning costs involved in removing my charcoal drawings – which, as even a police photo shows, will weather and disappear of their own accord, as was my intention with this work from the very outset.
Mr Keller, I ask you: What is your relationship to art?
On the one hand, artists are subsidized, but on the other hand not only not left in peace but even criminalized – in my case, after all, it is a criminal proceeding. I am left with the suspicion that what is being practised here is a kind of state art, in the sense that decorative, sustaining art-in-architecture projects are highly subsidized, especially with building projects that are widely rejected by the affected inhabitants, as previously with the Heuwaage[9] overpass and now with the Northern Bypass. And that experimental work, such as I have attempted to create, which does not seek to have any everlasting value and calls this value into question, is penalized with the argument that it is "criminal activity"…
Mr Keller, essentially you are suing me not because I drew on the wall with charcoal (to your mind: "damage to property") in an area that is temporarily a vast building site – to be consistent, you would have to sue every child who makes chalk drawings on walls (from the technical process angle exactly the same as my works). You are suing me because I displayed my opinion with my own provisional means directly at the place concerned – in my eyes a basic right in any correctly functioning democracy.
In expectation of your answer, I send you my greetings,
miriam cahn
P.S. Please find enclosed an interview from the BAZ [Basle Newspaper], which explains my work in more detail.

CITY COUNCILLOR
DIPL.-ING. ETH (Zurich)
Eugen Keller
HEAD OF BUILDING AUTHORITY
CANTON BASEL-STADT

Miss Miriam Cahn
Mörsbergerstraße 52
4057 Basle **Basle, 9 April 1980**

Dear Miss Cahn,

I refer to your letter of 21 March 1980.

In the meantime, the court proceedings of 1 April have taken place, at which we were represented by Mr Baumann, Head of the National Roads Bureau. I hope that you were able to see that it was not our intention to carry through an exemplary action here, but that we were concerned also to show our understanding in this particular case. The presiding magistrate understood our line of argument and suggested a compromise settlement, which you unfortunately did not accept. You will surely understand that nobody can accept uncommissioned paintings to be made on any structure. If they subsequently turn out to be a work of art, then the proprietor is at liberty to retain them.

Unfortunately, however, this whole business has a negative side. Graffiti sprayers who are not committed artists have completely different motives for presenting their statements in public. They carry out their night-time daubings using paint material that can be removed only with considerable effort and expense. The state has already had to lay out a great deal of money for this purpose. For this reason, I was also sad to hear that you were not prepared to refrain from uncommissioned paintings in future, although Mr Baumann's intention was to offer you an easy way out.

We have stated that we are prepared to leave your paintings in all places where they do not constitute a nuisance. There are indeed surfaces that have to receive a coat of paint later on and for which a rough subsurface is necessary to make the paint adhere. Besides these there are sections that belong to the German Federal Railway [DB]. As long as the DB agrees to leave the works in place, here too no costs will accrue.

Matters concerning the Art Fund come under the remit of the Education Department. This Department is responsible for setting and publishing the terms of the competitions. The Art Fund – whatever one's attitude to it may be – has repeatedly tried to support young artists, and so it is not quite clear to me why you refuse to enter for its competitions. It seems to me that this would be a better way to give visible expression to your views, because the painting of walls or pillars belonging to others cannot be left to the discretion of individuals. Nevertheless, it cannot be said that it was our intention to criminalize you. I think that we have demonstrated this by our actions before the magistrate and it remains for me only to hope that you can muster a modicum of understanding for our viewpoint.

Yours Faithfully,
E. Keller

WATCH ROOM
a large square room, the ceiling low, artificial light from above, 12 beds, 3 beside each wall, in the centre the medical orderly at the electronic control panel. he won't move away from his position since he must always be able to reach the alarm button.
– and what is this room called?
– observation room. Every ward needs its observation room.

onset of menstruation. having children, having a house, having husbands, and while the blood flowed out of me my legs overwhelmed by memory became weak, I pulled the blanket over my head ...

the soldier sits by the border underground in front of his computer + waits for the command ...

when i visited my sister in the clinic she told me about the effect of the depot injection: every minute had seemed to her like an eternity, she had been precisely aware of everything around her, every sound, every movement, everything, yet around her herself there had been an impenetrable mass, the inside had not been able to come to the outside, right down to the very simplest gestures and words. we held each other and cried. i wasn't able to tell her any single reason that would have made living worthwhile, not a single one. the trees, the countryside? the city, home, country? our parents, friends? job? politics? – she was my mirror: i just knew a few more tricks to survive.

WATCH ROOM 1982

miriam cahn
Mörsbergerstr. 52
4057 Basle
PRO HELVETIA
Dr Christoph Eggenberger

Dear Dr Eggenberger,
I would like to inform you that I will not be participating in the exhibition "Swiss Drawings, 1970–1980".[10] The reason for this decision lies in my work: I hang my works myself on site, in accordance with the given circumstances/time/space.
I accept compromises when the exhibition philosophy convinces me, e.g. "Feminism International" in Holland.
Your exhibition philosophy, however, does not convince me at all: I see here nothing more than a cultural showcasing of Switzerland abroad at the expense of the artists and not a communication of our work issuing from a position statement of the exhibition organizers. In terms of cultural policy, it is easier to choose 45 artists known for their drawing (there probably aren't many more) than to choose only a few, since in this way debates and position-taking can be avoided. This is not in my interest.
In the hope that some of my artist colleagues react similarly – I remain with kind regards,
Your Miriam Cahn

PRO HELVETIA
Hirschengraben 22
CH-8001 Zurich **Zurich, 6 April 81**

Dear Ms Cahn,
Your letter did not surprise me – following our telephone conversation – but it did disappoint me greatly. And for a variety of reasons.
Purely personally and purely at first blush, I feel hurt because precisely what you denounce is something that I never intended and never in the remotest way entered my thinking and something that I never advocate to our foundation board. We are not a ministry of culture: we do not act for reasons of cultural showcasing, to use your terms.
I hope that the sole explanation for your decision is that you do not know us well: I would be most pleased to come to know you personally.
You know that Pro Helvetia is giving financial support to the exhibition in Regensburg and also to the exhibition in the Lucerne Museum of Art: both are giving rise to discussions, to debates with the works of art on display and to a dialogue with the gallery-going public at home and abroad. With very few exceptions we never seek to be a showcase for Switzerland: we seek debate over and beyond the language regions at home and across borders with countries abroad. Your letter calls into question my entire – exhausting – work.
And concerning the Drawing Exhibition: it was not Pro Helvetia that first had the idea of taking stock of Swiss Drawing in the 1970s – it was the exhibition organizers who approached us with this idea, an idea which we have gratefully taken up and supported with

all means at our disposal. There is hardly any exhibition to which we devote as much time and effort as we are devoting to this one. Charles Goerg and Hans Christoph von Tavel are the initiators of the project and are also on the committee, together with Hans Hartmann, Dieter Koepplin, Martin Kunz, Pietro Sarto and myself.
All the artists will be receiving the finalized list of artists this week. The formulation of the thinking behind the exhibition is not included in this posting: the committee, with Charles Goerg in the chair, has tried to apprehend the phenomenon of "Drawing" in the 70s and in Switzerland. I can hardly imagine a more topical subject and am eagerly looking forward to their answer, the result, which will be on display for the first time in December in the Musée Rath in Geneva.*
I do not share your hope that other artists will join you in your attitude: so far, indeed, I have heard very different, highly positive opinions from that quarter.
In a committee meeting last week, we discussed your particular problem – that you hang your works yourself on site. Unfortunately, we cannot grant you this possibility at all of the exhibition's destinations; but we do have the provision that some artists can be allocated a room space, or a corner of a wall 3m x 3m or more, a space which they can organize in line with their own ideas and which can be re-constructed in that way in each exhibition situation. So, you need only to determine such a space and to detail in a model or sketch how you wish your works to be hung.
Actually, I don't want to talk you round to changing your mind at all. You are thereby making your statement and we are making ours with the exhibition. The word that provoked me into writing this long letter is just the showcasing at the artists' expense. You can ask many artists in our country and you will find that this is not the case by any means!
Yours faithfully – and in hope of an early reply,
Christoph Eggenberger
* I don't think that with this selection we are sparing ourselves debates and statements: quite the reverse. Many directions and many names are missing, and have to be missing, because otherwise you get an encyclopaedia but not an exhibition. I am convinced that this here does make an exhibition and a stimulating one, i.e. a good one too!

Dear Dr Eggenberger,
Many thanks for your frank letter. It shows me that my refusal leads to debate and controversy. I would like to expand a little on what I hinted at in my first letter. Art can scarcely be separated from politics if and when politics is experienced in individual terms.
Pro Helvetia supports projects involving cultural work abroad. Since Switzerland, as a so-called neutral country, is not very active in foreign policy, it shifts the latter to other levels, e.g. to economics and industry, developmental aid and, precisely, culture. With the

help of Pro Helvetia, Switzerland not only promotes Swiss art abroad but also operates the cultural and political showcasing of Switzerland. Where it is no longer primarily a matter of mediating Swiss artists abroad but of organizing showcase events, I speak of showcasing at the artists' expense.

For some years I have noticed that there is an increasing number of exhibitions that are assembled under largely nationalist criteria and are passed around between countries as a "multi-pack": the "young" Italians, the "new wild ones" from Germany, the "open-minded" Swiss (?) etc. – a tendency that is linked to the so-called "trend reversal", the political reaction of the past few years. These exhibitions often perpetrate a falsification of history: the 70s are damned as image-less, over-intellectual etc., politico-cultural utopias such as left-wing radicalism, social sculpture and feminism have suddenly disappeared and a general sigh of relief goes around the art world – there are "pictures" again (to be sold). Now, the Lucerne exhibition – despite its cumbersome title[11] – is neither a consciously historical or personal statement by Martin Kunz on the past 10 years, nor, with a few exceptions, could the artists show their work as THEY wished. Martin Disler's letter in the Tages-Anzeiger points this out. The result is a national Christmas exhibition with more elevated pretensions. I emerged from the exhibition with a sore head and with the feeling that here good artists – from Dieter Roth to Martin Disler – were being put through the mangle.

This exhibition is now travelling abroad. The image of Swiss art will once again be a mediocre one; again, quantity is being shown rather than quality. If even one of the better ones, namely Martin Disler, backs out in horror, that just goes to confirm my doubts on this type of exhibition-mongering from above.

I feel, unfortunately, that the Drawing Exhibition will be similar. 45 people are simply an imposition, if they are assembled merely for reasons of technique and medium (drawing).

I still have unhappy memories of the Pavilion of Drawings at the documenta[12] as far as the artists' drawings are concerned. Precisely drawings are often a PART of an artist's work. I have visions of 45 partial works travelling around and being misunderstood as wholes. And soon we will have again reached the point where artistic work is classified primarily in line with technical and medial criteria and no longer as intellectual work in this or that medium. There is no such thing as "drawing as a phenomenon", but only works in which more or less drawing occurs.

The exhibition in Regensburg, however, did convince me: it had a modest theme, "Aspects of Young Swiss Art"; after consultation with us artists,[13] the number of participants was kept low; we were able to set up the exhibition together with the exhibition organizer and so had specific debates on making art and making exhibitions – which is much more interesting than structures firmly fixed in advance. That brings me to my ideas concerning the support and promotion of Swiss art abroad: emphasis on WORKING abroad: guest lectureships, studios, studio exchanges, travel scholarships, exhibitions set up by artists and exhibition-makers on site, exchange projects of all kinds.

Well, I hope that I have been able here to make my standpoint somewhat clearer for you. The fact that the majority of artists does

not share my opinions tells me only that the “majority” is, as always, on the wrong track and at the same time – unfortunately – determines what goes on.
Greetings from the various movements,
Yours, Miriam Cahn

miriam cahn
mörsbergerstr. 52
4057 Basle **Basle, 10 October 82**

dear Hella Santarossa,[14]
many thanks for your letter. unfortunately, i will not be able to come to Berlin. however, i think your initiative is a very good idea, and so i will try here to put in writing what my thoughts are on this matter. "Zeitgeist"[15] is a sequel to "Westkunst",[16] documenta 7[17] and the Venice biennale[18] – all exhibitions in which the male artists and the few women artists are no more than stooges of megalomaniacal exhibition-makers, who want to make a name for themselves. in the case of "Zeitgeist" this was even taken so far as to order pictures in certain formats! (as can be read in "Der Spiegel"[19]). these exhibitions are really not taking any risk at all. if i look at the list of the artists invited, i can divide them into two groups: "safe" older artists such as Beuys, Kounellis, Penck etc.,[20] who make very fine works, but don't entail any risk, since they are very well known, and "safe" younger artists such as Chia, Clemente, Schnabel etc.,[21] who also make very fine works, but are members of this over-hastily launched painter generation, so that they too are already so well known that they don't entail any risk for exhibition-makers. women artists, however, do entail a greater or lesser risk, depending on the individual case, because they create works that cannot be pigeonholed – except politically.
why exclusively painting and sculpture? today, when making art includes each and every technique? i see it like this: painting and sculpture are traditionally embedded and hence "usable": in the living room, in a collection, in the traditional gallery, in the museum, in group or mass exhibitions. no more headaches over: how can i hang, collect this type of thing (installations, videos, performances, conceptions), how can i mediate it (installations, which need room-spaces, videos, which need machines, conceptions "without any images" etc.), how can i store it, how sell it, and anyway: what are these male artists and women artists out to achieve actually? the discussion concerning the interlocking of making art, living, mediating art, viewers and sales is suddenly as it were blown away, to make room once more for the traditional distribution: the artist produces, the gallerist sells, the art society director exhibits, the museum and the collector store and preserve, the media are satisfied because they can once again reproduce pictures and the lords and masters of the world are happy.
and the best way to keep this system alive and kicking is to puff up traditional techniques into THE means of expression in art and to devalue all others. in this way, painting and sculpture sell very nicely. so the discourse is no longer about why does this male artist/ woman artist choose this or that technique in connection with his/ her work, life and environment, but: which technique is most easily exploitable. and accordingly the old myth of the artist is revived, the myth of the male painter, the male sculptor who – in solitude, in seclusion, and in suffering – paints away at his pictures with a grand gesture, chisels away in fury at the wood, and for heaven's sake doesn't concern himself with his function as an artist in today's society – that could, after all, hinder him in the process of creation, that divine myth of the genius sustained by a patriarchal cultural tradition. women have no place here.
involuntarily and, one supposes, more out of cynicism, the makers

of the "Zeitgeist" exhibition have chosen exactly the right name for it, so manifesting a cosily dangerous acquiescence in the current situation, instead of submitting it to critical analysis as befits their function as exhibition-makers.
in this context it is clear why no women artists (one = none) have been invited. it is a conscious falsification of history: in the last 10–20 years, after all, women artists have brought a good many things into the open with their works. with their means (painting too, drawing too) they have taken a stand against their societal function; they have confronted and opposed traditional, patriarchal art and any over-cheap marketing of their work and have sought for new paths: as material, they have used their biographies, going to work on the non-history of women and using their bodies and spaces as their centre; as techniques they have used whatever is appropriate and as a weapon feminism.
what all these women artists have in common is that they are experimenting right across the established lines of all techniques, often viewing their woman-ness as the focus of their work.
the real question is whether exhibitions such as "Zeitgeist" make any sense. should a woman artist strive at all to take part in such exhibitions? basically, yes, for reasons of equality of opportunity and artistic freedom. but, following my experience at documenta 7, not at all costs. at d7 i came across cynicism and deep-rooted contempt towards women artists and male artists and their works, that is, the sheer opposite of the officially stated attitude of those running the exhibition – that they wished to provide a worthy framework for art. i also maintain that this unhealthy situation at the exhibition was recognized and i was surprised that more women artists and male artists did not decide to pull out. for me, pulling out of the exhibition was a logical consequence deriving from my work.
we women artists should definitely demand equal representation in exhibitions. precisely if and when i as a woman artist am sceptical towards current exhibition-making, i should definitely have the opportunity to try this out in situ, as should our male artist colleagues also.
i also think that exhibitions would look very different if women artists were treated on an equal footing with male artists.
well, i hope that your initiative will achieve something (even if it is only an undermining of old certainties).
warm regards, Miriam Cahn

1970–1980

completing training
travelling
forgetting training
travelling
occupying kaiseraugst[22]
women's movement
travelling
forgetting training
art
travelling
women's movement
art
going away
art

1980–1990

coming back
art
career
travelling
deployment of pershing II[23]
career
fulda gap[24]
art
travelling
career
going away
art
staying away
chernobyl[25]
career
schweizerhalle[26]
art
travelling
career
travelling
art
coming back
art
fall of the wall[27]

HfBK MUNICH
"Working Group on Aesthetics"

Munich, 24 February 1983

Dear Miriam Cahn,
At the Academy of Fine Arts in Munich, half of the students are women, yet in the teaching body there is not a single woman professor to act as an example and role model.
For us, therefore, it is a matter of urgent concern to bring your attention, as a recognized and successful woman painter, to the job advertisement for a Chair in Painting + Graphic Arts – see the attached copy – with the request that you apply for the post, if you are interested in taking up a teaching position.
If this is ultimately not your serious intention, we ask you nevertheless to apply – for tactical reasons, so that in the extremely patriarchal structure and mind-set of our Academy emancipation can be further promoted and advanced.
Your solidarity would be a major support for our endeavours, if only because the percentage of applications from women would thereby be increased.
In the first instance, all that is required for an application is a letter (CV, catalogues, perhaps photos), which could be followed up by a comprehensive dossier should the need arise.
Yours Faithfully,
Heidrun Schimmel

---

miriam cahn
mörsbergerstr. 52
4057 basle/CH

basle, 15 March 83

dear Heidrun Schimmel,
many thanks for your letter. i will not, however, be applying for this professorial post. and i will give you my reasons – firstly the personal ones: neither do i wish to become a professor with a fixed position, nor are painting and graphic arts my medium.
now to my reasoning concerning solidarity: it is clear to me that i would not get this post, or have only a very slight chance. that, however, would not be a reason not to apply. for me the reason is rather: is this post worth my solidarity?
your call for solidarity seems to me a little like the call for equal rights for women in the army – not so dire, of course, but similar. the impressions i have gained so far of german academies are so bad that the only remedy i see here is to shut down these things left over from the nineteenth century and to re-open them with an entirely new system adapted to suit today's technology – and, of course with a teaching body based on gender parity.
i think that your tactic for moving emancipation forward is wrong: first of all, one must examine whether the quality of such a position is at all worth a committed woman applying for it. the policy of taking one small step after another through the institutions has its limitations, on the one hand where it is a question of women and on the other hand where it is a question of making art. i think that as far as making art for women is concerned, emancipation can be better advanced with weeks, or circles or working groups such as you run at the academy and such as are being tried out at other

academies in germany. guest lectureships, limited in duration and hence more intensive and more independent than fixed positions, could perhaps assist the function of unsettling and so breaking open rigid patriarchal structures – at these ancient academies a revolutionary atmosphere needs to be created, but from outside, from "day-to-day life", compelling these long-established institutions to abandon their professorial demeanour, their "master-pupil" relationships, to define art anew and to open up these temples of the muses. putting it in concrete terms: if i now apply for this professorial post out of wrongly conceived solidarity i am cementing the present structure more than performing a revolutionary act in solidarity. i am cementing the idea that this institution of the academy is worth us women striving to become a professor in it – i am cementing the idea of men that such a position is so utterly "important" that now even women apply for it. we should boycott it, just as we boycott the military. we should organize campaigns against the fact that art in the academies has been taught in an identical way for almost a hundred years, the nude models should go on strike, the wives of these professors, the women should refuse to draw nudes, to assume traditional painters' stances etc. . . .
that's how I see it. your women's week was a small beginning along this path – i would be immediately prepared again to do something in this direction, because i am well aware that examples and role models, women as examples, are important for us, and precisely in academies.
but – from outside.
well, i could write pages and pages on these problems, but i hope that you understand me – warm regards
your miriam cahn

CLASSIC LOVING

dream: i was flying swiftly through the trees: my hands, my eyes were torn out of me by the hands that had been torn out of me.

in the morning i felt that my work had become to produce art. in the war and industrial spaces there was hectic over-production, a filling of the walls adapted to the exact dimensions of the spaces. in the manly part of my work i functioned like a rocket-builder or a computer expert, or a financier (ah! quel désir du pouvoir!), a warrior, soldier, mission completed, equilibrium of terror, the employment contract had become space = time = money.

classic loving: on the maternal side the dramatic, even melodramatic, powerless energy; on the paternal side the corresponding energy strategy, the maximum use of energy with the help of the most profitable technology, the work ethos; the whole a power system.

i for my part, however, watched, and it was impossible for me to do nothing, impossible de ne rien faire, classic loving, the classic active life, work as the only justification for existence today, work or death.

didn't i want rather to find something that i had lost, forgotten, that had disappeared? that could not possibly be looked for systematically? only by wandering around, errantry? erring, erreur, error, doing it wrong, here was my field, in the wrong, erroneous work and in its repetition in another conception of time.

now i worked on the womanly part of this work: forgetting the given spaces, i bent towards myself.

1982

Terry Fox
Postcard showing the 'Inferno' mosaic (Baptistery of San Giovanni, Florence) 28.1.86

CARO MIRIAM. GRAZIA MOLITISSIMO FOR YOUR ANNOUNCEMENTS AND LETTER! I HAVE BEEN IN USA FOR 6 WEEKS AND ONLY RETURNED TO FIRENZE 2 DAYS AGO. IT WAS SO GOOD TO MEET YOU IN HAMBURG AND I'M GLAD WE COULD MEET SO. I RECEIVED TODAY THE CATALOGUE AND AM HAPPY TO SEE YOU STANDING BEFORE MY WORK ON PAGE 66![28] YOUR NEW LIVING/WORKING SITUATION SOUNDS VERY GOOD. YOU SHOULD PUT YOUR BED OVER THE HOLE IN THE FLOOR THROUGH WHICH THE BOMB PASSED – I WOULD LIKE TO SLEEP OVER THIS HOLE ONE NIGHT TO SEE WHAT KIND OF DREAM COULD BE PRODUCED ... ONCE I DREAMED I WAS NOT FALLING (VERFREMDUNGSEFFEKT). NOW I AM A BIT WORRIED AS I HAVE VERY LITTLE MONEY AND NOTHING COMING UP. KNOW OF ANYONE WHO WOULD BE INTERESTED IN A SHOW OF DRAWINGS BY ME? THIS IS NATIONAL "PIZZA WEEK" IN THE UNITED STATES. IT WAS VERY COLD (-40 C.) WHERE I WAS BORN NOT NEARLY AS COLD AS REAGAN'S[29] HEART. WHAT A POOR AND BRUTALIZED COUNTRY IT HAS BECOME – I THINK EVERYONE WILL KILL EACH OTHER AND THE INDIANS MAY ONCE AGAIN LIVE THERE IN PEACE. PLEASE DO ME A FAVOR AND TELEPHONE TO 851*** IN BERLIN AND GIVE MY LOVE TO WHOEVER ANSWERS. GRAZIE! – I HOPE TO SEE YOU AGAIN SOMETIME I LIKE BOTH YOU AND THE MANIFESTATIONS OF YOU – TILL THEN – WARM HUG IN THOUGHT,
BACI! TERRY

---

gentile signorina/MIRIAM CAHN
c/o PRAXIS INC. 33 PAKENHAM STREET
P.O BOX 536 fremantle WESTERN AUSTRALIA 6160
10 June 86

"THE LOSS OF EVERYDAY SECURITY IS THE BEGINNING OF PHILOSOPHY"
Dear Miriam – well, at least you can say you have been to the very edge. I once had a good friend in San Francisco who was married and yoked to a sheep farm in Tasmania. Her husband left her after a few months and as she had no money, the only way she could survive was to wash clothes and cook for a group of sheep farmers. she also had to fuck them – so it could be worse ... I have a good friend in Australia, she is probably also in the Biennale or at least in Sydney. Her name is JILL SCOTT.[30] you should ask someone I think everyone knows her. She might be good company.
I almost came to see you in Berlin – in fact it was all planned as I should stay at Julius. I had an installation performance in Hasselt, Belgium, on 26 April, so did Julius – then we should go together to Berlin – I even brought a present for you. But then Kossuth came to stay with them so there was no place and I was told you

were very busy getting ready to go to Australia, and I didn't want to bother you. Das tut mir leid! ma un altra volta…

I hope you're feeling better now that you have work (?) to do in your "residence". I know how you feel exactly – that is why I chose to stay always on the fringe (?) of the art world – it's sometimes playing games in a way that can be too much and takes you along with it until you're not sure anymore if you're "that" Terry Fox or this one – at which point you have the danger to lose your base and become just like the others – which of course is what they want. In my way now I am working on drawings that are probably not interesting to anybody but me – but that gives me a lot of pleasure and freedom – but of course no money! ha ha.

I will go to Basle on the 5–10 July and do a video workshop in the garden of the Wenken Park. Then back to Florence. I have the gallery of Tina Bitterlin as a studio for 3 months as it is closed now it is a wonderful feeling to finally have a studio again – it's been a year of only a tiny apartment to work in – also the gallery is beautiful – on the primo piano with a balcony running all along it overlooking the Baptistry and the Duomo. It has a 4.5 meter ceiling so I am doing large drawings and some sculpture – I am also doing a series of drawings for the blind – very interesting to me – but also funny because it doesn't matter what they "look" like! Now that I can finally work again I'm feeling much better – also the weather has been 25–29 for 6 weeks and a nice breeze – primavera! I also am working on a piece with a wired (mirror?) for Beuys that i started as soon as he died but couldn't work on in my apt. its title is "DAL CIELO AL FUOCO" and the drawings for the blind contain the text of it. I will have a show here in this gallery in September and then in Tina's gallery in Basle 3 Oct – 29 Nov with a performance in the Museum of Contemp. Art in Basle for 13. Maybe this would be a time to meet? Here is an account of a woman named Ann Armstrong walking on a mountain (as you did) in Canada during a lightning storm:

"AFTER EACH STRIKE WE MOVED IN SILENCE FOR A WHILE, WITH ONLY THE TEARING WIND AND SLASHING RAIN. THEN THE ROCKS WOULD BEGIN A SHRILL HUMMING, EACH ON A SLIGHTLY DIFFERENT NOTE. THE HUMMING GREW LOUDER AND LOUDER. YOU COULD FEEL A CHARGE BUILDING UP IN YOUR BODY, OUR HAIR STOOD ON END. THE CHARGE INCREASED, AND ALL THE HUMMING SWELLED UNTIL EVERYTHING REACHED AN UNBEARABLE CLIMAX. THEN THE LIGHTNING WOULD STRIKE AGAIN – WITH A CRACK LIKE A GIGANTIC RIFLE SHOT. THE STRIKE BROKE THE TENSION. FOR A WHILE WE WOULD GROPE FORWARD IN SILENCE. THEN THE HUMMING WOULD BEGIN AGAIN…"

I hope you handle your Australian experience o.k. I always was interested to get there – please write to me

again at least when you're back home in Berlin.
Until then all best wishes, greetings and thoughts.
Love Terry

Postcard showing the sky-blue sphere in the Old Sacristy (Basilica of San Lorenzo Florence) 1987 (?)

CIAO BELLA!

– so what have i done to you, he asked.
– nothing, she said.
– men have problems too, he said, you can't just simply …
mais je savais ce qu'il allait dire! je l'avais entendu toute ma vie!
when my mother phoned, i told her that i didn't have any time; that i had a lot of work to do, that she shouldn't phone, that she shouldn't come to see me, that i didn't feel like it.

i had a lot of women friends and male friends whom i met daily. the more i worked, the emptier it became around me. the more i saw the connection between my work and my woman-ness, the more i worked. no escaping. no. the longing remained, to have a man for myself alone. but i didn't write any more: write to me! didn't phone any more: give me a call! didn't go round any more: when are you coming to my place? are you coming to my place?

i produce weapons: i throw white plasticine onto the black floor and call these pieces: women's weapons, projectiles, counterfeit weapons.
i draw lying down, crawling, crouching, with black chalk, dance on white paper and subsequently wash the dust from my body.
i dream that my hair is falling from my head in tufts like with the people from hiroshima. i am the first in whom the contamination of our region makes itself visible.

1983

basle, 18 june 84

dear mr Boudaille,[31]

thank you for the invitation to take part in the XIIIth biennale in paris.

i shall, however, not be a participant in this biennale: i have no desire at all to wander each year through one of these gigantic exhibitions; and I do not like the current international situation, in which always the same artists are chosen by always the same commission members for always the same events of so-called great international importance.

no, gentlemen, i will not be participating in your biennale: it is too easy for you to do this type of name-dropping without going out in search of less-known artists …

yours sincerely,

miriam cahn

and after mr Boudaille, while greatly regretting the misunderstanding, had sent me the list of invited artists with the information that this biennale was the first time that international art would be shown so comprehensively in France:

dear sir,

having read your letter, i had a good laugh: the list you have sent me corresponds pretty closely to the image i had in my mind of this “new” paris biennale. let’s say that i know almost every name at least: almost half of these artists have taken part in a biennale or a documenta or in westkunst or in zeitgeist etc. … look for the women artists – they do not even constitute 10%: as always in these gigantic, “important” exhibitions full of artists of “genius” you have invited a few alibi women, and i am fed up with playing the alibi woman.

i would like you to know that in basle, as in other cities with an artistic culture, there are at least as many women artists who produce good work as men – and, bizarrely, all these major “important”, “trail-blazing” exhibitions don’t give a damn …

please do not misunderstand me: i have nothing against the artists you have invited nor against their works, but against these forever same concepts of large-scale exhibitions where the attempt is made to combine the “old” with the “young” to see if “the young stand up”, and where the already intense competition between artists is pushed even further – because this system artificially pushes towards the point of hysteria tendencies which have nothing to do with art, working at art, but with money and solely with money.

and this is rather something to cry over.

greetings

m. cahn

To the new head of the Department of Education, Basel-Stadt
basle, 1984

dear Prof. Striebel,[32]
what you state in the Arts Section of the BAZ of 19 May 84 is the direst form of smear campaign against intellectuals. with a blind belief in science, you measure our artistic work in "bits": "nowadays, the full substance and message can be measured exactly". and you then arrive at the "objective" and intelligent result that if, when looking at a picture, you have to do the personal work of interpretation and of personal feeling, you prefer "to look at a blue door or a window shutter".
then do so. it is likely better for you to look at blue doors than to make public statements about our work, of which you quite evidently have not the faintest idea; or to get into an educated bourgeois fit of rage when standing in front of Barnett Newman's "day before one" because "there is no message".
what a tone, what language!
where you have no comprehension you immediately bellow "cliquishness"; then you subdivide people into "educated people, who should involve themselves in debate" and others – only, a few lines later, to give the professorial recommendation to theatre professionals to "adhere faithfully to the work as the writer or composer originally intended it". whereas how they do their work should be left to the theatre people themselves, even if it costs our – after all still democratic – city money. and what effect will your measuring of our Basle carnival night cartoons as having "100 bits of clear substantial message" have on the financing of museums, on the Kunstverein, cultural events and art scholarships? a more blinkered, backward-looking attitude is hardly imaginable.
like mr Bessenich[33] i think the outlook is grim, grimmer than he thinks. although not directly dependent on you, i am reliant on the cultural atmosphere in Basle in order to be able to work.
professor, from your seizure of power we can expect only negatives – we, the "others", the "cliquish", the unaccountable, with our "little clear substance and message", we, the "uneducated", the artists who cannot be measured in "bits". and when do you want to get rid of us, eliminate us, stamp us out?
your miriam cahn

Guido Bachmann
c/o Lenos Verlag
Wallstrasse 9
CH 4051 Basle **24 June 85**

Dear Miriam,

In 1972, after I had left Bern (for ever), I wanted to settle on Madeira, where, however, (see "Parabel") I could stand it only for forty days, up to 13 Sept. 72. On my return, I had the good plan of settling in Berlin; but I got stuck in Basle and am still hanging around here in the fullest sense of the word. I can't get away from the place: that's why, as agreed on the phone, I've been silent, because I haven't got anything good or new to report. Which means: my financial situation is in such turmoil that I can't turn a blind eye to it without getting a criminal record.

Your postcard, which I received last week, gave me new heart, however: the fact that you now want to stay on in Berlin will help you a lot along your way. I know Berlin well: I know how the place and its atmosphere can give one a boost. The people are less sleepy and much more critical. I think that the Berlin passages in my books capture the spirit of the place well.

Despite all the trials and tribulations, I am still at work on the epilogue. Meantime, however, I have finally ditched that duff can of worms I was working on when we came to know one another. I'm keeping strictly to my diaries (1964–1984): they are informative concerning the birth of the trilogy, i.e. the book of the book. After that I'll be liberated. In every respect. If I can still keep up this agony (till 1987), then I can be open again. If I don't keep it up, everything will remain a torso. But that wouldn't be artistically perfect either.

We'll meet up in August –
love, Guido[34]

PARKETT ART JOURNAL / ART MAGAZINE

Zurich, 11 June 1986

Dear Miriam,

Did you have a fine time in Australia? I trust that you're none the worse after the journey. And now I'd like to ambush you straightaway with my request. You remember, we talked a bit about it at our last meeting: I'd like to have Miriam Cahn in Parkett! My thoughts on this matter always revolved around questions like "how?" + above all "who?"... until I had the idea, dear Miriam, of asking you to do a so-called "insert" for us. That means, you would create 10–12 pages in Parkett – they could be printed on special paper and could also be "divergent-format" as a kind of "booklet-in-book" and, as an insert (=slide-in), they would be an independent, stand-alone UNCOMMENTED pictorial piece.

We have been making such inserts since the 6th number. Up to now, Lothar Baumgarten, John Baldessari, Robert Mapplethorpe and Edward Ruscha have created such pieces. Naturally I've always considered for this section artists who in their work have revealed an affinity to the medium of a magazine booklet – to leafing through pages – to offset printing etc. And now I'm astonished that I didn't notice earlier that this "insert option" seems absolutely tailor-made for you.

Now I'm really excited about it and would like to give you a ring soon and hear what you think. What I'd like most of all would be if your insert could make it into the September number.

So, hoping to hear from you soon!

Fond Regards,

Bice[35]

---

miriam cahn
danckelmannstrasse 31
1-berlin 19 west **berlin, 15 july 86**

dear bice,

many thanks for your letter and your request to create the "insert" for your "parkett" number.

unfortunately, i'm less than enthusiastic about the idea. in its style, "parkett" is the complete opposite of what i understand by an art magazine. it's also light years away from my idea of art and being an artist.

my work is created against the backdrop of feminist theories and is at the same time totally provisional in its techniques and self-understanding.

your magazine fits completely into postmodernism. it is very attractively designed (attractive in the traditional, classic sense), blends fashions with art and trends, brokers an (artificial) american-european axis without any awkward questions asked, and international jet-set tourism dances on your dance-floor – why not. now, when even a few collectors are collecting me and a few museums are purchasing and exhibiting me, it suddenly occurs to you that i also make booklets and series in offset technique directly from the original – and that this would fit nicely into your "insert" programme. that's not so very novel/witty and is moreover

superfluous from an informational point of view – i've already done about 10 such printed pieces, and the most attractive booklet, i reckon, is the one from the bonn museum of modern art.
"miriam cahn in parkett" (between you and me: do think it's right to talk to me in this advertising lingo?) – quite certainly NOT in an uncommented piece. i would be prepared to conduct a kind of dispute, but quite certainly not as an "insert", nor as a "nice" conversation, but well-prepared (not: attractive). how about (just as an idea on the spur of the moment) cahn-stalder-winteler-müller v. curriger-burckhardt-schenker-amann or something like that? what do you say?
no offence meant
greetings
miriam

dream parts, day-to-day life + work

i am circling slowly like a glider or an eagle over a landscape that is forever becoming wider. i hear a muffled bang it is an atom bomb in the newspaper i read that similar bombs have been dropped on zurich rome + paris. i let myself drift in the clear river the aborigine man drifts beside me + we make love in the water. in a town by the sea i stand on the quayside + see seals harbour seals large fish + other undefinable animals + point them out to the people i am the only person to see the dead child on the clear bed of the water. s. helps me by giving me a small dried fish and a longish object against my menstrual pains. we are standing at a crossroads binningerhöhe near basle aircraft rush past over our heads some so fast that we can hardly see them. my sister is carrying the shells which she found when bathing in mountain lakes. running i press my little tabby cat to my side. i know that alongside the federal german parliament in which i am the rhine flows through i see it large and lovely through the tiled wall of the waterworks. we are in a watery transparent landscape + m. collects plants + animals above all this wild wasp whose sting is admittedly not fatal but painful.

i dreamed of basle as a world city: that in broad daylight a black cloud rolled over the town + everybody ran in panic. i waited in an east berlin café until the cloud had passed.

i look down the road to the rhine in high spirits we run up this australian hill to colonial square we kiss we run farther up to the hilltop: here australia in the sunset there the beach + the sea. in my parents' house i look out through large windows and see mediaeval roofs hills and this large city in clear light i look at the rhine the house stands at the waterside i look into the clear green-blue water + to the boats. on this tropical island we run across european hills + pine trees forests with forest floors full of needles i hear the roar of the sea + see the tall grey waves with which i am already familiar. i run across the mittlere brücke a. lays the table for three we sit on the bridge eating it is summer southerly mediaeval basle as it may have been once.

a. told me that all the city's junkies were contaminated.

g. told me that she had spent the morning between 5 + 7 in panic.

my father told me that between 5 + 7 he sat in his house + didn't know how to breathe.

my mother told me that she had looked out of her window at the disaster + sent me a drawing. my father told me that many friends had phoned him up.

h. told us that he had survived only because he had acted inconspicuous like a mouse.

p. told me that at home between 5 + 7 he had opened the best bottle of wine + had sat there smoking + waiting.

r. told me that his colleague with the immaculate hair-style could suddenly no longer comb his hair.

while running i thought luckily a. is on holiday i thought now they're all going to die i thought i must immediately go there. a. told me the people stood on the bridge and looked down into the water.

swans + ducks + seagulls were swimming in the river, the water was flowing through the town. later i looked down into the water + saw nothing.

i work in a woman's rhythm:
24 days work, 6 days rest or:
25 days work, 5 days rest or:
26 days work, 5 days rest.
during my absence little animals run through the black dust + leave their pathways behind them.

 i work with the energies of a woman: "ovulation works" during my ovulation, "menstruation works" before my period.

i have these two spaces: DUST + WATER
using a knife i scrape the black chalk into dust, the remainder i chop into little pieces as housewives or chefs do, mixing it with the dust + forming a heap, i strew the dust over large white sheets + lie crouch kneel while working on paper.
i fling the watercolours: magenta, blue, yellow up the stretched paper, imitating volcanos or A- + H-bombs, the colours flow slowly down and mingle.

READING IN DUST – strategic places

Zurich, 27 February 86

Dear Miriam,

dear christoph,[36]
although I'm sure it was well meant, your letter made me angry.

actually, it just confirms what i had already suspected from your review: a somewhat effusive, completely unpolitical and highly sentimental attitude towards art and artists ... admittedly you polemicize against the art "scene" (x-artists etc.), but it obviously also puts such fear into you, or at least influences you so much, that you have to distance yourself in this somewhat childish way (with the word x-artists, which I, to be honest, find insulting). so intimidated that you name no names? and at the same time the pretension of being factual?
that, I would say, is politics not to say almost realpolitik.
well, that brings me to my main argument: what you call ideology is not ideology at all. feminism is a specific approach to life, a way of living, a theory, a praxis, a way of seeing etc. – namely as a product of woman-ness (this in contrast to beuys's way of seeing). and one of my intellectual positions, which was certainly influenced by the pragmatic demand of the 70s: "the political is the private, the public is the personal", is in total contradiction to your way of thinking of separations between the person and the "work". and by the way, not only to your thinking but also to the general public opinion about art, what art is, what artists (i.e. male artists) are supposed to be, namely something withdrawn, aloof, someone unworldly, a genius, not concerned with the lowly areas of EVERYDAY life (and also: politics), men who perfect their "work" in secluded, occlusive artists' studios ...
well, chia, cucci, kiefer, dahn, lüpertz of course and a few others do have this very traditional attitude – disler as well has a tinge of it, however much i value him. these men also often make pronouncements with which i as a woman artist cannot identify at all: they make reference to patriarchally oriented traditions and aesthetics which i wish to have nothing to do with – after all, these are the aesthetics of prevailing power. for my taste, too little is being called into question here.
beuys, acconci, gerz, vom bruch, stalder, müller etc. are, for me, artists who at least call the aesthetics of prevailing power into question; part of this is the questioning of the distribution of power between man and woman; a new interpretation of corporeality, a questioning of what constitutes an image-likeness, a search for a new image of the human being-man/woman. it is not (or: not only) a matter of producing a lasting "work", of painting, sculpture or suchlike, but of images altogether in our, from our, with our time
what is striking is that the former group uses traditional techniques so to say exclusively; most then also become very rich (which I wouldn't bother about), but above all, they act like rich people (which really gets my goat), because there too the tradition of separations between man and "work" makes itself evident ...
whereas the latter group often flips around in a variety of media (which is more in line with the present time) and can be less plnned down to this "i am a genius" attitude of the rich artist, because, thanks to the techniques they use, they either don't earn anything or, if they do, they use the money for further projects (e.g. beuys etc. ...).
it is undoubtedly for these "others" that I feel affection ...
my role-models, however, are unequivocally women artists: rosenbach, export, lassnig, christa wolf, chantal ackerman and many other women in a variety of areas. they go much farther than the "other" artists – because they involve their woman-ness in its

full radicalness, polemically, personally, privately, politically and above all aesthetically. the techniques are right across the board, the content is partly brand new – and ages old (birth – death – children – menstrual cycles). brand new, because finally seen from a woman's point of view, and ages old, because these themes are actually part of being human.
you contemptuously call this comprehensive work "ideology" – and so unmask yourself as an unconscious bearer of ideology. I think that you haven't got a clue, have never seriously concerned yourself with the work of women artists, women academics and scientists, women writers, women film-producers etc. no, when you hear people insisting on woman-ness and the woman's point of view you have in your mind's eye the cliché of the "women's libber" – and that then closes down YOUR open-minded vision.
i, however, do not accept this attitude in an art review which even presumes to call itself factual or objective. because it is neither factual (you quite obviously lack cultural information) nor objective: via your criticism of my work you quite candidly and hence below the belt express your antipathy, not to say your hatred of these "women's libbers". i am not at all concerned for mild treatment, or, as you put in your timorous way, for diplomacy, but really and truly for factualness, i.e. for KNOWLEDGE, and I demand knowledge of art critics – it is your function to INFORM people and, lord knows, that does not exclude a personal attitude to the matter – but here too the writer must KNOW what writing is. your timorously nebulous, highly art-historical way of writing probably matches your general attitude and approach to art – namely, a traditional one.
well, enough said.
i'll send a copy to elisabeth[37]
warm regards,
miriam cahn

j-f-müller **27 december 86**

dear josef-felix,[38]

a new typewriter! well, now i can write to you about my "doubts" – they're not doubts but, what is worse, boredom. by that i don't mean necessarily the "man/woman" idea and creating an exhibition in itself, but perhaps the idea of the combination: your work – my work. it is too easy. you are so quickly in agreement with everything i say. and i say such a lot, after all, and jump around so much in my "pool of ideas", and above all "woman-ness" is central, absolutely central to my work, whereas i think that with you "man-ness" is also central, but that it just tends to be embedded. of course, this bed is damn prickly and bumpy and askew and slippery – but it is a bed. being critical and radical is part of being a MALE artist; being critical and radical is equally part of being a WOMAN artist, but there is no bed, no history for us to lean on – and that makes the nature of our radicalness totally different. women artists have nothing to lose because there was nothing there.

it was a very good thing that i came to visit you and that we talked so thoroughly – indeed, with map exercises (i love military expressions) – about our idea of such an exhibition with HANDS-ON REFERENCE to our works. i have come to understand your work fundamentally better having been in your studio – the atmosphere there, st gallen, how you live etc. i liked a lot, and i love your work. only, i have come to see that previously i understood it "wrong" – your work is not as complex as i thought at first: it is quite direct, also from the point of view of method and procedure.

well, all of this doesn't speak against our project, after all. what does speak against it is my feeling of boredom. i have come back from st gallen with the feeling that, for sure, i have come to know you more closely and your work better. but as for the issue women artists / male artists, woman / man not a jot. then i thought: once again i have played mummy and he the little boy – once again i have continually raised questions, played thought games, and he has profited. that, admittedly, is putting it a little simplistically and brutally, but for me it's true, and it happens to me again and again. sure, it would be an attractive exhibition, but not an intelligent one. attractive – we've both got that "at our fingertips", haven't we, but is it also interesting? precisely BECAUSE our conversations and map exercises went as they did, i don't find them interesting any more and the whole thing bores me.

it's difficult to understand something like this at present – at first, i also thought it good; but every time i think about this exhibition, i am overcome by boredom, and that's the truth.

well. one might think that something could be constructed on the basis of this mummy / young lad thing – which, of course, is also a man / woman thing. but i reckon that there's something wrong with that, deriving from the nature of my work and the nature of your work. what, i don't know either – at any event it would be a reduction. and that, i think, is it in a nutshell: i've always got this feeling of a reduction instead of an expansion – as you can see, i'm trying all the time to circumscribe my unease about this whole thing, but probably it's above all what i'm calling mummy / young boy. i simply don't want that. i feel very ill at ease about it.

i still think the idea is a brilliant one – but not with the two of us. perhaps we could consider doing it with "several"? i don't know.

at any event – let's stay in contact and i'd be pleased if you came to berlin.
greetings and kisssss.
miriam

miriam cahn
danckelmannstrasse 31
1000 Berlin 19 **berlin, 19 february 87**

dear prof. dr striebel,[32]
in 1981 i was taken to court by the building department because i had worked on and in the section of motorway near the badischer bahnhof: always at night, i drew signs and made drawings in charcoal on the various pillars, in tunnels, overpasses, underpasses and in ill-defined sites created by the motorway architecture – “my” area, i believe, covers kilometres.
if you go in search in this area – on foot of course – i presume that you will still find a few such drawings and signs.
now the art credit commission, of which you are chairman, invites me to embellish, to “style” this same motorway – i should please fetch the plans from the same building department that took me to court in 1981.
does the art credit commission actually still notice what it is doing? that is the political aspect. in addition, there is the aesthetic aspect, if it can be separated off at all:
if the art credit commission were informed about HOW the artists to whom it issues invitations work, then their choice would turn out differently. or, putting it the other way around, if it invites people such as me or dillier or stalder,[39] then the commission must come up with less firmly defined areas that correspond to our work.
shaking my head in disbelief, i can only say that evidently nobody on this commission has concerned himself with my work – because i work exclusively with provisional materials such as chalk, paper, video, plasticine etc. and i work in a “performance”-like manner, through my body, in spaces (by which are meant also political spaces) and following a woman’s cycle. (all this can be read up in more precise detail in my catalogues.)
the commission presumably thought that i am a motorway specialist precisely because of the above-mentioned work (its title, by the way, was “my woman-ness is my public part”). probably, however, nobody on the commission knows this work. for me, a motorway is an intolerable place in terms of urban architecture and the ecology – a place which, at that time, provoked me to work ILLEGALLY and on foot (in contrast to LEGALLY and by car), WHEN, HOW, + WHERE i wanted, and WITH the risk of being caught, as also happened, namely on christmas eve, the feast of love.
i get the impression that the commission wants to “appease” me by allocating me the task of “embellishing” an underpass. i make you and the commission a counter-proposal: go and look, on foot of course, for the remaining drawings and signs in “my” section of the motorway and purchase them from me – why not? the police can assist you with their pictorial archive.
with kind regards,
your m. cahn
copies to: kunstverein basel, mr stumm BAZ,[40] stampa,[41] monica dillier and other artists.

PEDESTALS + THE ATTEMPT OF THE NATIONAL GALLERY, BERLIN, TO OBSTRUCT AND PREVENT GIACOMETTI

berlin, 1 november 1987

dear herr honisch,[42]
when i enter the berlin national gallery, the building designed by mies van der rohe, i see on the right a white-painted shed, in which slides are shown. on the left the sculpture by max ernst, a friend of giacometti, has been unnecessarily and heedlessly pushed to one side. in the middle, the figures for the "chase-manhattan-plaza"[43] under glittering light on a gleaming white, 5–10 cm high dais.
in the centre of the exhibition hall on the lower level, between the chairs, stands "der karren" ["the chariot"] on two white pedestals placed one on top of the other. three spotlights shine brightly down from above the head of the woman on the chariot, and the chairs are standing with their backs to the entire work.
walking through the exhibition i am forever seeing pedestals: pedestals with and without perspex hoods, pedestals with glass hoods, pedestals with hood fixtures but with no hood, pedestals on boards, pedestals with rails above or below, pedestals on other pedestals, pedestals on daises of various heights – i even encountered a dais made of green resopal ("frau ohne arme" ["woman without arms"]); one pedestal has been given a sheet of cardboard shoved between it and the sculpture ("kopf diegos" ["diego's head"]), and the sculpture "drei schreitende manner" ["three men striding"] is for some absurd reason standing diagonally on its pedestal.
sometimes the pedestals are standing in work groups on white-painted daises, which prevent me from walking around the sculptures. they are often pressed so close to the wall that it seems the national gallery consists of WALLS WITHOUT SPACE. since everything is painted gleaming white and is brutally lit from above, i can scarcely see the surface, the patina, the skin of the works on display; the garish light falls onto the sculptures through the edges of the perspex hoods, cutting them to pieces: i saw two of the tiny figures standing in three perspex hoods inside one another on perspex pedestals which are in turn standing on one of these white-painted pedestals. "DAS BEIN" ["THE LEG"] IS THE ONLY WORK THAT IS STANDING DIRECTLY ON THE FLOOR. thus, giacometti's figures have not only had their skin removed, but have been deprived also of the possibility of standing and of making their striding movement.
giacometti and van der rohe – the entrance foyer as a SPACE WITHOUT WALLS with its carefully chosen materials and its special light. positioned directly on this beautiful floor, giacometti's women would stand, the dog would run, the men would stride. van der rohe's "grey" light would lie gently on the skin of these figures. van der rohe's "almost not" building would form a unity with giacometti's "almost not" figures.
herr honisch: an exhibition, of whatever kind, does not consist only in acquiring the finance, managing loan contracts, transport, insurance, catalogue etc. creating an exhibition means a passion for the work of making art, for the art of seeing and displaying, and for the work of conveying knowledge and insight.
of all this there is nothing here: this exhibition looks as if first of all the sculptures were counted, then the same number of pedestals were fetched from the store room, then the works were distributed

– any old how – onto the pedestals, sometimes with, sometimes without a hood, put now here, now there, then switch on the light and the exhibition's done and dusted.
this slovenly attitude shows me that not only are you indifferent to giacometti's work but also to giacometti as an artist who mostly set up his exhibitions himself and who, with the help of his brother diego, changed the patina of his figures if the conditions of space and light called for it.
now he has been dead for more than 20 years and you don't even take the trouble to reflect on how his work can be communicated TODAY. this confirms me in the belief i have always held that art mediators who are not in the least interested in contemporary art also do an injustice to the works of dead artists.
neither do you visit artists' studios, nor are you curious about experimental approaches. you probably have scarcely any contact with contemporary male artists or women artists and are therefore not aware of how we work today. under the pretext of proximity to downtown berlin you have banished the space for current-day art to the hideous site of the grundkreditbank. in this way, you don't have to concern yourself with things that offer a challenge to art history and can avoid inside your own institution confrontations which would prove intellectually and artistically fascinating.
all this has an impact on your exhibitions, in this case on the giacometti exhibition. in your institution, you do only two things: ADMINISTER AND SHOWCASE. and for the director of an art museum that stages temporary exhibitions that, to my mind, is too meagre.
your miriam cahn
P.S. copies sent to the TAZ berlin and to mr thomas wulffen[44]

to Barbara Gross[45] **berlin, 12 april 87**

dear barbara,
many thanks for your letter – i am, of course, pleased that you like my new works.
nevertheless, i sometimes really cannot understand you: after all, we have discussed so often about how i see the "art world", how i exhibit, what i think of the art trade, of museums, of private life – how i see all that.
and now once again you come and ask me whether i would like to have an exhibition in your private house, and i'm seriously beginning to wonder whether you took any notice of and took seriously those discussions we had together.
to put it again briefly: i am fundamentally opposed to exhibitions in private houses – they are, quite simply, a shoddy compromise. a nineteenth-century idea (salon), a hole-and-corner semi-public, a cosy non-debate among "friends" and, above all, "typically female" – faffing around in private because you basically haven't got the courage to open a gallery.
if we women artists were to work like that, we would still be reduced to producing small formats at the kitchen table, in an acute plight, trapped between kids and kitchen and husband, making hastily sketched, diary-like art, financially dependent on the husband etc.
today, however, the situation is that we women can work as WE want – we can become women artists, we can run galleries, we can work as we want – only, we must really want to, because the difficulties are still there, but they can be overcome. our work absolutely must be public: otherwise, we actually fall back into the nineteenth century, and back to the kitchen table.
so please: don't try to tell me that an educated woman of around 40 with 1 child cannot open a gallery with all its odds and ends and bits and pieces and, for sure, financial difficulties – you quite obviously don't want to. i am also coming to believe that you haven't come to terms on the information level with the problem "gallery-art trade-mediation-avant-garde". to put it somewhat nastily: it is simply cushier as a private person to do a bit of collecting, a bit of haggling and higgling, a bit of being feminist, rather than actually building up a place of mediation, not least mediation of ideas.
look, i'm being so caustic here because people like you get in the way of the still few interesting places of mediation that do exist. an example: if you buy something from me and then sell it on to, e.g., some museum person, without moreover telling me in advance, and i naturally think it's for your collection (which, moreover, is how you put it), then the communication between me and this museum person = nil. very cosy: this museum person doesn't need to have any contact with the oh-so-irksome artists. he or she doesn't need to come into the artist's studio. the consequences are often completely absurd inquiries, with me first having to enlighten the people about my work from scratch, having to invite them to come to my studio, if they understand at all why I am getting so "het up".
for me, an interesting place of mediation is a place which museum people or other people use as their first port of call when they want to make a purchase, to make a purchase but then also receive reliable information and be handed on – to the artists; i.e. a kind of complex service supplier. and as a matter of course, the supplier keeps me as a producer fully up to date.
look, i've got nothing against you exhibiting your collection in

private – it's no concern of mine and I don't find the idea interesting. i cannot prevent you at all from selling works from your collection – but I am not in agreement with such private dealing. among other reasons it pushes up prices and is beyond my control. it is precisely what in economics and politics is known as a "grey area".
perhaps you don't understand why my nerves are suddenly so on edge. above all, it's because i have the feeling that all of our conversations have come to nothing. since i feel some affection for you, however, i am also writing you this letter – and since it's a matter of concern to me that women artists should be mediated in a fully qualified manner.
warm regards,
miriam

Edition Gross
Ms Miriam Cahn
Danckelmannstr. 31
1 Berlin 19 **12 May 87**

Dear Miriam,
Your reproach that my activities take place in a private house is, of course, accurate. But you know also that my work is in the process of development. First there was the edition on women artists, which is still the main emphasis of my work today, now focussed on Mapplethorpe. On the other hand, my daughter was always there and she always necessitated a professional compromise – I used to work full-time. I wouldn't want to have any turbo career at her expense. This consideration is perhaps not so understandable for those who have no children, but there are obligations here that I cannot push heedlessly to one side. The same is true of my relationship to my husband, whose work has up to now always tied us to this place in the country.
I have tried to make a virtue out of necessity, not in order to propagate a nineteenth-century idyll, but to enable events to take place here on the level of a personal relationship and the opportunity for more intensive discussion and debate. In the first place, therefore, my own house could not be and was not to be a place for the art business, but here people from the art and cultural worlds were to meet – and this in a very similar way to any gallery, only with the difference that the people brought more time and leisure to encounter art and the woman artist (if she was present).
[…]

to Silvia Bächli[46] **berlin, 17 september 87**

dear silvia,
i tried to catch you in basle, but it didn't work + so now i'm writing to you. i went into your exhibition in the kunsthalle + would like to write to tell you what i think of it.
my first impression was disappointment at the exhibition as a whole: not that what was hung there was, say, "bad" – but the overall atmosphere was, for me, very hesitant, very non-courageous, a bit "what-i-can-show-i'll-show". a bit playing-it-safe, all that.
if any, then it was guido's[47] works that addressed the situation in the kunsthalle – and also the publicity value of the kunsthalle. moreover, his works contained the element of there being something more to come and one doesn't know in what direction – that is, a kind of future in the work itself, an intellectual tension that interests me, even if his work is fundamentally foreign to me.
your works, on the other hand, are fundamentally akin to me – by which I mean that the theme and the manner of the work is closer. + there it just frustrated me that there was not more there – i had this déjà-vu effect. i.e. i didn't see anything more in this exhibition than some 1 1/2 years ago in your studio.
it may be my own fault. i thought: exciting, these large pictures, all the more exciting in view of the kunsthalle, these high difficult airy spaces, exciting too that, when you switch from these small (private) formats to the large (private?) formats, what happens then.
what happens when YOU begin to work on the floor, what happens to YOU + is it visible.
when i pace around your rooms (in the kunsthalle), your easy-goingness almost gets me in a rage – precisely because i see inklings which are going in a direction that could be hugely exciting. i got this impression most, as an intimation, with your "breast pictures" in the little room – there i sensed something that cost a bit of an effort on your part, perhaps showing breasts full frontal, perhaps breasts at all. the small room showed me a little your potential energy, showed me that the interesting aspect in this work lies at the point where i do NOT know what it's leading up to. precisely when one is as "skilful" as you, the danger, after all, is to work as one knows how – it's what one can do. (i'm now seeing how tricky it is to express this point) – in brief, also in the way that you hung these works – somewhat shamefacedly – there was something new.
which made it all the less comprehensible that you had hung the other rooms in your "old manner". sure, every sheet is ok, the relations between them ok, as a complete whole it's "attractive" – but not "flawed" enough, too "attractive", design (not the individual sheets but the whole thing) and very very playing-it-safe. it is as if, in your case, working on the floor had had no effect whatsoever on the works done on the table – and i can't buy that story. or they were older works (didn't look at the dates), and if so i don't think it's the right thing to show "old" works like this in such an exhibition – you're not so old after all …
i was also a bit disappointed by the big pictures. there were so damn few of them and i'd expected a whole deluge (that's the way i am), newer, bigger, where you dare to lose yourself and to make "errors", where the twisted, warped element that comes out in your work, for me, especially in the bodies (or better: parts of the body) could be expressed even more twisted, more gnarled, more

frightening, more moral, more rigid, or the release, liberation from it. in short that it becomes – in whatever direction – more radical, more existential, more wrenched from need.
there are intimations in the shadows behind the things in the big paintings, and precisely these shadows make me all the angrier, because they point to an energy in you that you simply don't dare to use – why actually? what have you got to lose?
the technique (or rather: the procedure) that you use has the inherent snag that it betrays everything, that one cannot hide oneself + that an easy-going, cosy approach becomes IMMEDIATELY visible. why: working on the floor always means WANTING to lose control, i.e. to abandon oneself to the procedure or the material inasmuch as one CAN not know what it (the material) will do. it will do what it wants, but THROUGH you as an individual, as a whole being, and there precisely is that something one doesn't know. more interesting + more exciting, but also more dangerous, because this procedure is a kind of dialogue between your day-to-day life, everyday life in general and you, a kind of "questioning" and the answer is sometimes shocking – oh, I can't put it in words. at any rate, through working on the floor you are pretty radically and uncontrollably confronted with yourself (+ what i call "world").
in your exhibition rooms i asked myself the question: do you want this at all? if yes, then – sorry – you'd have to work much more. if no, then it's the wrong procedure.
so, that's that – of course, it would have been better to talk, but by the time i come to basle again i'll have forgotten or have only a hazy idea of what i wanted to say to you – + your work essentially interests me – please, don't you too fall into this "swiss" prosperity-born cosiness.
kiss,
miriam

Basle, 25 October 87

Dear Miriam,
Your long letter was, I can't say a "pleasure" to read, but nevertheless: you took the exhibition seriously and write what you think.
Despite your disappointment that there was "no more to see than last time in the studio", I think I can discern interest. Your letter has set me thinking. My answer has been a long time coming – besides, I've been away for 3 weeks in the meantime.
There are a few points that I see differently. Painting breasts was/is highly sensual. Even if the women do not seem particularly strong. The positioning of breasts and arms as I often observe it, expressing an attitude that can be found In many women. Painting breasts costs me as much of an inner effort as painting feet or street lamps. Why you should find this completely normal, classical hanging of pictures in a row shame-faced beats me.
The "old" way of hanging still interests me. The flickering of space, the unstable equilibrium. The almost-touching-propping-up-holding-up-attracting-looking beyond-repelling. Attract, connect, release, accelerate; brake, shove, brace, arouse, entwine. And the beholder

in their midst, drawn into the restless motion of the waves.
As far as the date of the small drawings is concerned, they are all from 86/87 (they were no old ones among them: "motifs" have a certain length of life and change slowly over this period).
As far as the large ones in the 3rd room are concerned, you really did see almost all of them in the studio a year ago. I had to add two older ones (84 + 85), because the large new works (I've got quite a few more) rejected and assailed each other so much that it was impossible to hang the room differently. A wider range, more, as you would like to have seen, was an impossibility with the sheets available (all full frontal, the white of the paper combines with the wall and if the sheets came too close to one another, the result was a 3rd picture for the eyes).
I would be pleased to talk with you about our methods of working (e.g. floor) and our works. Writing, to be sure, is a precise means of expression, but many unspectacular points slip between the lines.
I trust that cosiness born of prosperity (nowadays possible anywhere) will not befall me.
Warm regards,
Silvia

PRO HELVETIA: invitation to take part in the exhibition in the Louisiana Museum of Modern Art, Copenhagen **berlin, 9 march 88**

dear mr durschei,[48]
many thanks for your letter + your invitation to take part in the exhibition in the louisiana museum. i will, however, not be taking part – and for the following reasons. once again, this is a typical pro helvetia multipack-CH exhibition: always the same names, neatly and pluralistically distributed across the media (as varied as possible), across the languages (all national languages if at all possible), and across degrees of celebrity (well-known and less well-known well mixed). In the process, however, you have strangely forgotten the gender quota (too few women artists! too many male artists!). anyway, an average bunch is guaranteed + hence a boring exhibition that says nothing either about the artists or about the exhibition-makers. nice and neutral.
if you were really concerned to promote swiss art abroad in an informative way, then it would be better to make ongoing SMALL group exhibitions over a number of years + above all solo exhibitions – with well-known, less well-known, recalcitrant, different, maverick etc. artists.
the experience of, for example, the "stiller nachmittag" ["quiet afternoon"] exhibition in the kunsthaus zürich showed me that things can't go on like this anymore.
in these multipack exhibitions, there is no room for a complex and commercially scarcely viable artist such as rémy zaugg,[49] for example – although he is well-known internationally. nor for recalcitrant people such as guido nussbaum. rut himmelsbach + silvia bächli are still treated as if they were beginners. etc. clara saner[50] hardly figures. etc. no, it's always the same packet that gets the nod: raetz-disler-stalder-cahn-fischli/weiss-müller + a few more "garnishes". i'm sick and tired of it – once or twice is quite enough.
so, before i definitively write myself into a rage, i'll break off at this point + send warm greetings,
your m. cahn

Artworks for the main auditorium of the Hochschule St. Gallen
Lis Keller
Kunstverein St. Gallen
Otmarstr. 3
9402 Mörschwil **17 January 89**

Dear Miriam Cahn,
Our Commission sat yesterday and it is a matter of importance for me to report on their deliberations.
The cycle of works on the entrance wall met with spontaneous approval. Some members of the Art Commission had difficulties with the wall opposite. To some, the wall seemed "overloaded" with two works; for others, the format of "Bergsee" ["Mountain Lake"] seemed too large altogether in relation to the space.
We then studied variants.
1) The smaller work on the left, hung asymmetrically on its own
2) "Bergsee" on its own
Variant 1 seemed to be a possibility.
Variant 2 did not meet with approval, inasmuch as the picture "cut" the wall too severely. All those present were very taken with "Bergsee" in itself.
Since we could not come to any agreement, I suggested for the wall a third possibility, which I would like to present to you as a proposal:
Entrance wall: as suggested, the impressive "female cycle", (which, by the way, comes out wonderfully against the grey concrete wall)
Wall opposite: two works of medium-sized format (comparable to the smaller of those hanging at present from the "male form canon")
I tried to explain your manner of working to those present and spoke also about the exhibition strategies that led to this dichotomy. The people were fascinated by the idea and immediately authorized me to talk to you about it.
I would like to do this in the first instance in writing, so that you can consider the matter in peace and without any pressure.
It is of very great importance to me that we find an ideal solution and I would like to devote all my energy to this end.
I am, of course, very keen to hear your reaction.
With kind regards,
Elisabeth Keller

---

miriam cahn
strassburgerallee 68
CH-4055 basle **basle, 19 january 89**

dear ms keller,
many thanks for your letter – only, that's no way of going about it. if i come to st gallen and hang my works, then that is binding. i presented the commission with two suggestions, as mr guyer[51] certainly told you: the one that hung there, and a variant with only the landscape and the series opposite. if i arrived at this result with these two possibilities then there are reasons for it which are

founded in my work – so, please, don't YOU rack MY brains for me – and, moreover, i don't need any instruction on the fullness or emptiness of spaces.
however, i accept the fact that the commission does not want these works presented in that way, and i am prepared to come up with something else, conceivably with different works – as long as something comes to my mind. i am prepared to do this, however, only if the commission stops considering the approx. 10,000 possibilities which could well be brought together from my work over the past 12 years – instead of taking a close, considered look. if, therefore, i am to come to st gallen again to make an installation in this space, the commission must decide whether it wants the present proposal, the second, or the one that has yet to be hung or not. AND NOTHING ELSE – unless it decides to go shopping at stampa and to hang the works itself, which, however, doesn't seem to me to be the scheme you conveyed to me.
your proposal using "old" works is out of the question – from the point of view of your own scheme (involving artists with new works) and from the point of view of my work – and leads only to even more confusion and lack of concentrated thinking if the decision has to be taken by a commission.
i think it is easier if 1 mediator operates between the commission, myself and stampa: in this case, mr guyer, who was present at the hanging and is hence better informed.
so, we'll be in contact again – as long as i and mr and mrs stampa come up with something that makes sense.
greetings, your m. cahn
P.S. copy sent to mr guyer

torture pictures in may 2004
when i see the nonchalantly smoking female soldier who is walking a prisoner on a leash and looking at him with a disparaging smile i see after the first dismay caused by revulsion valie export walking a man on a leash through the streets of vienna. if in a film I see the world trade center in the background, i automatically switch my mind to attack and the collapse of the 2 towers and think at the same time of my own earlier works.

put valie exports pictures of her performances on display today: what would they show? a document of the 1970s? a private s/m thing? a feminist fable? a predictive anticipation and hence a confirmation of art as avant-garde? a primordial symbol (things were always like this, all human beings are like this)? at any event just looking at exports work would bring to mind the topical pictures of the woman soldier with the leash.

something similar happened to me when putting together an exhibition with earlier works: in the 1980s i naturally used the symbol of the world trade center as a political and feminist critique. and now this building, which had always been an icon, had been attacked in real life and destroyed. in the exhibition in madrid shortly before the outbreak of the 2nd gulf war my works on the world trade center took on an unintentionally topical and terrible significance: had i "foreseen" this? no. was it a primordial symbol? perhaps. buildings are primordial symbols, but high-rise buildings are historically linked to modernity. pleasure at producing these giant drawings and the portrayal of the skyscrapers? of course. and primarily. a feminist fable? yes, and tied to the then time (division into male and female worlds).

and now this "topicality" of the picture material, which with export and myself takes on by historical chance a significance that was never so intended, apart from the fact that interesting art always changes anyway in the eyes of its beholders. today we look at goyas "desastres" with modern war reporting in mind. but what does it mean when i myself have to look at my own art in a consciously historical way because the justified ideological critique of the 1970s and 1980s period has taken on such utterly perverse forms, since it has slipped from thought into action. because word/picture have suddenly become real in the sense of a copy, of the document of a genuine act like a snuff porn film that can immediately be broadcast all over the world. it is as if goya had prompted soldiers or even himself to commit atrocities so that he could reenact / simulate them later.

so i look helplessly at my warships, offshore oil rigs, world trade centers etc. their only valid statement is their beauty. if i exhibit them, then as a document of my helplessness.

torture pictures in may 2004

when i see the nonchalantly smoking female soldier who is walking a prisoner on a leash and looking at him with a contemptuous smile i see after the first dismay caused by revulsion valie export walking a man on a leash through the streets of vienna. if in a film i see the world trade center in the background, automatically the pictures of the destruction of the twin towers are switched on in my mind and i think at the same time of my own earlier drawings of the world trade center.

put valie exports pictures of her performances on display today: what would they show? a document of the 1970s? individual s/m behaviour? feminist critique of pornography? a predictive anticipation and hence a confirmation of art as avant-garde? a primordial symbol (things were always like this, all human beings are like this)? at any event anybody looking at exports work would recall the pictures of the woman soldier with the leash.

something similar happened to me when putting together an exhibition with earlier works: in the 1980s i naturally used the symbol of the world trade center as a political and feminist critique, as a symbol for capitalism run wild and US hegemony. and now this icon has been attacked and destroyed. in the exhibition in madrid shortly before the 2nd gulf war my works the portrayals of the world trade center took on in the context an unintentionally topical significance: had i foreseen this and thus been a priestess of an avant-garde? was it a primordial symbol? was it personal pleasure at producing these giant drawings and the portrayal of the skyscrapers? a feminist critique of the "male world"?

and now this topicalization of images which for export and me myself gain by historical chance a devastatingly false significance – or perhaps not? what does it mean when i have to look at my own art in a consciously historical way because the justified ideological critique of the 1970s and 1980s period has slipped from fluxus-flowing thinking/feeling/testing/performing into final ultimate action/execution? because word/picture has suddenly become a real document of a genuine deed that is as final as dying? in an aesthetics of tame picture mobiles – "hi-mum-hi-dad-look-how-i-am-doing-well", from snuff porns or hollywood spectaculars that can immediately be broadcast all over the world in real time?

it is as if i would really have to hack off peoples limbs in order to be able to paint them like that. it is as if i would have had to have seen dying and dead people in reality in order to be able to reflect on dying and death.
it is as if goya would have had to prompt soldiers or even himself to commit atrocities so that later he could produce his "desastres".
it is the complete rejection of any form of imagination.

torture pictures in may 2004
when i see the female soldier who is walking a prisoner on a leash and looking at him with a contemptuous smile i see at the same time valie export walking a man on a leash through the streets of vienna. if in a film I see the world trade center in the background, automatically the pictures of the destruction of the twin towers are switched on in my mind. at the same time i think of my own earlier drawings of the world trade center.

put valie exports pictures of her performance on display today: what would they show? a document of the 1970s? individual s/m behaviour? feminist critique of pornography? a predictive anticipation? art as avant-garde? a primordial symbol (things were always like this, all human beings are like this)? at any event anybody looking at exports work would recall the pictures of the woman soldier with the leash.

something similar happens to my works: in the 1980s i naturally used the symbol of the world trade center as a political and feminist critique, as a symbol for capitalism run wild and US hegemony. and now this icon had been attacked and destroyed. in my exhibition in madrid shortly before the 2nd gulf war the portrayals of the world trade center took on in the context an unintentionally topical significance: had i foreseen this and thus been a priestess of an avant-garde? was it a primordial symbol? was it personal pleasure at producing these giant drawings and the portrayal of the skyscrapers? a feminist critique of the "male world"?

and now this topicalization of images which for export and me myself gain by historical chance a devastatingly false significance – or perhaps not? what does it mean when i have to look at my own art in a consciously historical way because the justified ideological critique of the 1970s and 1980s period has slipped from fluxus-flowing thinking/feeling/testing/performing into final ultimate action/execution? because word/picture has suddenly become a real document of a genuine ultimate deed that is as ultimate as dying? in an aesthetics of tame private picture mobiles – "hi-mum-hi-dad-look-how-i am-doing-well", from snuff porns or hollywood spectaculars that can immediately be broadcast all over the world in real time?

it is as if i would really have had to experience war, have had to hack off peoples limbs in order to be able to portray them like that. it is as if i would have had to have seen dying and dead people in reality in order to be able to reflect on dying and death.
it is as if goya would have had to prompt soldiers or even himself to commit atrocities so that later he could produce his "desastres".
it is the complete rejection of any form of imagination.

in writing this text i hardly manage to capture the eeriness of what is going on here. if exports performance or my drawings seem today to be either an anticipation or a historical document, this could be one of the reasons for the recent development of art in the direction of docuphotography or commissioned art: the idea that only those things are true that have been "experienced", used, purchased, that are "reality" and naturalistically recognizable. everybody knows that torture is universal, but the picture of the woman soldier with her victim as a dog is supposed to be reality because produced by the perpetrator, is supposed to be truer than the picture of exports performance. our pictures are fiction/art, not documents, and hence implausible and useless, thank goodness. for the truth that speaks out of the woman soldiers holiday snap and the concomitant moral outrage worldwide are two sides of the same coin: the refusal to combine information and knowledge with imagination, the refusal to think in aesthetic terms. of course, everyone knows that even the justest war is cruel, that torture is always used. but why does this knowledge not become outrage when faced with the pictures of goya, of export and countless others? because they are art?

i call this "the aesthetic revenge of the proletariate", a concept that occurred to me when for the first time i watched stefan raab instead of harald schmidt. ballermann aesthetics – the woman soldier is now a star, even if a negative one. probably she will be able to capitalize on it.

torture pictures in may 2004

when i see the female soldier who is walking a prisoner on a leash and looking at him with a contemptuous smile i see at the same time valie export walking a man on a leash through the streets of vienna. if in a film I see the world trade center in the background, automatically the pictures of the destruction of the twin towers are switched on in my mind. at the same time i think of my own earlier drawings of the world trade center.

if the pictures of valie exports performance were put on display today, everybody would recall the holiday snaps of the woman soldier with the leash.

something similar happened to my works: in the 1980s i naturally used the symbol of the world trade center as a political and feminist critique, as a symbol for capitalism run wild and US hegemony. and now this icon had been attacked and destroyed. in my exhibition in madrid shortly before the 2nd gulf war the portrayals of the world trade center took on in the context an unintentionally topical significance.

and now this topicalization of images which for export and me myself gain by historical chance a devastatingly false significance. perhaps even their destruction. destruction of the felt thought by action. because word/picture has suddenly become a document of a genuine ultimate deed in an aesthetics of tame private picture mobiles – “hi-mum-hi-dad-look-how-i-am-doing-well”, from snuff porns or in the case of the twin towers of hollywood spectaculars that can immediately be broadcast all over the world in real time.

it is as if i would really have had to experience war, have had to hack off peoples limbs in order to be able subsequently to portray them like that. it is as if i would have had to have seen dying and dead people in reality in order to be able to reflect on dying and death.
it is as if goya would have had to prompt soldiers or even himself to commit atrocities so that later he could produce his “desastres”.
it is the complete rejection of any form of imagination.

if exports performance or my drawings seem today to be either an anticipation or a historical document, this could be one of the reasons for the recent development of art in the direction of docuphotography: the idea that only those things are true that are “experienced”, used, purchased and naturalistically recognizable. everybody knows that torture is universal. but the picture of the woman soldier with her victim as a dog is supposed to be “more real” because it is produced by the perpetrator, is an “aesthetic revenge of the proletariate” via todays technology of instant reproduction. perhaps benjamin is pleased, perhaps however he is turning in his grave.

of course, the comparison of export with the holiday snaps of the woman soldier is false. the only parallel is the gesture: woman walks man on a leash like a dog. exports walking of the dog man through the streets of vienna was in its time a voluntary revolutionary manifesto; the mobile phone greeting of the woman soldier was a record of her job as a demonstration of power. yet anyone who does not have this information to make a distinction will not distinguish, because the final image is identical – woman walks man on a leash like a dog.

it could just as well be a recording of a performance today, which however instantly transmitted worldwide and received actually only by the art-loving public would not lead to a moral outcry like the picture of the woman soldier. thank goodness or what a pity? weakness of art or weakness of so-called "reality"?

when i saw the first holiday snaps of torture i could have bet that the first thing mister rumsfeld would do would be to ban mobile phones with cameras. and thats what happened. today pictures are the strongest medium of all, but only self-portraying docu-aesthetics. just as before modernism photography destroyed paintings function, so today art is changing its function, which does not mean that it itself is being destroyed, on the contrary: everything starts all over again, anew. beuys with his social sculpture, warhol with his 15-minute stars, fluxus with dissolution-and-zen aesthetics, zeitgeist performance and video with and for "everyone" have come to an end reaching their final point. all over again and anew is certainly not to limp along behind docu-aesthetics as in the annoying last documenta. anything but. all the image possibilities that are precisely not applicable and usable in the social or political or aesthetic spheres, that are actually in general and in themselves not applicable and usable.

torture pictures in may 2004

when i see the female soldier who is walking a prisoner on a leash and looking at him with a contemptuous smile i see at the same time valie export walking a man on a leash through the streets of vienna. if in a film I see the world trade center in the background, my mind automatically switches on the pictures of the destruction of the twin towers. at the same time i think of my own earlier drawings of the world trade center.

if the pictures of valie exports performance were put on display today, everybody would recall the holiday snaps of the woman soldier with the leash.

when the world trade centre was attacked i was reading "plateforme" by michel houellebecq. in this context the book unintentionally became well-nigh prophetic. so now this symbol of the economic hegemony of the USA much-used in the 1980s had been attacked and destroyed in reality. in my exhibition in madrid shortly before the 2nd gulf war the portrayals of the world trade center took on in that context an unintentionally topical significance.

and now this topicalization of images which in export/houellebecq/cahn (and others) gain by historical chance a devastatingly false significance. perhaps even their destruction. the destruction of the felt thought by action. because word/picture has suddenly become a document of a genuine ultimate deed in an aesthetics of tame private picture mobiles – "hi-mum-hi-dad-look-how-i-am-doing-well", of snuff porns or in the case of the twin towers of hollywood spectaculars that can immediately be broadcast all over the world in real time.

houellebecq was accused of racism and fascism because one of his characters in the novel talks himself into a hatred of islam. these critics failed to distinguish between a character in a book and the person who wrote it, what prevailed was the usual, popular, makes-good-television, vulgar psychological opinion that art is good only when it is "real", i.e. stemming from experience, i.e. autobiographical. the writer was thus denied any powers of observation, analysis, distance, description, imagination, and actually all that goes into the entire complex work of making art.
it is as if i would really have had to experience war, have had to hack off peoples limbs in order to be able subsequently to portray them like that. it is as if i would have had to have seen dying and dead people in reality in order to be able to reflect on dying and death.
it is as if goya would have had to prompt soldiers or even himself to commit atrocities so that later he could produce his "desastres".
it is the complete rejection of any form of imagination.

exports performance, houellebecqs novel or my drawings seem today to be either an anticipation or a historical document and not a possibility and offer. this could be one of the reasons for the recent development of art in the direction of document: the idea that only those things are true that are "experienced", used, purchased, seen and above all naturalistically recognizable. everybody knows that torture is universal. but the picture of the woman soldier with her victim as a dog is supposed to be "more real" because it is produced by the perpetrator, is an "aesthetic revenge of the proletariate" against the complexity of interpretation via todays technology of instant global reproduction. perhaps benjamin is pleased, perhaps however he is turning in his grave.

of course the comparison of export with the holiday torture snaps of the woman soldier is just as false as the equation of houellebecq with his characters. the only parallel is the gesture: woman walks man on a leash like a dog. exports walking of the dog man through the streets of vienna was in its time a voluntary revolutionary manifesto; the mobile phone greeting of the woman soldier was a record of her job as a holiday greeting and a demonstration of power. yet anyone who does not have this information on the difference will not differentiate, because the final image is identical – woman walks man on a leash like a dog.

the most exciting thing of all today in art is differentiation through information. no: one picture is not like another. despite the vast quantity of pictorial material and the technology of its dissemination. i insist that one picture is not like another, i insist on differentiations, on re-flection, re-thinking after the first felt shock due to déjà-vu. things do not become "true" only when the individual experiences them as "real". i reject formulations such as: i cant judge that, i cant imagine that etc. and above all the expressions so popular over here in (swiss) german: "ich für mich" or "i for myself" (if somebody else is speaking) and the "wie" or "kinda" expressions especially popular among women: "ich bin wie krank" or "im kinda ill" (is she ill or not) "i see kinda nothing" (does she see something or not) and the heightened form: "i kinda cant judge that", "i kinda cant imagine that"…

torture pictures in may 2004
when i see the picture of the female soldier who is walking a prisoner on a leash and looking at him with a smile i see at the same time valie export walking a man on a leash through the streets of vienna. if in a film the world trade center is in the background or is missing, i automatically see the pictures of the destruction of the twin towers. at the same time i think of my own earlier drawings of the world trade center.

if the pictures of valie exports performance were put on display today, everybody would recall the holiday snaps of the woman soldier with the leash.

when the world trade centre was attacked i was reading "plateforme" by michel houellebecq. in this context the book became prophetic. so now this symbol much-used in the art of the 1980s had become an icon attacked and destroyed in reality. in the exhibition in madrid shortly before the 2nd gulf war my old world trade centers became in that context unintentionally topical.

the topicalization of images by historical chance destroys our work through the topical competition of documenting a genuine deed in an aesthetics of tame private picture mobiles, of snuff porns or in the case of the twin towers of hollywood spectaculars. pictorial documents that can immediately be broadcast all over the world in real time.

houellebecq was attacked because one of his characters in the novel talks full of hatred about islam. this criticism fails to distinguish between a character in a book and the person who wrote it. the usual, popular, makes-good-television, vulgar psychological opinion that art is good only when it is "real", i.e. stemming from experience, i.e. autobiographical, denies the writer any powers of observation, analysis, distance, description, imagination, actually all that goes into the entire complex work of making art.

it is as if i would really have had to experience war, have had to have seen dying and dead people in reality in order to be able to reflect and work on dying and death.
it is as if goya would have had to prompt soldiers or himself to commit atrocities so that later he could produce his "desastres".
it is the complete rejection of any form of imagination.
it is the "aesthetic revenge of the proletariate" via todays technology of instant global reproduction against the intellectual complexity of interpretation. perhaps benjamin is pleased, perhaps however he is also turning in his grave.

of course the comparison of export with the holiday torture snaps of the woman soldier is just as false as the equation of houellebecq with his characters. the only parallel is the gesture: woman walks man on a leash like a dog. exports walking of the dog man through the streets of vienna was in its time a revolutionary manifesto; the mobile phone greeting of the woman soldier was a record of her job as a holiday greeting. yet anyone who does not have this information to make the differentiation will not differentiate, because the narrative is identical – woman walks man on a leash like a dog.

yesterday i watched a film about being blind. a girl, a professor, an athlete, a social worker and a voice specialist talked about their perception techniques. The girl painted pictures for another blind person who could still see shadows. The professor described exactly the way to his university, the athlete was a model for the voice specialist, who makes sculptures. the social worker creates perception programmes with his visually impaired clients and in his free time goes jogging with his dog on a short leash. the athlete trains with a colleague to whom he is tied by a short cord attached to his hand.

the professor, who became blind through an illness and so knew what seeing is like, described the difference like this: when he feels around something with his hand or his stick this can happen only one thing after another. in his mind he then fits this felt information together to form a space, which takes time because of the technique of feeling around. seeing, he said, is the grasping of surroundings "at a glance", very fast, which makes the grasping of surroundings through the other senses to a certain extent superfluous. feeling faces on the other hand, he said, was superfluous because in contrast to voice and smell it offered no information and was moreover too intimate.

the social worker described his stick as a part of his body, something like a car for car-drivers, who could feel exactly the length and the breadth, the spatiality of their car in motion like their own body, e.g. when parking. he said it was similar for him as a blind person when moving around with his stick. if he went jogging with his dog beside the river, he preferred to do so alone because friends who could see would describe to him things he didnt want to know about at all e.g. a garbage bag floating in the river. in contrast to sighted people he didnt want to know about the garbage bag in the river because he couldnt get it out of his mind again and it took on an importance and dimensions that impaired his enjoyment of jogging beside the river.

the girl painted bubble-shaped forms, above the blue sky, below the blue water and the brown earth, growing out of the earth green shapes, partly framed in black, and as with every child these were very precise things and stories: a fish, trees, particular flowers, waves in the water and so on. there was not a single difference, not even in the sureness and swiftness of painting, from other sighted children.

in the darwinist sense seeing is for human beings the swiftest technology of survival. thats all.

torture pictures in may 2004

when i see the picture of the female soldier who is walking a prisoner on a leash i see at the same time valie export walking a man on a leash through the streets. if in a film the world trade center is in the background or is missing, i see the pictures of the destruction of the twin towers and think of my own earlier drawings of the world trade center.

if the photographs of valie exports performance were put on display today, everybody would recall the holiday snaps of the woman soldier with the leash.

when the world trade centre was attacked i was reading "plateforme" by michel houellebecq. the book became prophetic through the event. this symbol much-used in the art of the 1980s became an icon destroyed in reality. in the exhibition in madrid shortly before the 2nd gulf war my old world trade centers became in this context unintentionally topical.

the topicalization of images by historical chance destroys our work through the competition of the document of a genuine deed in an aesthetics of tame private picture mobiles, from snuff porns or in the case of the twin towers of hollywood spectaculars. pictorial documents that can immediately be broadcast all over the world in real time.

houellebecq was attacked because one of his characters in the novel speaks full of hatred against islam. this criticism fails to distinguish between a character in a book and the person who wrote it. the usual, popular, makes-good-television, vulgar psychological opinion that art is good only when it is "genuine", i.e. stemming from experience, i.e. autobiographical, denies the writer any powers of observation, analysis, distance, description, imagination, actually all that goes into the entire complex work of making art.

it is as if i would really have had to experience war, have had to have seen dying and dead people in reality in order to be able to reflect and work on war, dying and death.
it is as if goya would have had to prompt soldiers or himself to commit atrocities so that later he could produce his "desastres".
it is the complete rejection of any form of imagination.
it is the "aesthetic revenge of the proletariate" via todays technology of instant global reproduction against the intellectual complexity of interpretation. perhaps benjamin is pleased, perhaps however he is also turning in his grave.

of course the comparison of export with the holiday torture snaps of the woman soldier is just as false as the equation of houellebecq with his characters. the only parallel is the gesture: woman walks man on a leash like a dog. exports walking of the dog man through the streets of vienna was in its time an aggressive revolutionary manifesto, the woman soldier's recording a kind of holiday greeting, showing that she feels good in her job through the exercise of power. yet anyone who does not have this information to make the distinction will not distinguish, because the narrative is identical – woman walks man on a leash like a dog.

yesterday i watched a film about being blind. a girl, a professor, an athlete, a social worker and a voice specialist talked about their perception techniques. the girl paints pictures for the social worker, who can still see shadows. the professor describes the way to his university while walking. the athlete is a model for the sculptures of the artist/voice specialist, who teaches actors how to apprehend their body and space via the sound of their voices. the social worker creates perception programmes with his visually impaired clients and in his free time goes jogging along the river with his dog on a short leash. the athlete practises his sprints with a colleague to whom he is tied by a short cord attached to his hand.

the professor, who became blind through an illness, described the difference between seeing/not seeing like this: when he feels around something with his hand or his stick this can happen only one thing after another. in his mind he then fits this felt information together to form a space, which takes time because of the technique of feeling around. seeing "at a glance", he said, was a human beings swiftest and best technique of survival for apprehending space. he would, he said, have had to forget the process of seeing completely in order to be able to use the other senses in line with their qualities. feeling faces on the other hand, he said, was too intimate and in contrast to voice and smell offered no information.

the social worker described his stick as a part of his body used to apprehend space while walking something like the way car-drivers felt their car as a part of their body when driving. when jogging beside the river, he said, he preferred to be alone with his dog, whose movements were information for him just as the river gave him orientation through its sounds and smells. sighted people however would describe to him things he didnt want to know about at all. a garbage bag floating in the river would when described become so big in his mind that he couldnt get it out of his mind again and it impaired him when jogging. anyway, he said, the description mania of sighted people when faced with blind people was colonial.

the girl painted a light blue strip above, and below a greenish oval with dots on a dark blue background and a brown strip out of which green things were growing upwards, and in addition vertical and horizontal black strips. while painting the blind child described to the blind man what she was painting, and as with every child these were very precise things and long stories accompanying them. i saw no difference in the portrayal, the sureness, concentration and swiftness of painting from sighted children, whose pictures i do not understand without their interpretations of them. what i see are offers, possibilities, configurations.

torture pictures in may 2004

yesterday i watched a film about being blind. a girl, a professor, an athlete, a social worker and a voice specialist talked about their day-to-day lives and demonstrated their survival techniques for a life without sight.

the girl painted a picture for the social worker. the professor described the way to his university while walking. the social worker created perception programmes with his visually impaired clients and in his free time went jogging along the river with his dog on a short leash. the athlete practised his sprints and runs with a colleague to whom he was tied by a short cord attached to his hand.

the professor, who became blind through an illness, described the difference between seeing/not seeing like this: when he feels around something with his hand or his stick this can happen only one thing after another. in his mind he then fits this felt information together to form a space, which takes time because of the technique of feeling around. seeing "at a glance", he said, was a human beings swiftest and best technique of survival for apprehending space. he would, he said, have had to forget the process of seeing completely in order to be able to use the other senses in line with their qualities. feeling/palpating faces on the other hand was too intimate and in contrast to voice and smell offered no information.

the social worker described his stick as a part of his body used to apprehend space while walking something like the way car-drivers feel their car as an elongated part of their body when driving and manoeuvring. when jogging beside the river, he said, he preferred to be alone with his dog, whose movements were information for him. the river gave him orientation through its sounds and smells. sighted people however would describe to him things he didnt want to know about at all. a garbage bag floating in the river would in their descriptions become so big in his mind that he couldnt get it out of his mind again and it impaired him when jogging. anyway, he said, the description mania of sighted people when faced with blind people was unpleasant.

the athlete spoke of his feet as tools for a liberating suspension of gravity. because when running they were for a short moment always both in the air. moreover through his movements he could apprehend the exact length of the dirt track and perhaps even the space of the arena. although he had won the bronze medal in the paralympics he was, he said, clear about the fact that he could never run faster than his partner, to whom he was attached by a short cord.

the girl painted a light blue strip above, and below a greenish oval with dots on a dark blue background and over it a brown strip with green configurations growing upwards and various black lines and edgings. while painting the blind child continually described to the blind man what she was painting, and as with every child these were precise things and long stories accompanying them. i saw no difference in the portrayal, the sureness, concentration and swiftness of painting from sighted children, whose pictures i do not understand without their interpretation of them. what i see are offers, possibilities, configurations, pictures.

ART/WOMAN Project on the Thematization of the "Feminine" in Art
Anna + Bernhard Blume Cologne, 8 April 89

Following the nomination of the psychologist Ms Adrienne Göhler to be the new President of the HfBK,[52] we as initiators of the planned two-semester lecture/workshop programme "ART/WOMAN / Project on the Thematization of the Feminine in Art" find ourselves confronted with an ideologized situation that leads us to provisionally suspend the project.

It seems to us no longer guaranteed that our commitment to an unbiased and long-term problematization and pedagogical reinforcement of the specifically feminine in art will not be instrumentalized and hence abused by the supporters of this candidate.

Precisely in our capacity as artists committed to feminism, we must protest against a situation in which the evident and – we fear – irremediable ignorance of this candidate concerning the complex phenomenon of art (as evidenced in her trial lecture, which has unfortunately only now been made available) should be objectively concealed and subjectively compensated for by the politico-moral avowal of "being a feminist".

Anna + Bernhard Blume[53]

---

miriam cahn
strassburgerallee 68
CH-4055 basle basle, 14 april 89

dear anna and bernhard blume,
i am not in agreement with you abandoning the WOMAN/ART series on the grounds of the current discussions surrounding the election of adrienne goehler. the "professional" protest letter with its telephone-created and hence imprecise collection of signatures from celebrities in the art world conceals massive hostility towards women – and this has no place in your programme?
yet it TOO is a constituent part of the "thematization of the feminine in art".
i have read adrienne göhler's trial lecture and i see nothing at all to justify this outcry from the "academic" art world. i would consider it at least normal for adrienne gohler to be given the opportunity to try to do the job of director in her way – things cannot get much worse at this fossilized academy. every other candidate would have had this opportunity too – and hostility to women is NOT the problem of women.
what I also find Intolerable Is your anxiety that we, the invited speakers, and thus your idea of "WOMAN/ART" would be "instrumentalized by the supporters of this candidate".
how influenceable and stupid do you think i am actually?
when i come to an academy to present my work, then i do just that and don't allow myself to be "instrumentalized". THE FACT THAT my work makes connections between woman/art and these age-old misogynous incriminations launched under the pretext of a lack of qualifications is something that I would naturally include for topical reasons – and this you are afraid of?

or are you afraid – I hope not – of the “academic” art people, who in the analysis of the topic WOMAN/ART come off just as well or as badly as the “other” people?
since your retreat leaves the students once again devoid of information about the various types of feminism and art, and since your reaction enrages me, i am still prepared to take part in your lecture series – not in the never-never-land of the future but NOW.
greetings, your miriam
P.S. copies sent to adrienne goehler and the academy’s student union.

miriam cahn
strassburgerallee 68
CH-4055 basle **basle, 30 july 89**

dear adrienne goehler,
many thanks for your letter – and warm congratulations on your appointment and "admission to the stables" (horrible german phrase).
you are right to say that male dominance over aesthetics must go. the stupid thing is just that, for the time being, i really do not want to have a teaching post, not even in the form of a visiting professorship. the reasons for this lie in my work: at the moment i cannot possibly combine this form of "rhythmical, cyclical" working – my work procedure – with a pedagogical, teaching stance: it simply can't be done.
on this issue, i am absolutely "old-fashioned", and i think i am still too young for it – could well be that i become a good teacher later on.
in the catalogue which i have sent to you or your office, there is an answer i wrote to a similar inquiry from munich – an answer which, if i read it again today, is only in part true for me now: at that time, i considered these old academies to be more or less as hopeless as the swiss army – namely absolutely superfluous and not worth women applying for. – today, i still consider the swiss army superfluous, but academies should have as many women teachers as possible only not precisely me at the present moment.
experience shows that even the most "open-minded" men in the art business can think of the names of only 2–3 women, be it for major exhibitions or as professors. for this reason, i'm sending you here another list containing "my" women artists, i.e. i consider each of these women to be of high quality and each interesting in her particular way.
what i would find interesting, however, and would do without hesitation would be contributions to topic-based events or symposia or whatever – also in interdisciplinary form, which would, after all, be an obvious approach for your academy. by now, there are women architects and women graphic designers, feminist art studies, perhaps women engineers, women photographers etc., etc., etc., who could be brought together under certain topic headings that re-define the concept of work in the context of woman-ness. the point is that it is not enough to have more women professors – we must get it into the brains of men AND women that, for about twenty years now, working as a woman has been something new, perhaps, who knows, something trail-blazing for the future. who knows?
in my experience with academies, what is missing above all are impulses from outside – and that would be my ticket: a swift jump into the lukewarm water of the academy, and then off i go again. (i assume that the warm receptions i get from audiences at my public lectures result from precisely this procedure.)
well, again i wish you all the best for your start and steady nerves and plenty of strength – with warm regards,
your m. cahn

ACADEMY OF FINE ARTS HAMBURG
der präsident (crossed out) die präsidentin
4 August 89

Dear Miriam Cahn,

Thank you for your letter and your congratulations/ good luck wishes, which I shall certainly need.
I have still to track down the catalogue that you kindly sent – I have unfortunately never received it.
As you can imagine, I am disappointed that the wonderful women always react so seriously and reflectively at the point where men do not have the slightest difficulty – namely in their self-evaluation.
You will certainly soon receive a letter from a woman literary scholar. I will be most interested to hear what you think of the idea.
At any event, I look forward to meeting you sometime and perhaps, after all, to enlisting your services.
With warmest regards,
Your
Adrienne Goehler
P.S. Many thanks for the excellent list of women!

THE SUBTLE ABYSS: Sexuality/Body Image/Language in Contemporary Feminist Art
McLellan Galleries in Glasgow **Basle, 7 August 89**

dear Hilary Robinson,
thank you very much for your letter. but I am sorry, I can't participate in your project. I think this sort of feminist exhibition is 5 to 8 years too late – the last one "kunst mit eigen-sinn" in vienna 1985[54] showed very clearly the end of this sort of feminist show. this doesn't mean for me that feminism is out of art – on the contrary. but for me lucy lippard, hélène cixous, luce irigaray are the very important "grandmothers" of feminist aesthetics, but today is today. I am sorry: my english is too bad to explain it exactly: "today is today" means: after 20 years of very much working by feminist and women artists it is high time for museums to include women artists in their programme with the same normality as men-artists – and not: "let's do a feminist art-exhibition" – and then over the years again nothing moves, because we had our minority exhibition. and it is high time for us women artists to be more demanding about shows and not to be glad about everything we can get – just because we are women and have to be grateful to show – just because we are still discriminated against – no, that is not my way. I hope you understand.
sincerely yours,
miriam cahn

braunschweig university of art: invitation to apply for a professorship in painting **basle, 22 november 89**

dear h.p. zimmer,[55]

many thanks for your inquiry as to whether i would like to apply for a professorship. just as much as you and the female student representatives in the appointment commission, i consider it a disgrace that in braunschweig as well there is only one woman professor among the teaching staff. the stupid thing is that i myself have no wish at all to have a teaching post: from the point of view of my work, i cannot possibly imagine having a professorship – the way in which i work cannot be combined with the attitude and stance of a teacher. that may not be the case for ever and a day, but it is at the moment. on the other hand, what i do really enjoy doing from time to time is delivering a guest lecture about my work – preferably in a context in which the wretched situation concerning the absence of women professors and the very few internationally renowned women artists is thematized. i know that this sounds contradictory: on the one hand, kicking up a great fuss about the backwoods-like conditions in the academies and then oneself always refusing when one might have possibilities of gaining a professorship. but for me politics is really being able to do what i want to do – and not any wrongly conceived acts of solidarity.

i'm including, however, a list of women artists whom i consider good and whom you could ask just as well as me.

with warm thanks and wishing you good luck,

miriam cahn

Postcard of the Cathedral in Ancona
12 September 84

Miriam, Thanks for the photos. THEY LOOK INCREDIBLY GOOD! You've hit the nail on the head here if I might put it like that. They're lying in front of me and that's where they'll be staying for some time. I must purify myself in your storms.
A big hug,
Your Jeanchristophe[56]

Postcard: Barbara Kruger, "Your every wish is our command" **5 January 86**

Dear Miriam,
Today I was in Baden-Baden and went to see your FINE (!) exhibition.[57]
The astonishing thing is how you are becoming more and more "pictorial" and perhaps it won't be so long before you are painting black pictures. That's not wishful thinking on my part, not at all! Precisely your small works seem like a beleaguered breast breathing in and out.
The custodian was very much on his toes and kept a strict eye on me while I was taking slides. On the day your exhibition opened I was in Madrid. Actually, I wanted to go today with E. Kaufmann,[37] but then it didn't work out. I wish you good health and joy in the New Year and remain with a firm kiss Your Jeanchristophe
(Secretary of the M. C. Fan Club)

3 December 87

Dear Miriam,
Here are the slides returned. Many thanks for them. Was able to put them to good use.
Once again, we're totally and utterly involved in the Christmas Exhibition, this time even with a MUBA trade fair hall[58] included ...! (The 1st floor is being renovated).
Hope things are well with you. Now that you've been living so long in my city of birth, you'll soon be saying: "Icke bin eene Berlinerin"
A kiss from Jeanchristophe

26 January 88

Dear Miriam,
I think we need to understand one another properly: feminism as understood today is a form of the ideology from the late 60s and 70s. I think it is important – or, it was important for me – not to associate R.M. with the ideology, which is also foreign to her as a member of the younger generation.
But I'll talk about this with her. Thanks for the tip-off
I'm very pleased that you have read the programme ... (How many do?)
A kiss from Jeanchristophe

Postcard showing a detail of the statua del Tevere
6 July 89

Dear Miriam,
You send me a lion with bared teeth and I send you a man with gruuuesome lips. Imagine him giving trying

to give you a French kiss …
Thanks for your postcards. Paid a quick visit to Basle – unfortunately only very brief – but saw your work in the Stampa Gallery, and so have an idea of what you are producing. See that you're immersed in the basic research stage and am really curious about what will emerge. Hope to get in touch soon. Many fond wishes from your Jeanchristophe

postcard of Bernhard Blume, "Im Wahnzimmer" ["In the madness room"] 19 January 90

You know, Miriam, it's strange how our thoughts "cross". Found your text very striking. (But resistance is forming.)
Many fond wishes from
Jeanchristophe
P.S. Thanks for the appealing rebarbative "dry" invitation

3 February 91

Dear Miriam,
You know, I am always glad when you write me a few hefty lines. This war,[59] Miriam, is the product of an unspeakable colonial policy, which is now decades in the past. Saddam Hussein is a rogue. In 1963, the Kuwaitis bought their freedom from the Iraqis for the equivalent of DM 330 million, just for the sake of peace and quiet, because Iraq had no claim to these "few square kilometres". Here in Germany there are many anti-American demonstrations. I am not against the Americans. As long as there is injustice and injustice has been done, collective memory will always hit back, and that means war, in whatever form and with whatever means. War is unspeakable, like hitting someone. What does one do when somebody wants to be hit? Because as the person who's been hit he can give the other person the blame? Do you understand? Miriam, we'll do something together. At present I'm under dire pressure. We're opening on 6 June. On 14 February I have to deliver a talk to the SPD council members in the Town Hall on the exhibition hall project. Keep your fingers crossed for me. The money's getting tight. But for us too there are possibilities, on a limited scale. We'll make a room – and tremble together.
A firm hug for you from your
Jeanchristophe

5 January 1992

Dear Miriam,
Have never thanked you for your Kunsthaus Zürich documentation. This I now do and thanks too for the greetings with the super cactus drawing!
There is still no final decision on our exhibition hall and so in approx. mid-year I will do as follows:
[elevation drawing of the planned room]
This means that we are getting a large, but also difficult room space because there is a) no right angle and b) the parquet floor surface is laid out relative to an imaginary point. I have had a model constructed and would like to show it to you. IT WOULD BE WONDERFUL IF YOU COULD DO SOMETHING HERE. Best of all

would be: straightaway in summer for a few months. But I don't know if that's possible if one hasn't seen the space and if the wall – i.e. the new wall – is not yet in place. You'd have to judge that yourself.
TELL ME WHAT YOU THINK.
I'd also be pleased to send you an official letter of invitation to come and assess the situation on the spot.
A fond kiss from
Jeanchristophe

FAX an Miriam Cahn N.Y.C.
001/212/533 *** **7 February 92**
Dear Miriam,
I think that you can install your work here from 25 May onwards.
Then you can start here, so to say, with the documenta.
...
A firm kiss from
Jeanchristophe

STADT FRANKFURT AM MAIN
MMK Museum of Modern Art
Invitation to the Opening of the New Exhibition Spaces on Saturday, 6 June 1992, at 18.00 hrs.
Dear Friends of the Museum,
On 6 June of this year, the Museum will be exactly one year old. In January, we presented eight new exhibition spaces; now there is again a larger number. Szenenwechsel [Change of scene].
In the central hall, 57 Penguins by Stephan Balkenhol will be on display. In an adjoining room, we will be showing works by Richard Artschwager, Ed Ruscha, Bruce Naumann and Rosemarie Trockel. On the mezzanine floor, Barbara Klemm will be showing the third part of her exhibition with photographs on "China and India". In the triangular room on the intermediate level we will be presenting a multi-part work by Miriam Cahn. (The Pop Art from the Ströher Collection remains on the same level but moves into the Museum's newly-designed western part.) Further rooms house work groups by Jochen Flinzer, Andreas Slominski and Thomas Bayrle.
It would be a great pleasure to welcome you to the Opening of the New Gallery Spaces in the Museum of Modern Art (MMK), Frankfurt am Main, on Saturday, 6 June 1992 at 18 hrs.
Yours Sincerely,
Jean-Christophe Ammann

1 February 93
Dear Miriam,
Yes, you're right: we talk our heads off and already it's there in the newspapers to read ...
The name of the donor who helped us to purchase your work-group is IGNAZ BUBIS.[60] He did so on the occasion of being awarded the Ehrenplakette [Badge of Honour] of the City of Frankfurt am Main on 21 January 93.
I didn't want to tell you this on tape and last week I didn't

get around to it ("Szenenwechsel III" [Change of Scene III]": re-hanging, re-arranging, guided tour for press, guided tour for the Friends of the Museum (100 people), Opening Night on Friday (600 people) ...).
A firm hug,
Your Jeanchristophe

basle, 18 may 93

dear jean-christophe,
here's something that happened to me yesterday: one of the most interesting female museum directors gave a talk about her work. I've known her for thirteen years and love her way of speaking in public: she walks to and fro slowly and with great concentration; her eyes and her expansive arm movements underscore her words, which are a very personal language in the sense of the personal = the public, the private = the political. she passionately loves her job of being a mediator of art and working together with her women artists. this comes through in her talks, which are highly precise and informative.
she was talking about the assembly and construction of her museum, the museum of modern art in frankfurt. she spoke humorously about the political wrangling with the lady mayor, the female head of the culture department and the construction office, and about amusing misunderstandings in the struggle with the woman architect for better exhibition spaces (this female architect took offence at the description of the stairway as a "via mala", until she herself saw the via mala gorge); she spoke about her exhibition space strategies evolved in close co-operation with the women artists, about issues of money, space, publicity and other matters that go hand in hand with her unique collecting policy for this museum – in short, her talk was a pleasure.
she also showed slides of the individual exhibition rooms and of works by a selection of women artists and, in an informative and personal way, she analysed the works and underlying attitudes of women artists such as hildegard baumgarten, andrea slominski, maria stumpf (i really love her work) and stefanie balkenhol. and i also found interesting her interpretation of reinette zaugg ('hier, dort, ici'), whom i perhaps don't love but now understand better.
in comparison to other collections of contemporary art, the frankfurt museum of modern art contains quite a few men artists; in the "szenenwechsel" there were unfortunately too few or no young ones – is that a result of the so-called "backlash", with which you are familiar? however that may be, in the selection she made for her talk i was the only male artist represented, which is on the one hand an honour, but on the other hand a source of anger, because that turns me into an alibi or token man, which, one hopes, is not her intention. what really offended me, however, was that when she cited the title of my work she made such a characteristic lapsus: "1 male month" became on her lips simply "1 month".
where was underlying attitude, the method, the physicality, the heart of this work? the male cycle element, which determines the way the room was hung? Is it SO difficult for her to utter the word "male"? was it habit, after she had spoken throughout her entire talk of women artists? (a procedure i'll never grow accustomed to because in point of fact it makes no reference to me.)
wounded in my masculinity – and hence unsure of myself – and hence ineptly I tried after the talk to make clear to her that this is

no way to go about things. her lovely dark eyes looked down at me in friendly fashion as if i came from mars.
i am writing to you because as a fellow member of our gender and as a fellow sufferer you are familiar with such situations. i am writing to you because you know that i don't believe in understanding between man and woman, but in the observing, seeing, precise perception by men of women (and vice versa). in my new works I am trying precisely that – this, i hope, new seeing, observing by men of women, and in fact the more i work the less i understand …
kiss! Your CATO

postcard: Ludwig von Hofmann (1861–1945), 'das verlorene paradies' [paradise lost] 31 May 93

Dear Miriam,
As you can see, your wonderful letter has left me totally deflated. Once again, you have hauled me over the coals and rightly so. Many thanks and fond greetings from
Jean-Christophe

(letter to Monika Dillier) 14 June 93

Dear Miriam,
I referred to you in a kind of sudden "inspiration" …
Many fond wishes
JCH

Dear Monika,
Thank you for your letter, which was a great pleasure. Everything you say is quite right, but that would have been a different topic. In SUCH a talk, I have to put myself into the position of the artists. If I choose this or that work, I can also MUSE over it, and I would like to do so in line with your wishes.
You know, Monika, I think – putting it very subjectively – that women today have the greatest drive. They deal with intimacy in such a matter-of-fact way that the men get the wind up. I experience this in the art history seminars – three of them – that we host here in the Museum. Women are and remain my Great Hope, and some time or other that must come through. The women – the young ones – are miles ahead of the men – not only the young ones (I correct myself) – but in the fine arts it is still hard to substantialize this. The drive is looking for the appropriate form!
If SUE WILLIAMS[61] writes in a letter, "When I piss on your face, I expect a 'Good Morning, how are you?'", then at first she can only write it, and only wants to write it, because there is no other form for it, since any other form, apart from the written, would probably be anecdotal, just as the much celebrated Louise Bourgeois,[62] whom I also admire, is anecdotal much too often.
If a woman says, "I want to fuck you" (to a man), she scares him right to his innermost being – and men today are in large part scared – but what FORM do I give to this "I want to fuck you"? (You understand, Monika, and you know me well enough, that these are metaphors.) If there is a form specific to women, then

MIRIAM CAHN has supplied a not inconsiderable part of it. She doesn't see what she does, because women do not see their sexual parts, unless they take a mirror like Anaïs Nin. A man, on the other hand, has his "apparatus" IN FRONT OF HIS EYES and IN HIS GRASP. I think that this is a major difference anthropologically. Many fond wishes to you, Monika, and
Warm greetings,
Jeanchristophe

il fait très beau [glorious weather]

Dimanche le 28. juin, [Sunday, 28 June] (1993 ?)

Dear Miriam,
Warm thanks for your drawing, was very pleased to receive it. However, I never spoke of "time-sex?"... No idea what that is. Tantric 6 hours / 12 hours union? For me that would be beyond Good and Evil – (for you too, I think). I never said anything about "Sex is a time-bomb" nor about "time is a sex-bomb" or "bomb is a sex-time" or "time-sex", nor again about sex being related to time as time to sex, or sex + time = mc2 (or sex times time = size x speed squared (when the orgasm hurtles through the brain at the speed of light).
I think one can talk about such things, best of all with Stampa when he's clambering up a rock-face, or with Gilli[41] when I've protruded my Dracula teeth again and her sweet blood is flowing through my centuries-old veins.
Have just been in Barcelona, co-awarded the Olimpiada Cultural Sculpture Prize to Siah Armajani, was at the seaside with Judith, then back to Barcelona (lecture and seminar), showed extensive SLIDES OF YOU – holy smoke, nom de bleu – all in 10 days, Judith's coming back on Tuesday, she'll be very pleased at your book. Today, Sunday, I've been dealing with the post – nibbling away at the Mont Blanc massif, and it's been huge fun to write to you. A smacker from JCH.

(with photo-portrait of m.c. by Rolf Kleinstein)

8 November 93

Dear Miriam,
Didn't make it to your exhibition[63] in Zurich after all. Many thanks for the wonderfully attractive catalogue. We've got terrible financial problems here. Absolute state of emergency.
But, as you know: "A la guerre comme à la guerre" [We'll just have to muddle through]
No running away from responsibility!
A firm embrace
Your Jeanchristophe

FAX **basle, 10 march 94**

dear jean-christophe,
as thanks for the trouble you took with the recommendation (it worked, i'll be in offenbach next semester), here's the draft plan, which i like because it's a "pupil-work-avoidance" plan and contact sheets with – a very few – of the latest works i've been making.
the gloves are merely the tools, cotton gloves with emery paper glued on, with which i make my 'sculptures' (if wood, then also

carving) and also very thin copper and aluminium plates, which peter kneubühler[64] then prints. a few are also illustrated here and i really wonder whether you see the difference these printed things and the others. the coloured things are partly painted – pigment/ water + a 'carrier' such as egg, glue etc. depending on circumstances. all the dust particles that arise when working with the gloves I keep and they are then also rubbed into the paper or combined with the 'carriers' depending on the case. and, of course, always also chalk/pigment. Content remains: unnameable – lying – sarajevo – WAS MICH ANSCHAUT [see pp. 131ff.].
of course, there is much more than pictured here. it would be good – but of course there's no hurry – if you could come and look at it all.
and otherwise: how are you doing? and Judith?
greetings + kiss,
miriam

GRAND HOTEL BEAU RIVAGE INTERLAKEN
10 September 94

Dear Miriam,
We are here over the weekend, celebrating my parents' diamond wedding anniversary. Thank you for your letter. Didn't know that you're in such a bad way, or rather already on the mend. My best wishes for a steady recovery from your complaints accompany you. And those of my parents, whom I've told about you.
Miriam, we'll have to postpone your room from January 1995 to June 1995. I have to bring something forward as a matter of urgency. Perhaps that's not such a bad thing in view of your slipped disc. At any event you'll be in the annual programme for 1995. As far as the performance is concerned, we can talk about it. At any event, I've learned something about it from what you've told.
Please take great care. Let the phase of healing be HEALING. I embrace you, and my parents and Judith send their heartfelt greetings. Your Jeanchristophe

Postcard: Christine Bernhard ? (handwritten)
20 May 95

Dear, truly dear Miriam. My heartfelt thanks for the grand and convincing effort you put in. Today, I took "my" students to study your works, for a whole hour, and it was really intense. I read your book with great enjoyment on my journey to Venice. It is very gripping and revealing because all of the figures, without any exception, are INCORPOREAL creatures, who busily go about their everyday lives and become entangled in emotions like elves: pleasure and pain with no bodily echo. A firm embrace Your ICH

Postcard: Frida Kahlo, 'Two Nudes in the Wood' (1939)
24 August 96

Dear Miriam, all the best of luck in London. We've made a note of your address. Now your big, black tree is hanging downstairs in the triangular room with Ruthenbeck[65] and his heaps of ashes and some pictures by Axel Kasseböhmer,[66] which are surprisingly related thematically. Last Wednesday, I did a guided tour

of the three of you for – oh heavens, 200 people. Was well received. But it's a real struggle for me to overcome my weaker self and inner resistance. It's damp here.
A firm hug, take care, Your Jeanchristophe

28 May 97

Dear Miriam,
I'm so pleased about the choice of pictures we made. It is simply FINE.
Can you please send me the PHOTOS and the "final price" (would be good if it could be in DM).
I'm writing to you for one thing because I'm hugely pleased and for another thing because I've already started on the "Fund Raising". (I've already got 15,000.)
Customs dues have to be added to the price because CH is not in the EC. So we'll have to make a favourable CUSTOMS PRICE.
Fond greetings from
Jeanchristophe
Your "drawing" is already hanging in my office ...

18 June 97

MIRIAM
TREASURE!
Thanks for your Letter and suggestion (verrry good!)
Erich Ganzert, my restorer, will be getting in touch with you.
A kiss from
Jeanchristophe

FAX

to: Jean-Christophe Ammann **maloja, 14 july 97**

dear jean-christophe,
am thrilled! + will be standing there on 27 oct. ...
i have rented a flat in maloja, where I also work – tel/fax 081/*** for the next few weeks
(drawing of mountain peaks) the prize is just fantastic, am still over the moon
kiss, miriam

FAX

an : ammann **basle, 9 september 97**

dear jean-christophe,
today I chucked your pictures into the depths of the official transport system – did you also have to sob so much at Diana's funeral procession?[67]
kiss miriam
(drawing: I throw the pictures into an abyss)

Karl-Ströher-Stiftung
Frankfurt am Main **29 July 97**

(handwritten): Prize-giving Ceremony 27 October 1997 The pictures will be on display probably from June 1998
DECISION OF SELECTION COMMITTEE
The Board of Trustees of the Karl Ströher Foundation has decided to award its Prize for the year 1997 to Ms Miriam Cahn. The Prize money is DM 20,000. In addition, the Foundation will purchase from Ms Cahn works of art to the value of DM 20,000, which will be made available on loan to the Museum of Modern Art,

Frankfurt.
Frankfurt, 14 July 1997
Ulrike Crespo
Rainald Pohl
Dr. Jean Ammann
(handwritten):
Miriam, dear,
If this is okay by you, we can do things as follows:
DM 40,000.- Ströher Foundation
DM 30,000.- Nassauische Sparkasse
DM 20,000.- Friends of the MMK

DM 90,000.-
Fond greetings from
Jeanchristophe

FAX **maloja, 10 august 97**

dear jean-christophe,
coming back to the ströher prize and the financing of the purchase of my works by the MMK:
the way YOU suggest is NOT possible.
with the 1:1 exchange rate sfr-dm I have already given you approx. 20% discount. and it's absurdly abstruse if, in addition, I am to help finance the purchase of MY works with 20,000 dm of MY prize – no way, absolutely not.
the way I now see it is as follows:
you drum up another dm 20,000 so that the bill then looks like this:

purchase dm 90,000
prize money dm 20,000
----
total cahn dm 110,000

or I supply 1–2 pictures fewer – with you, of course, choosing which:

purchase: dm 70,000
prize money: dm 20,000
----
total cahn: dm 90,000

there are no other possibilities. I am an ARTIST, not a sponsor of the MMK – with all respect …
please get this mess of YOUR making in order again –
kiss, miriam

FAX **basle, 17 march 98**

dear Jean-christophe,
I'm looking forward to 28 May – it's great that by then your pictures will be hanging.
now the following issue: I have problems myself to hang 12 pictures in a room. normally I hang "many", "full", "too full", "too many", and there's a reason for this, namely the provisional, transitory element, the idea rather than "the work", and this is also true for the oil paintings, where actually I dissolve the oil-painting-ness, just as previously I dissolved the so-called drawing-ness through the sheer size and quantity.
how to proceed in your case: the best thing, I reckon, would be to go ahead in a pretty "cool" way, as things have turned out, i.e. YOU hang the 12 pictures in the room, because it is YOUR choice made from a pretty large pile in my studio. that's also the interesting thing about these new works, that the act of choosing makes the

"exhibition" in contrast to the earlier works, which were more determined by me.
find it still difficult to explain what the difference is to previously; at any rate, the oil paintings are somehow "more social", i.e. if someone chooses from a pile of works, as you did, then at the same time the "responsibility-for-hanging" (phrase just invented) is transferred to you – to you personally, not to Mario[68] or anyone else. and this a big difference to the room of my works that you also have – there, the "responsibility-for-hanging" lies with me.
another attempt to explain: when last summer I did the exhibition "I as human being" at STAMPA, the following happened: gilli and stampa chose in advance a relatively large pile from the huge pile in my studio and then we hung them in their exhibition rooms. I tried to hang in my mutually dissolving manner and that didn't work in practice. I then left it to the two of them and that way it did work, and it wasn't foreign to me, but it was simply different. a kind of trust that seems to the distrustful animal I am very human – and so the exhibition title turned out to be absolutely spot-on, although I couldn't know that in advance …
does that make sense to you? I simply can't explain, no more than you probably know why you chose precisely these 12 pictures from that huge heap … and that's precisely the interesting thing, which we make something of for this bank evening, don't you think?
e.g. like this: you (not mario) hang the 12 pictures in this fine, closed exhibition space. I come along as the "inspecteur des travaux finis" [building site inspector], and in the evening we can talk about it in front of these bank people – I think that this entire procedure (artist's studio – choice of pictures – mediation with/without the artist's co-operation) is interesting. In addition, I then have something to do on this bank evening, and don't have to just stand around in a dumb representational role – which I utterly hate …
this is just a kind of basic idea – we can do things differently, am open for anything, except for representational rubbish …
on 27 September 98 I am being awarded the käthe kollwitz prize in berlin + opening of the exhibition in the akademie der künste, where I'll be showing the latest stuff in one of these strange exhibition spaces.
kiss and looking forward to doing something with you again.
miriam

---

postcard: Max Ernst, 'hausengel' ["house angel"] with the additional words 'JCH dances for Miriam …'

2 February 98

Dear Miriam, When I saw my thumb, I was reminded of Max Ernst's "Hausengel" from the year 1937 … (Not good associations as far the pictorial comparison goes). I was very pleased to get the small picture and send you heartfelt thanks.
A hug and a kiss,
Your Jeanchristophe.

---

21 March 98

Miriam,
I'm choosing squared paper, so as to get the strong emotions into order as you would like. I'll do my best!
Whether I can do justice to your ideas I don't know. At present I tend towards a "conservative" conception of the presentation of your works: each work a small

nuclear power station without radioactive radiation. I'm preparing myself inwardly. The hand with the thumb looks at me every morning. I move my thumb and practice with my thumb. Everything you have sent me is hanging on my walls so that I can practice – in mind and in movement: "Do you get it?" Today is my mother's birthday, on 21.03.98 she becomes 85! What will we do if we reach that age some day?
Miriam Cahn invites JCHA to a cup of tea: "Can you still remember back then ...?" "Listen, do you still make pornographic drawings ...?"
Many fond wishes from Jeanchristophe

pink paper **11 October 98**
MIRIAM
1) Congratulations on the prize, thanks for the catalogues
2) Mario Kramer said that your room in Berlin was absolutely the best thing he had seen in the framework on the Berlin Biennale etc.
3) Bob Haozous is an Indian chieftain and he looked at your poster on an Indian reservation. Frau Dorothee Peiper-Riegraf[69] wrote down – sort of – what he said.
A kiss from Housi-Chrigu
In response to your request, I gave Bob Haozous the MMK's Miriam Cahn poster.
"I choose the female form simply because I think that we are all related to the earth in the male-female way. Reproduction is male and female and the pregnant woman is a symbol of the continuous ... Just the thought of a woman, combined with a structural material, a structural shape really seemed like a contradiction. It's the contradiction I really loved about the piece ... The breasts again are very important. The print you gave me of the lady with the breasts, the Swiss lady – it's just beautiful! It's a symbol of differences. It's a symbol of rebirth, of sharing. How much closer to the earth can you be than feeding someone from your body ..."

fax
richter cahn
sils
waldhaus silsersee
haus: tita carloni **maloja, 15 november 98**
dear jean-christophe,
a few days ago, I zapped on your head by chance, and since I was naturally pleased to see you here in maloja, I stuck there (3sat).
on kippenberger:[70] I considered this exhibition to be approximately the meanest and falsest thing that can be inflicted on an artist who has just died – namely to deliberately show only one part, selected by technique and thus, precisely with kippenberger, to destroy the context, the heart of his work, by stylizing him in schoolmasterly fashion into a "painter", in order to show that he was "nevertheless" a good artist ... and you fell for it and are now wild about his painting. to my mind, kippenberger was always too much the "paris bar german artist" of the 1980s. but this exhibition is a pillaging of the dead and robs him of his selfhood.
and now to the other source of annoyance (apart from heisig,[71]

who is completely beyond the pale, as you said in the sole redeeming moment in this broadcast): richter.[72] I know, I know, as soon as anyone talks in germany about nature, landscape or – even worse! – the alps, there are only 3 possibilities: the green party, caspar david friedrich and berchtesgaden.
why, please, should richter's landscapes be "sweet" or "kitschy" and not other pictures of his painted in like manner? because they are landscapes and hence nature? and why should he not stick photographs of his young wife with their child next to third reich extermination photos, if it is in the context of his overall material work ATLAS?
richter is an artist of the unportrayable EVERYTHING, and thus at all events topical and interesting and here I have no desire to listen to your jabber limited to questions of taste, personal preferences and self-righteous political correctness. your round-table discussions don't even have the intellectual level of the "literarisches quartett", which is at least eloquent, witty and malicious, and therefore as the case may be amusing to watch, even if one doesn't agree at all.
no way, no way, jean-christophe, what are you up to in this schoolmasterly talk session – sometimes no mediation is better than such wretched mediation …
here are 2 cuttings from today's NZZ,[73] where there was by chance an excellent article about richter, and then to conclude: when I go walking here in the mountains, absolutely out of season, no tourist, no skiers, nothing, only perhaps if one's lucky animals, when I'm here in and around maloja, where I live and work for half the time, then I know that richter is right.
from the NZZ:
The key thinking on this is supplied by one of Richter's jottings from the year 1985: "Let something emerge instead of creating it. So no assertions, constructions, attitudes, inventions, ideologies – in order in this way to arrive at the actual, the richer, the livelier, at what is above my understanding." A few months later, Richter called this "painting like Nature", a timeless process of becoming and being. It was, he stated, not any plan that drove him to paint, but the enjoyment of letting something emerge, "in the expectation that an image turns up, puts in an appearance". The intention-free procedure takes up a long-forgotten, "primordial" artistic act, rediscovered only in the 20th century – that of discovering an object or a form.
In 1992, Richter placed 43 small-format painted-over photographs in the glass cases housing mementos in the Nietzsche House in Sils-Maria, and in addition placed a steel sphere in the Nietzsche Room. Hanging opposite the entrance was an offset print of the photographic transformation of a mountain range into a sphere, produced in collaboration with Sigmar Polke in 1968. The polished steel sphere in the Nietzsche House was one version of a multiple, each copy of which had the name of a mountain peak in the Grisons engraved on it. The sphere, which Richter viewed as the "most idiotic perfection", was to be an ironic underscoring of the fictive transformation of the mountain range and to evoke the association with Nietzsche and the eternal recurrence.
kiss, miriam

letter with photo of a wood by Otto Steinert (1964)

glued on **7 November 99**

Dear Miriam,

Thank you for the wonderful reportage. Looks magnificent. Yes, sure I'll come by again. It will have to be next year. Now I have to go straight to the garage in Geneva, am getting an approx. fivefold bypass inserted, to soup up the engine from 8 to 12 cylinders again. Am just back from Argentina; I, who had never ridden before, sat every day on a horse. The "lady's" name was Diabla and she treated me in a very civil way. A hug from your Jeanchristophe

700 YEARS SWISS CONFEDERATION
CANTON ZUERICH
ARTISTIC STYLING OF THE WESTERN FAÇADE OF ZURICH MAIN RAILWAY STATION
Frau Miriam Cahn
Strassburgerallee 68
4005 Basel **Zurich, 5 December 1989**

Dear Ms Cahn,
We refer to your telephone conversation of today with our juror Dr Harald Szeemann[74] concerning the artistic styling of the western façade in the historic hall of Zurich's Main railway station. Please find enclosed a few documents from which you can gain a first impression of the task involved.
We would, of course, be most pleased if you were to decide to take part in our public artwork competition and remain
With warm regards,
Fritz Brühlmann
Secretary
Enclosures: plan of the western façade 1:50
1 on-site photograph
prospectus of Zurich main railway station
2 newspaper cuttings

basle, 26 december 1989
dear fritz brühlmann and dear harry,
many thanks for your invitation. I am honoured, but do not understand why you should ask precisely me, given that my art is always done on paper and is highly provisional, and if it does take place in a public space then I choose the places solely by myself and do my work "illegally".
moreover, having looked at the photograph of this attractive glass frontage in the station I was – once again – enraged that artists should here produce an "artistic styling" – after all, it's perfect as it is – there are no aesthetic reasons for a "public artwork competition" for this attractive glass frontage: the sole reason is prestige.
don't you see this?
warm regards,
miriam cahn

Zurich, 29 December 1989
Dear Ms Cahn,
What can we say? Of course, we are disappointed at your refusal, and we cannot do the work in the main station "illegally".
Concerning the photograph of the attractive glass front. I think it's just that the photo is too attractive. It shows, after all, only a very small extract of the entire hall and in this extract the glass frontage seems more or less well-proportioned. But not when one is actually standing in the hall. Then the "hole" in the western façade seems harsh.
Concerning prestige: you're probably right that this is involved here. Only, who could deny that this human, all-too-human need is not also there in the background with many museums, art patrons and collectors. It can,

after all, be used to the great benefit of art.
Wishing you all the best for the New Year, I remain
With warm regards,
Fritz Brühlmann
Harry on the phone: “after all, you could try something different …” [addendum of artist]

harry szeemann
FAX
miriam cahn
giessliweg 81
CH-4057 basle **basle, 28 october 99**

dear Harry,
have been to see your cheerful end of the world in the Kunsthaus Zürich[75] – FINE! As a great fan of Meidner,[76] Pynchon,[77] the disaster film etc., I am, however, a bit offended because my work would have fitted this exhibition …
You invite me to participate in exhibitions that are "wrong" for me and NOT to those that are "right" for me – do we want to go on like this all through life? now, when we're getting older?
warm regards + greetings, miriam
PS. by fax, because you're bound not to look at your post until 2002 …

BAZ letters to the editor
p.o. box 4002 basle
miriam cahn
strassburgerallee 68
CH-4055 basle **basle, 30 may 90**

first the yowling against the 700th-anniversary boycott of the small WOZ, then the baying against the former BAZ culture editor, peter burri – what a magnificent culture editor we have!
matters of content are dashed aside over columns in a pseudo-jaunty flippant style – blows below the belt are dished out: intelligent readers can escape from these articles only with a gulp! and a groan!
the only thing that interests stumm is scandal – but not, for example, in the French sense of "scandale", which represents a vigorous and philosophical version of discussion – oh, no! stumm is interested solely and exclusively in his own vain self, in his self-produced scandal.
nothing against self-representation! but information, self-critical distance, intelligence and ironic diction are way, way beyond stumm's horizons.
regrettably, we are compelled to endure these feeble-minded pieces from a self-appointed front-rank critic – the BAZ is basle's only major daily newspaper and hence the power of reinhard stumm knows no rivals and no bounds. thus, the arts section reflects the bleak cultural climate of a city that has nothing more to offer than navel-gazing braggadocio.
this city has got the newspaper it deserves.
miriam cahn

super 8 films

i owe the idea of making films to a mouse that was scurrying in panic along the platform in the charlottenburg subway station – so fast that its legs became invisible as they whirled. this scurrying would have become a film. i would have liked also to film the movement of the little animals that crept in my absence through the black dust and left their tracks behind them.

the animals, plants, the weather, the streams, rivers, lakes and seas, the mountains, hills and plains give shape to the moving pictures, to the film, through their own movement. i intervene myself as little as possible. the personal element is the excerpt, my breathing and the moment at which i film. i position the camera and everything moves past it, or i follow an animal that is going on its way. as i do so, i breathe. breathing is like the blinking of an eye – the slow closing and re-opening of the aperture.

i cut only a little, because movement is chronology. montage is the chronological gluing together of the 3-minute pieces.

arnold dreyblatt[78]
postcards
Miriam Cahn
Praxis Inc.
33 Pakenham St.
PO Box 536
Fremantle, West Australia 6160
"Budapest" 1986

Miriam, just back from tour in Holland and concerts now in Bethanien and record come out – I am really confused so much travel – N.Y. was better this time – I realised it's my home + I had more distance – I ran around with Hungarian friends to Russian part of Brooklyn and I was ok and I could see everything so clear there sometimes – now finishing last concerts and then I must move out to Arndtstr 35 1/61 by end of July. then maybe I go east – the last tours were so boring. I don't know what to do + for now nothing with Who's Who. Zinnober[79] asked about you (send them card) ALL IS BULLSHIT I had a great shoestune from an old Turkish man here
Love Arnold

Miriam Cahn
Danckelmannstr. 31
1000 Berlin 19
RFA Allemagne
"Liège" 1988

Miriam,
I don't know if you're back yet from Canada – I've cleared out my garden + it's very nice here now – eating + drinking with Terry – + working on solo music and pictures for my home movies – you should come + visit sometime in the summer – it should include a weekend for the local music scene.
Love, Arnold
Terry Fox address:
58 Rue Pierreuse tel - 3241-***

MIRIAM CAHN
Strassburgerallee 68
4055 Basel
Switzerland
"LUGOSI LASZLO" – a good friend
"BUDAPESTI NEONOK 1986" 1989 (?)

Dear Miriam – I missed you in Berlin by only 5 days – after mad travel thru Hungary, Romania, Bulgaria then Anatolia to Syrian border then Hung again, CSSR to friendly Berlin – which was a surprise because – can you believe it – I felt at home! It went ok in Linz – better in music than with the pictures – but as first time I felt satisfied + I made solo piece – but now all problems again – try now in Rotterdam to get support (want to move as soon as possible) + if not Brussels Köln or back to Berlin – the wandering Juden! + I want to get a video camera because this slide thing I made for Linz is a dead end. Otherwise IT'S A FULL TIME JOB NOT BECOMING INSANE! I would like to visit you after I get

settled – you can still write to Belgium – until further notice!
Love, Arnold

Typed letter **1990 (?)**

it looks like we missed each other again – i think that i arrived in berlin just after you left – Eva Maria gave me the dates when you would be in Berlin but i guess she thought that you would be coming later
I'm going to New York for a month after travelling continually since sept – i haven't been in one place for more than two weeks since then
so i'm a little dizzy
I have some commissions for pieces to be performed in Holland in June
and then I was offered a really good place in Berlin – an old girlfriend (and her boyfriend who's from Zinnober) will get a renovated loft in Kreuzberg by Oranienpl and want me to move in – i can rehearse in a big renovated kellerraum and its cheap and really luxurious and will be ready in July
so i guess i do it
i miss the east
and after the french, belgians and dutch i love the germans after all
anyway i learned my lesson
it's no point to look for a home
and it looks now like slowly Zinnober is breaking up and they're going to come out one by one – maybe not all but some of them and they will come to this loft
so it's a little bit family
except for the Republikaner
i'm 35 years old and ready to compromise
(but don't tell anyone because i applied for DAAD and i don't want them to know that i would come anyway)
Gabi (the leader of Zinnober) will come to Basle in a few weeks and i gave her your address
i hope you're ok
maybe after i'm settled in summer i could come and visit you finally and we could go to the mountains
i've never been in mountains like that
in Dagestan in the Caucasus there are mountain Jews living like goats but it's hard to imagine
love, arnold

Miriam Cahn
Gissliweg 81
CH-4057 Basel

"rheinsberg nach 1900" **1996**

Dear Miriam, Thank you for the three books, coming at the same time as the Sandoz Ciba Merger! The books are really beautiful – and it was a great treat to read in English – so personally suddenly dreams, family, life and death! I guess we are all getting older! Hope to meet you again someday. I will make a big project in Copenhagen this year for the Kulturstadt Europa! Maybe you come (end Nov.) Love, Arnold

31 November 85

Dear Miriam,

Thank you for your letter. Yes, the staging of the Fassbinder play[80] has caused a stir – and rightly so. As you can imagine, I am wholly on the side of those who are obstructing its performance. I am glad that the Jews are refusing to accept this, in a consistent manner and without any rioting. In this matter, it seems to me totally irrelevant whether the author wanted to be anti-Semitic or not. The reactions prove that the play can be understood as anti-Semitic. And that's the point at which tolerance stops. It's too serious a matter to be decided by the literary smart set.

What is happening here again is precisely what Hitler so slyly insinuated: the rich Jew, as speculator and extortionist, is responsible for the sins of capitalism. He becomes the scapegoat for the capitalist system. By exterminating the Jews, you solve the "social question". This "terrible simplification" was one of the major driving forces behind the Nazis' success in 1933.

And today, once again, this type of negative image is being asserted. It must be nipped in the bud. And if the author is being misunderstood, then that's HIS mistake. The political climate today is hot enough anyway – think of the big successes scored by parties that are against the "foreigners" and that are ALWAYS also fascist: in Israel, in France and now also in Geneva and Lausanne …

I think it's a good thing that, as you say, the German intellectuals are being "ambushed by history". If that wasn't the case, then one would have to be astonished at their blindness, obstinacy, obtuseness. But precisely the fact that the events of this century are continually in their consciousness, lurking and nagging, makes me relatively optimistic about Germany's future at present. So, I am very definitely of the opinion that tolerance stops with anti-Semitism. It's not the same whether a writer "owns up" to his homosexuality, or his alcoholism or his voyeurism – or to his anti-Semitism. Because, whether he intends it or not, the latter can have a long-distance effect and, whatever form it takes, a highly dangerous one.

There is a point in your letter that interests me. In the field of literature and poetry you seem tolerate a far broader range of opinions, statements, philosophies etc. than in the fine arts. Yet the word always has a stronger effect than the image, more unlimited and time and entering the human mind. Especially on the stage (Schiller is quite rightly cited here: "The Theatre as a Moral Institution". And that's why I find Heidegger, Ezra Pound e tutti quanti great minds who flirted with fascism suspicious.

After all, you demand a clear standpoint from the creative artist and accuse the Abstract Expressionists of lacking commitment (which I don't quite agree with). But we don't want to discuss that today.

You are of course quite right to say that an exhibition that wants to show German art in the 20th century cannot simply leave out the Nazi period. On the other hand, it's damn difficult today to find anything good about the years 1933–45. This total absence is an undeniable phenomenon of art history. Most good artists, whether Jewish or not, emigrated and the others went into inner emigration. So what should one put on display? The weak late pictures of Heckel, Nolde and Dix?[81] Or loathsome Nazi art such as the muscle-men of Arno Bräker? Where can they be found? If I had to make an exhibition, therefore, I would reserve a room for "1933–1945": photographs of Nazi architecture, a statue by Bräker, any "attractively" painted portrait of Hitler, Goebbels or Göring, and alongside them emigrant art: a powerful Beckmann, a Freundlich[82] and a Max Ernst.
Unfortunately, they don't allow me to …
Phew, this letter is already far too long. Our congratulations on Sydney, Baden-Baden and Bonn (information from Stampa) and we hope to come to the opening of the exhibition in Baden-Baden. Is the date 12 September correct?
How have you solved your housing problem?
Next week I'm flying to New York for a few days, to speak as an expert on forged Greek jewellery (satanic stuff) in a trial; travel paid. Then in mid-October to Heidelberg to give a talk and to attend the inaugural lecture of Luca Giuliani.
Much love from
your old
Dad[83]

thomas struth: “when herr flick says that he wants to brighten up the history of his family by making a gift of art, I feel that I’m being appropriated.”
gerhard richter: “names are being bandied around, values and qualities are being asserted – and actually all that is being demonstrated is how easily and quickly someone can nowadays stack up a so-called high-end collection. with a bit of money, almost anybody can do it.”
hans haacke: “his collection was funded in part by slave labour.”
marcel odenbach: “what disturbs me about this collection above all is that it has been built up by a tax-dodger, who is now being celebrated in berlin on the grand scale.”
and many others consider it INCOMPREHENSIBLE that flick has made no payment to the compensation fund for forced labourers. (quotations from the TAZ in the ZEIT)
incomprehensible?
the real scandal is that flick does not pay into the fund and is thus continuing the family tradition of his grandfather. slyly he dons the absolution cloak of the “greatest contemporary art collection” and “donates” it to the city of berlin. immediately there are debates about the problematic form of this donation, about iwan wirth as its seller, about flick the tax-evader, about kin liability, and about the quandary brought about by the involvement of the artists: pavlov’s dog[85] is barking, the outrage remains in-house, yeah, that’s how it is, it’s all as gerhard richter says. and thomas struth. and marcel odenbach. at last a few artists who speak up at the last minute. in flick’s case, however, I find these critically intended objections negligent, because, for one thing, it is not about our art world, but about the fact that flick doesn’t pay into the compensation fund and thinks that buying and showing contemporary art would wash him whiter than white.
flick the ageing playboy urgently needs new publicity. nowadays, being “controversial” is the best advertisement of all. “controversial” catapults flick into a pseudo-intellectual milieu that gives a knee-jerk public reflection of conditions in the art scene so gifting flick cost-free advertising. hans haacke, who always takes on the function of the admonisher, does not fail to pop up either – and so my artist colleagues can find incomprehensible something that is in fact very easy to comprehend.
there is a lamentable lack of distinction made here between problems in the art business, art as work and the interpretation of the past. flick, after all, is not saatchi,[86] or schmidheiny[87] or whatever the names of these big-time collectors may be who sometime, someplace make a so-called donation so as to save (taxes, storage) and to bathe in the public gaze with the help of art. and the scandal is not that flick comes from a horrid family, but that in contrast to his brothers and sisters he refuses to make the unspectacular reparations and, moreover, offers contemporary art as a substitute for religion, as absolution. flick has the historic obligation to make direct financial reparations – there are no two ways about this – even if, due to the sheer inflation of wrong-minded commemoration, we’ve all grown weary of these correct issues.
instead of gifting him publicity, we should quite simply ignore flick and his collection. once he has paid into the fund, the lad can, as

far as I am concerned, do just what he likes with his millions.
miriam cahn

 re-considered escape ways

i reconsidered my surroundings, i saw my surroundings in a different perspective, i thought of escape ways, vanishing points, refugees, refuge-seekers, people fleeing, horizons, views from above, views from below, landscapes, townscapes, territories, perspectives. suddenly i had to go to madrid just because of the avenidas, i could also have gone to buenos aires or N.Y. but i went to madrid also because of the meat-coloured city, madrid meat-city.
on the way from basle to ZH airport by train i suddenly saw the familiar landscape anew, i laid out lines, horizons, thought really in spatial terms and became very tired in the process, brain-tired, laid out nets from the train as it travelled, as in a computer model everything was disturbingly new as at birth. i could just as well have travelled back from the airport to basle again. a precipitate birth, at the same time the impression of a circle closing.
i thought also of my taking flight my flight movements out of my surroundings, my somehow insipid surroundings. i reconsidered my friendships, which tended to be a kind of unvarying objects in a territory, closer or farther away depending on my point of view in this terrain vague. they were fixed points, way stations when walking when running, roof constructions, protective buildings, standing around in the territory. it was advisable to have several. the more i re-considered my escape ways the better.
i thought also of refugees, these people cast into a landscape and into a territory, who had no buildings to stop over - + rest, nothing, no fixed points, no places, no roofs, nothing, they had only themselves if at all. my escape ways were roofed-over by the privilege of freedom. I neither had to flee, nor to reflect on taking flight. I didnt have to do anything.
but throughout my life i have forever been dreaming of terrains with buildings, objects, sculptures, things which when dreaming in youth i flew over in fighter planes and which when dreaming today having grown older i stride over and across. stand around there. walk around there. stroll around there. stand there by chance and stroll, gazing, observing.
dreaming is self-definition, dreaming is drawing, painting, making music, writing, walking, running, thinking, breathing. when one is dreaming everything is moving is really true not graspable but portrayable. dreaming is taking hold of, is the movement of taking hold. dreaming is the work of taking hold/evading/running/fleeing, the work of slipping away, the work of taking flight.

i know the closeness of very many years ago: my old mother calls me today: -mon bébé, ma chérie- and i call her then: -ma vieille-. she is years ago i am now. ma vieille, mon bébé, ma chérie. thus the beauty of my childhood comes full circle. circle, round, without space but with duration. my mother sends me drawings with 5 trees, green, with violet trunks, their crowns oval leaning to the right as in the wind I/L/O/V/E and underneath a green circle with YOU written in it. she always sends me new and highly concentrated coloured circles, very beautiful circles, simple beautiful concentrated circles, ma vieille.

we are waiting for the next catastrophe. catastrophe = terrorist act = suicide attack. assassins are coolly observing and analysing our surroundings. what the WorldTradeCenter was for america, the murder of theo van gogh is for holland. hollywood image USA + european intellectual image, USA + europe, exactly observed, the weak points analysed for the purpose of destruction. the weak points analysed dissected and subsequently transposed into a perfect strategy of annihilation. i understand the will to disappear in suicide, to merge into absolute nothingness, to no longer want to be, to be nothing. but i utterly and totally really reject the act of suicide as a strategically deployed weapon as a tactic of the absolute, as the purpose of cool destruction. today suicide attacks strike at the heart of our societies, of my surroundings, which bear in themselves the possibility of failure, of the imperfect, the insipid, the democratic, the individual, of just living along, it doesnt matter, it is unimportant, it is my flowing, fleeting culture of changing standpoints, perspectives, horizons, points of light and escape ways. unbearable for suicide attackers. after all it would mean that their point of view is only theirs, their small human point of view, personal, individual, not divine, large, general. i fully understand suicide, but not a suicide attack with its extremely cool intelligence and extreme stupidity of feeling.

re-considered escape ways

new years eve, engadin, friends. someone says: -this shop has started selling kosher goods to orthodox jews thats fine but the jews are not to my liking. not to my liking? was i not to this persons liking? did she know that i was a jew? i was unable to react, my mood had taken a nose-dive, these were my friends, these were my jews. my jews were not to peoples liking. these were my friends. my friends and my jews.

pretty soon after midnight i drove back and saw these brightly-lit festivities, too gaudy, too bright, my good mood had taken a nose-dive, i plunged down into the dark valley, into the deserted dark Bregaglia Valley, with every bend i felt better, until i got to my place, got home, to one of my workshops, home into the dark. at night i dreamt of a yellow animal that was walking on a shelf from top right to bottom left and looked back at me with a severe glance. i lay beneath the animal like a child looking out from its bed at its cuddly animal toys.

for several weeks i had a terribly bad conscience towards my jews. i hadnt defended them. i hadnt asked, hadnt questioned my friends: -am i not to your liking either, am i not to your liking like my jews-. it was just that nothing had come into my mind, there was this paralysis, an emptiness, from which i couldnt come up with anything, couldnt do anything, paralysed i shovelled food into myself, anaesthetized, detached, turned into stone.

assuming my friends had answered, assuming i had asked them whether i wasnt to their liking either, assuming like my jews: i wasnt like that, not the same, not orthodox, not with stockings and a wig, not garbed in black no, that wouldnt be me, so i wouldnt be not to their liking my friends liking what would i be then? in spite of cahn not not to their liking like my jews, in spite of miriam cahn therefore to their liking, since not not to their liking like my jews? so were my jews my jews if i was without religion? without a jewish mother? in the eyes and minds of my friends i probably wasnt a jew because i didnt show appearance + existence like my jews. so i probably was to their liking i dont know because i didnt ask. perhaps having asked such a question i would be as little to my friends liking as my jews. my jews remain my jews. my jews are my jews, even if i never belong to a congregation and am not a zionist. my jews are my jews.

re-considered escape ways sarajevo writing in trains

in the period of the ceasefire before dayton i was invited to sarajevo for an exhibition. my works were driven over mount igman, i flew from zagreb to

 sarajevo in a military transport machine. the offices of the unprofor were attractive thanks to the absolute absence of any so-called interior design, the plane was a flying factory workshop, in the middle the material, we human beings at its outer skin firmly strapped. i was the only civilian. – why i was flying to sarajevo? – been invited, am exhibiting in sarajevo, am an artist. – the soldiers from various military -+ aid organizations looked extraplanetarily gobsmacked at this answer.
coming from switzerland and from civilian life sarajevo was inconceivable. the drive in the white-painted civilian car disguised as a UN vehicle through this space of the destroyed, through this destroyed urban space, the spatial quality of driving through this town, the spatial experience of this destructive rage, the space the speed of the driving recalled the TV pictures, i remembered the outstanding buildings, the newspaper, the hotel, the new quarter by the airport as spatial fixed points, shattered buildings, destroyed, eliminated, barely capable of serving their function.
then obala: a wild crowd of young people who had just been celebrating the end of their first sarajevo film festival + crying + laughing + smoking drinas + boozing, were drunk on the magnificent success of the festival. next thing: my exhibition. a number of these very young men worked in daytime as video – film + art specialists and at night as soldiers in the army defending sarajevo. actually i set up my exhibition with soldiers.
i was given accommodation in the same building on the uppermost floor, the block stood by the river, through small holes in the unprofor plastic sheeting i could look at the mountain, and i assume that over there soldiers of the besieging army were looking at us, observing us, a thought i immediately suppressed. there were sandbags in front of the obala which perhaps gave a bit of protection, protected us a little. in the obala there was a nervous little dog, who protected the people in the obala from intruders by barking wildly. this little guard dog "ticci" (its face twitched even when it was asleep) was a token/icon of the situation: all the people there were somehow TICCI, they all seemed normal young people, young adults, whose impairments became visible insidiously, revealed themselves to me little by little, bad teeth, pallid skin, unwashed hair, cracked nails, twitches, tics. they took great care with their outfit, the fact that benetton had opened a branch meant for them normality, even if they were not keen on benetton. normality meant the best possibility of survival, normality meant civilian life, meant urban civilian life, meant going out, meant dressing decently, meant giving shape to life. i went with them to the central cinema through the completely dark streets, into a completely dark cinema, forgotten the film, doesnt matter, the sudden lighting up of the screen, sometimes interrupted by total black, by complete darkness.
doing an exhibition meant normality meant inviting international artists. out of nothing they had constructed an attractive functional exhibition space in the academy by the river after their first had been destroyed by shell fire. carefully they unpacked my things, every smallest little bit of sticky tape was peeled off, preserved, every piece of packing material was folded up. subsequently we installed the exhibition just as fast professionally as anywhere else in the world. the opening was set for 13.00 because of the soldiers and the electricity; the invitations were delivered by hand direct to the houses and flats. at the opening i had a nice conversation in french about art with the serbian general of the defending army. it was a pleasantly intensive and brief opening. it was fine.
at the only kiosk open in the basarča i bought a map of the city "sarajevo and surrounding area". on the cover which had been reprinted during the war the usual tourist attractions could be seen as ruins. i got one of the obala soldiers to mark in the demarcation line of the besieging army. only then

did i become really, spatially, aware of what work this raggle-taggle defending army was doing to preserve their city. i thought of the maps of “basle and surrounding area”, of feldberg, belchen, blauen, gempen, tüllingerberg, grand ballon, which could likewise form a siege - + demarcation line.
a young video artist told me in a dispassionate voice that he had several times exchanged dead bodies and body parts with the enemy up in the hills. this lad had a very well-trained body, coming from civilian life i naturally thought of sports training. perhaps he was commanded, picked to exchange bodies and body parts with the enemy in the almost impassable mountain territory on account of his well-trained body acquired in civilian days for sporting reasons. perhaps however this job had hardened his body.
only in the shower in the hotel room in zagreb did the feeling of menace fall away, only when i was no longer in this besieged city did i actually, physically, become aware of this feeling of menace.
back in basle those around me reacted reticently when i began to report, steered the conversation onto other topics or manifestly let their attention drift away. my friends looked past me. although they considered me remarkably courageous. for them however rejecting war meant not thinking of wars. to them i was “occupying” myself with war, cahns got a tic about war, must be because of her history - + biography constellation. doing an exhibition in a besieged town didnt interest anyone although art as a token of normality is very interesting, should be of interest, art as a token of normality just as draculics poem[88] with the bus stop and the boring fact that the bus comes punctually every day means normality, day-to-day life.

i think that possibly, perhaps after this return home i decided, took the inner decision, really, emotionally, internally, as a feeling decided, took the decision, from within, emotionally, really, to observe, to study my surroundings, to study how my people lived and spoke. to listen to their language exactly and to evade the supposed embraces of solidarity especially of women, these women around me who refused to think farther than war-is-mens-business. some of the men around me refused to think farther, because in this system of war-is-mens-business-and-hence-bad they logically did not want to be the baddies. the attitude of my people was final and fundamental: -we cant imagine it. so they didnt want to know about my week in sarajevo either. but when the USA ended this european war with war, yes, then my small-town luminaries were against the USA, simply, traditionally, fundamentally, an intellectual closed system, us, enclosed in our well-being, punctual buses, punctual trains, electrical, hot water, everything normal, normality and a cosy refusal of using, treasuring the privilege of normality to think and feel in all directions. we are not forced to lug bodies and body parts in almost impassable territory and to exchange them with the enemy. we have the privilege of the normality of day-to-day life, we, we can reflect passionately, vehemently on what it means if a young video artist has to exchange body parts at night, this foot belongs to my corpse, this hand to yours.
while i am writing the panoramic train is winding its way through almost impassable territory. tunnels alternate with glimpses down into ravines, across to castles and historic railway bridges. indians, germans and asians enthusiastically contemplate and photograph/film the beautiful landscape. with every ascending loop the green of the trees becomes more filigree. in st moritz i will get into my car and drive home along the lakesides.

 re-considered escape ways writing while watching television

i dont read these texts after writing them. i think of them, memory, commemoration, recalling these texts. the sarajevo text as recollection perhaps self-important, conceited perhaps, self-image, self-indulgent. self-sufficient. suicide self-killing suicide attack freitod [free death, autocide] death by one's own hand, hand + hands. the WorldTradeCenter and the view of the two french documentary film brothers who by chance became involved in 9/11, their view from the ground, the worms eye view of the tower into which the first aircraft hurtles: the one brother was just filming a gas leak on the ground + and with presence of mind and professionalism thrust the camera upwards when the fireworker assisting him heard the plane. everybody the entire world saw those few seconds. later the firefighters in the tower lobby try to assess the situation by intense listening, harking to the building, listening to the injured building. they hear a sploshing, the sound of the bodies falling onto the lobbys projecting roof. on television i see nothing except men in firefighters uniform listening intently and hear the sound, the noise, the specific acoustic phenomenon of the human body impacting after a fall from a great height.

in 2005 i try to imagine in a drawing the last thing these human beings saw: the urban canyon of the street, the suction, the vanishing point in the street. leaping into death the last but autonomous decision really the autonomous ones own the last personal decision against terror, the individual neutralization of a suicide attack by killing oneself? the height of fall. imagining falling in a drawing. the viewpoint of the pilots, who were manoeuvring these planes and flew into the towers corresponded to the viewpoint of my early youthful giant-scale drawings, gliding dreamily and flying over landscapes and towns. 9/11 a dream turned into horror. in 2005 i HAVE to draw the perspectives, vanishing points horizons and standpoints of the others, drawing differently from the ground, from the viewpoint of someone jumping from the tower, looking down from the circling helicopters. i not only have to, something compels me. something compels me to reconsider everything afresh while drawing. being older compels me to think again about my old works. my old sad mother compels me. my silent sister compels me, i have to draw while thinking about it. compelled i have to think again about perspectives.

my jews are my jews who are just as foreign to me as all human beings as anyone as all families as all groups as all male friends as all female friends. but they are my jews and are not to be considered not to someones liking, nobody around me should be allowed to consider them not to his or her liking nobody should pigeonhole anyone or others in that way, be allowed to consider them as a whole not to their liking, as a people, as a tribe, as a race, no-one around me should be allowed to think or do or say that no-one should be allowed to call my jews my jews apart from me no-one should call jews jews apart from me or jews only jews are allowed to consider themselves not to their liking me my jews only i should be allowed to consider myself.

how i detest hate that, how i hate that and especially when i say it myself i hate this pigeonholing. it is better much better much much better to consider all human beings foreign i actually feel that all are foreign neither like this nor like that but foreign, always. that is the better state of affairs, a state of affairs a state of mind, of contemplating, observing, seeing. a state of a continual motion of seeing, a fluid state of seeing, always.

nevertheless my jews are my jews, they are my jews, a state of belongingness felt not lived, a feeling of belongingness, a feeling of belonging without day-to-day life without effects without community without belonging. if need be, perhaps, but but perhaps not i prefer to belong to the jews who are not to peoples liking than to the others who are to their liking, to the others whom they seem to define as to their liking, obviously seem to see themselves as to peoples liking in contrast to those whom they call not to their liking, my jews, obviously.

re-considered escape ways
whenever i think about the foregoing texts i have a feeling of badness, a feeling of something not true or not real, unreal because an attempt to capture something in words, and nevertheless the feeling of being able to achieve this capturing, a specific capturing only through writing. a creeping up upon. a condensing, a writing out, writing as an interim technique, as a procedure between image and sound, through the flow of writing tending to sound, through the filling of the pages tending to image. but i do not capture the content any more than with drawing/painting/photographing. Or as a waldau[89] patient says on television: -bim mole ischs problem was molsh …-
bim schribe ischs das problem was schribsch,
[when youre painting the problem is what do you paint …
when youre writing the problem is what do you write] what and which sound + rhythm. my jews are my jews is a how, less a what i can dream up my jews, dream of them. in a similar procedure to dreaming i can paint. in a somewhat more intellectual way i can as a commentary draw while dreaming. writing is somewhat more intellectual commenting is brain-driven training and perhaps possibly in the end possibly takes everything away by defining, destroys the condensation of dreaming. however, because i also dream in sentences + words, i could by means of dreaming as a procedure condense sentences + words.

a chance computer event led me to this hand-pncl-eraser way of writing. when travelling i take a notebook along. writing by hand is quick, i can erase words + sentences speedily and dont subsequently read my texts. but the proximity of pencil to drawing is frighteningly close and yet not drawing, i would never draw when travelling by train and outside or wherever, because drawing is an intimate process. writing by hand, however, is not. nobody sees anything except illegible signs legible only to me. this nothing is the wonderful thing about writing this terrible nothing, this nothingness is the wonderful thing about writing writing in such a notebook is nothing.
probably possibly perhaps art too is nothing. the object, the left-over thing, the image, this something that just exists away in its nothingness is a contradiction that has occupied me all life long that determines my life. i bear with pride the responsibility for my production of nothing, producing nothing is the best thing one can do today, nothing is the opposite of annihilation, nothing is a declaration of war on annihilation.

re-considered escape ways
suicide, self-homicide, self-killing, suicide attack freitod [free death, autocide], the virgin suicides, jean améry, death by one's own hand, freitod. freitod is for me the finest of words. free death is of one's own free will freely

 chosen free autonomous. freely i give myself death, i invite death to put an end to me i think my death i enact my death i plan my dying i kill myself i have lived enough freitod autocide the final point of the individual, to me myself of the self, i myself choose, the reasons are unimportant, the possibility of choosing, perhaps choosing, deciding this, only i, i alone decide, the choice, the decision, to decide, to act, i, the last time, to decide, decide alone, decide from the sum of life individual lonely alone, decide from the sum of my life, depart, only i i only i. the opposite of the suicide attacker, who merging with a higher power disembodies himself, disembodying innocent people casts into death human beings who have not so chosen human beings innocent people guilty only of being human snatches them away to death from the guilt of being human lording it in the name of a greater lord punished for their human flawed guilty sinful being being human being a self. lordly, lording it, disembodies himself and others, casts off the body that makes him a flawed human being, in disembodiment believing to have to prove that there is no such thing as individuals with a beginning with a birth and an end with death believes he must prove lordingly prove that through his deed there is a godlike power that justifies casting people into death, subordinating himself to the higher power the higher the attacker believes to be doing the right thing for all he determines what all have to do in the name of a power that has degraded him into a nothing into a tool a machine into a weapon. in his annihilation he annihilates them all, all that is, that is so. that wants to be as it is. that is. that might be. he believes he knows that his act will be rewarded in the world beyond. his higher power sells him his act, his suicide, his suicide attack as the goal of his life, as an ascent out of his unclear, imperfect, paralysing, poor being, his inchoate, impoverished, feeling-flung, flung, asocial being into social recognition. his power works on him, with him on his perfect training to become a deadly weapon, works with him, on him towards his existential dissolution as a social act, as a social deed, his suicide as a social deed that is for the benefit of all, is good for all, his power works on him and with him and just so long until he is a completely perfect nothing, a vessel that believes and whose sole content is the belief that he a perfect nothing will after his death become a myth a martyr to a cause an ideology a belief, his perfect nothingness, his shaped, perfect nothingness is the cool perfect deadly weapon of his lords and masters.

re-considered escape ways + heartless families + suicide sister

i wont write about my sister i wont write my sister, i wont describe my sister but perhaps my sad mother my mother who during the entire drive from the weekend cottage to home tried to jump out of the car. every time that she began to open the car door during the drive i ferociously held her firm from behind with my strong youthful arms, embraced her strongly from behind i embraced her from behind while my father tenaciously doggedly tried to drive home frantically fast as fast as he could tried to end the situation as fast as possible this desperate screaming questioning screaming questions attacking questioning of my mother as to the sense of life and reaching out again and again for the car door. no idea why my father didnt simply stop perhaps probably theyd have come to blows probably it would have taken even longer until at last at last he could have delivered this woman his wife my mother to the clinic at last at last no more this despair at last able to have escaped from this situation in that way my father had the driving wheel in his hand at least he clasped the driving wheel doggedly desperately driving father while i again clasped my mother from behind with my strong youthful arms so that she couldnt throw herself out of the moving car. no idea whether my sister was sitting beside me, my little sister because younger still a child and watching us adults desperately heartless adults. no idea i have really forgotten completely and heartlessly. i have quite simply forgotten her. i was so utterly concentrated focussed on my mothers movements specialised in observing in observing what kind of movements she made so that i could youthfully with my strong arms prevent her from behind from leaping out of the car that i have completely forgotten whether my little sister was sitting beside me. even today as i write i cannot see her sitting beside me in the car, no idea although actually logically she must have been sitting there i cant see her no idea and this flow of writing doesnt entice her out either, she doesnt flow out i cant see her she has no place in this situation heartless if i had seen her i would perhaps perhaps have done something different from holding my mother who perhaps was going to jump out of the car perhaps if i had seen my little sister if she was sitting beside me i would have held her in my strong youthful arms would have protected her against these terrible adults these heartless adults would have held her ears shut before this screaming of these heartless adults these desperate people despairing of themselves acting helplessly and heartlessly. no idea whether my little sister was sitting beside me. i was sitting on the right behind the front passenger seat and to my left i dont know i dont want to and cannot see and no idea, i had to concentrate heartlessly in this jungle fight extreme concentration was my chance of survival, concentration on the fight. no idea where my little sister was.

doctor: -do you draw better when you are happy or when you are unhappy?-
female patient: -when i am unhappy.- (klinik waldau / waldau clinic)

re-considered escape ways
how i hate waking up early immediately this writing in my mind early gloomy gloomy words + sentences which line up one after the other ready to be written, rows, series of sentences + words firmly sung into my mind, sound in my mind, soundmind, staying in mind, perfect writing, song, perfect, in its sequence in its successions of notes in its beauty, yet yet yet in this body of sound remaining soundmind, thrusting through the gloom of the too early, precisely not dream image remembered but writesound lying with the body of sound mind perfectly executed, made music with repetitions, trills, clusters yet yet gloomy forever in words + sentences of gloomy content wretchedness of content set to music body of sound as accompaniment, as background music as muzak unbearable sometimes many times yet yet also a pointer to possible procedures. what good luck that my computer has got bust and compels me to write like this by hand with the pncl + eraser + sharpener what luck lucky chance that compels me to write by hand to complete a movement on the one hand close to drawing on the other close to violin-playing closer to me than the delicate hammering tapping stroking of the computer keyboard. writing by hand with the pncl reproduces the sound of my mind writing by hand creates the tone/sonority/sound of my thinking my felt thinking it is the sound of the manner of my thinking.

re-considered escape ways
i assume that people who throw themselves from buildings do not see their surroundings. they do not see the urban canyons squares the other

 buildings from above. the people who threw themselves from the WorldTradeCenter the people falling the people letting themselves fall acted in panic in despair they plunged out of the windows fleeing from the flames the fire their decision was burn to death burn to a cinder or plunge plummet fall thud to the ground with that moist sound that i first heard in the film the document of the two young french film-makers. as a viewer at home i heard this sploshing the damp sploshing sound i heard together with the firefighters i heard this moist sound at home watching the firefighters who in this film again and again in the lobby of the one tower gave orders harking to the sounds of the assailed tower and seemed only gradually to grasp that this moist sound was the impacting of bodies of tumbling falling human beings on the projecting lobby roof of the tower of the WorldTradeCenter, which, as i watching the film at home 1 year later in contrast to the firefighters already knew, would soon break, cave in, collapse. even if the images that i had seen 1 year earlier live on television with the entire television-viewing world and the concomitant ceaseless shrill alarm bell will forever be lodged in my memory, it was this moist sound of the impacting bodies of fallen people tumbled from a great height fallen a sound that was later the actual sound of this disaster. hearing this sound 1 year later when following the reticent structure of this european docufilm only hearing it and not seeing, not having to see but having to imagine with the help of this moist sound having to being compelled to imagine what this noise provoked and evoked was insight, my recognition of 9/11, of now, of today, of contemporaneity. i was always working in the knowledge of this sediment with the feeling sound-feeling of a change that would show itself later sometime somehow. this noise, this sound-horror had to show itself. i absolutely really had to store this tone, this sound. this music of dread. this unmasterable, moist, muffled noise, this sploshing.
writing is ordering. writing on the train writing in trains writing when travelling is a sliding ordering. when one is travelling through regions, terrains, landscapes, towns horizons, vanishing points, standpoints dissolve. perspectives shift so swiftly as you rush along that i am forever having to re-assemble those spatial networks in my mind as i look out into the territory. when writing in trains on the move. tune, song.

the hatching stroking drawing with pncl is new. repeat with harder softer pncls hatch crosshatch across it without forgetting the perspective the horizon the vanishing point and the terrain to be portrayed, things standing around lying around unclear things running around. hatching makes a sound, especially when the pncl runs over a resistance like the edge of the paper. hatching is on a finer level the same as formerly the striking of pieces of chalk on the floor against those giant sheets of paper, hatching is concentration, felt thinking, hand - + mind performance. hatching is sound.

i think of my mothers circles of the similarity in process procedure: she draws presses with coloured crayon again and again hatching layer over layer. her circles the colour is concentrated condensed by the fine hatching and her circles are a testimony to concentrated work. she drew her circles in her room in the psychiatric clinic, at first disjointed, then gradually condensing into compact circles, gleaming, coloured, these circles show me my mothers possibility the possibility and the tragedy of my sad mother. for my sad mother it is impossible to believe in herself, for her it is impossible utterly and totally really not possible to imagine her circles as art, she values art as the highest of things and her circles and her circles therefore valueless and her circles therefore nothing, occupation, nothing. my sad mother very so utterly much my sad mother set herself and others such

utterly extremely high standards, evaluations that she can, will never ever never attain fulfil, unattainable everything, everything made unattainable by her volition, destroyed by her ambitions, so that perhaps at most this life-essential concentration on her circles remains and even, although, because her work on her circles is life-saving, life-sustaining, life-essentially beautiful these condensing life circles remain for her nothing, unimportant, valueless, disposable. no idea why my sad mother has to believe unwaveringly in this evaluation.
my wild mother believes nothing at all, but knows instinctively, wildly, musically that she is an artist, my wild mother blessedly my wild mother instinctively wildly she draws her circles in the psychiatric clinic and elsewhere my wild mother draws her circles when she feels lonely instinctively she draws against the world instinctively she knows wildly about the importance of concentration on a purposeless piece of work compellingly compulsively against compulsions on a work of expression.
my sad mother believes that her sadness is connected to her instinctive wildness, sadness stems from her wildness, untamed, believes that her instinct, wild, untamed, is to blame for her sadness, guilt, because forever breaking out, wild, wicked, beautiful, untamed, inventive. her possibilities can be united only in her beautiful circles in these condensed signs, in real condensed signs, in possible images of her life, of her possibilities, of a condensed escape limited to simple circles, these circles her possible still feasible statement of my poor mother.

actually but really actually i wanted to write about myself wanted about my work my working writing and compare actually compare myself with my mother really see in the comparison who i was and how i work in comparison to my mother compare with my mother distinguish in the comparison compare as a feeling myself with my mother compare find similar as a feeling as a wild sound-feeling of similarity of kinship of mother to daughter inheritance of feeling inherited possibility of works inherited procedures executed beyond the possible, beyond the possibility, inherited procedures of work, of working. not as a possibility only but as existence, but every day, but my life long. i inherit her ability without her. i inherit her wild ability. i am her brood, she my animal mother. ma vieille, ma chérie, mon bébé.

2005

30 December 87

Dear Miriam,

Talking of Aryanization. We emigrated in 1933 already. Uncle Heinrich Oppenheim had emigrated to Zurich as early as 1931 and urgently advised us to leave the country. Then we had a financial backer by the name of Morgenroth, the brother of a friend of Nonni, an industrialist and collector. He wanted to rescue his money in the form of collections purchased in Germany. These we were able to transfer to Switzerland. So we emigrated. At first, we wanted to go to Bern. In Thun we had old family friends by the name of Stämpfli, who were members of the Bernese Burgergemeinde[90] and thought that Bern was THE place. But this didn't work out. In order to gain a residence and work permit difficult negotiations had to be conducted with the authorities through a lawyer. The man recommended to us, Dr Brunschwig (Jewish), declared gruffly that he was against emigrants from Germany populating Switzerland – the situation of the Swiss Jews, he maintained, was already difficult enough. There we stood, Nonni, Erich and I, totally crestfallen. That was in Summer 1933. Now, we were advised to go to Basle, where we also had acquaintances. And there we were successful. In March 1934 we began our numismatic business in the Aeschenvorstadt. (By the way, I spent 1 August 1940 with the delightful ageing Stämpflis on Lake Thun ...).

Emigration was a decision we did not take long over. Since 1930 we had seen and experienced enough to have no illusions about our future in Germany. One of the great mysteries about the history of the 1930s is the blindness of German Jews, who let themselves be deprived of their rights and robbed of their possessions and still remained in Germany.

Up to 1935, I still went quite often to Germany on business, the last occasion being an auction of Greek coins in Berlin in February 1935 – coins from the Hermitage in Leningrad, auctioned by a Jewish coin dealer!

In 1935 came the anti-Jewish laws. Up till then, our firm in Frankfurt had muddled along in a rough and ready way. My Uncle Julius, a local patriot and convinced German, died wretchedly from cancer of the oesophagus. The firm went into the hands of its book-keeper, Frau Button. The house at 55 Niedenau was sold to a butcher.

After the War, we could have claimed everything back. But we couldn't imagine being owners of a business and a house in Germany again, carrying on lawsuits against rapacious "Aryans", who had enriched themselves, and conducting running battles with compulsory tenants in the run-down house – silly from a financial point of view; others came off better. The house had remained undamaged in the War and must be worth a king's ransom today. But I don't regret having

been silly – so much for our "tale" in brief.
The article in "Der Spiegel" is a very good one. The very fact that it has told you things that you didn't know shows that it was necessary! The fact that industrial and trading companies are celebrating the 50th anniversary of Aryanization (and falsifying documents into the bargain) is a bloody scandal. I am sure that certain readers of the article will say: 'Well, once again we see that before the Third Reich the Jews had all the levers of the economy in their hands.'
But that is just not true. Certain branches of trade and industry – livestock, hides and skins, department stores – were strongly Jewish, but not the major industries, and in the banks the Jewish influence had diminished in the 1920s already.
The current wave of remembrance of the shame and ignominy of the Nazi years is a good thing. And another good thing is that heads are rolling, such as that of Herr Hofer.[91]
When I can, I read memoirs of the 1920s and 1930s. The origins of Nazism have still not been sufficiently researched. In THAT respect, by the way, Golo Mann's[92] otherwise unlovely memoir is important. Canetti,[93] on the other hand, yields little.
Many fond greetings and kisses from your completely two-eyed
Dad

From: Miriam Cahn
To: Katharina Dunst
Subject: BOOK **19 august 2016**

dear Kathrin,
here, for a start, is the list of the already printed pieces, and another one, which I admittedly have but which is not so great…
saluti
miriam
<printed texts from catalogues.docx><überdachte fluchtwege.txt.copy.doc>
Sent from my iPad

From: Katharina Dunst
To: Miriam Cahn
Subject: BOOK **15 September 2016**

Dear Miriam
So, now I'm back from Ljubljana and a Getty Summer Institute at the SIK-ISEA, from the exhibition on Kreis 48, which drew a lot of visitors, and from the Fantoche Animation Film Festival.
At last I have read your text from the year 2005. What did you mean, however, with your "but which is not so great…"? – I found it interesting and read it with unbroken concentration from beginning to end.
The question as to what energy, enablement or disability, what parts of the old life are transferred to the young and new life and what is filtered, is something that interests me greatly.
The passage in the car, where your mother wants to jump out, you hold her tight and, in the process, fail to notice your little sister, seems very familiar to me.
When my little sister had a fall and died, I too was very focussed on my mother and her feeling of hopelessness. Her inability to move on attached itself like black veils on the inside of my eyelids and I really just wanted to get away from it. I could feel the disablement that came from her and strove to drive it, and thus also my mother, out of me or just to run away. No, not run away: I chose the struggle against her.
The focus was on my mother because one's dependence as a child naturally takes this direction.
What counts in such situations is survival and it is probably the desperate attempt to escape that makes one forget all else.
For her it must have been terrible. It meant that she had lost more than one child.
On the other hand, she was also forced to take a decision – whether she wanted to get on her feet again and start afresh or not.
Yesterday, I also went to the Manifesta[94] in the Helmhaus.
I think that, as Sagri says in her article in the TAZ,[95] curatorial tasks, budgets etc. are far too little talked about and were yet far too present in the parameters of the exhibition.
I was astonished at how obediently the artists had taken the premises on board – perhaps because of the

money?
In the Helmhaus there was a work by Leigh Ledare[96] on view, in which he had chosen a psychotherapeutic setting for his work. Based on age, gender, ethnicity or social status, he had chosen twenty-one Zurich participants as, so to say, an average local society.
Together with the psychologists they form a kind of demographic microcosm of the City of Zurich.
Hair-raising, but good! I have an allergic interest in psychotherapy because I sense something unhealthy in concentrating on negative emotions. And in point of fact there were pronounced and hence hurtful animosities within the test group – based on negative feelings, prejudices, aesthetic dislikes etc. – which were set off reciprocally and were actually thematized.
Paranoid! And once they have been expressed these things have to be tracked down. They can't be sucked back inside again.
In your text about Jews being found unpleasant and you transferring this to yourself, I don't fully understand you either.
Is it a question of a general feeling of solidarity with parts of society ostracized on account of diffuse negative emotions?
And finally, should I try to digitalize all the already printed texts from the catalogues you've named?
Are there any that take priority?
Warmest Indian summer greetings,
Kathrin

From: Miriam Cahn
To: Katharina Dunst
Subject: BOOK **15 september 2016**

dear Kathrin,
oops! a misunderstanding: it's not my text that I consider "not so great", but the technical aspect – it was digitalized from the printed copy back in the digital stone age and so doesn't look so great. Today, such things are bound to be much better ... the text comes from the catalogue "überdachte fluchtwege", which contains these various "clusters" of typographic whole-page-blocks. and in general: I don't evaluate my texts – they're just there.
and super what you write about your mother and your sister etc. in and around such events one becomes a fighter, which is good and okay, even if they always stick in one's mind as a history and, as you so nicely write, as shadows/veils behind one's eyelids.
but a good psychotherapy does not do what you describe – limiting itself to relying on only negative feelings. on the contrary, it works with feelings and the reflection on them, as they show themselves, no matter whether they are so-called negative/positive or unclear. evaluation is not permissible in this work on the human psyche – if it is done seriously. and sure, all types of things come to light here! and therefore the work should be done under conditions of medical confidentiality, and not run as an "art project" in the manifesta. how vain! of the therapists and the people who agreed to this situation! but it fits our selfie society and so in that sense is not completely wrong-minded as art intending to be topical.
and now for the jews: the text refers directly to the piece that is

prominently placed first in the catalogue: 'my jews'.[97] you can see the yellow animal that I dreamt of, the divided house, which is connected with a typical story that my father told me:
at the funeral of a pious friend he had to sit alone on the other side of the aisle. why? because his name is cahn = cohim = priestly caste. formerly, they used to sit in different buildings. The 'integration' variant is a building with a gap running right along the roof. even my devout father did not know this. and I not at all.
for non-jews, it is hard to understand that it is not a question of how religious one is, but rather that one remains a jew forever. with a name like mine in any case. the text refers to the situation which all of us jews are familiar with: you are in a gathering, friends, and then a casual, unthinking remark is dropped concerning the jews – be it that they seem to be especially good at dealing with money matters, or are sexually especially active, are super at languages, so-and-so and this-and-that, and, precisely, are not likeable. would anyone nowadays simply say straight out, "I don't find blacks likeable"?
through this piece of work "meine juden" I have learned to react in such cases and to point out to these people that these are anti-semitic remarks. the text refers to my conflict concerning the fact that even friends make anti-semitic remarks and above all to my paralysis in reacting because they are my friends. the text ends, after all, with the words: my jews are my jews, which does not at all mean that I am a such-and-such jew, pious, orthodox, areligious, assimilated etc., but only what it says.
yes, and now to the practical side: digitalize all the texts I have sent to you – as I have said, I have no preferences. currently I am typing out the letters, and here there are only 2 possibilities: if it bores me while I'm typing it, the letter is discarded, if not, it stays in. I am doing no editing in the sense of abbreviating or whatever. but – and here you come in as an internet archaeologist – there are sometimes letters where, while typing them, out I no longer know exactly what it's about (exhibitions, inquiries, names of people and institutions). Should I send you an example, so that you can see what I mean?
so,
wishing you all the best!
saluti
miriam

i would not be

i would not be if i not not i i too but not at all if.
i would not be only not i i too i would not be. i am because. i am i i too because if.
i would not be if my mother had not met my father i would naturally by nature not be i would not be.

my mother from paris have to flee fly my mother refugee. my mother daughter sister with her younger siblings from paris have to flee to the south. my mother put by her parents my grandparents in panic on a kindertransport on a children's train in panic from paris to southern france in panic before the german enemy their own children alone on the kindertransport to the south to their uncle in panic. my mother eldest daughter alone have to care for her siblings. my mother with her siblings swiss refugees on the kindertransport. my mother in paris born raised panic before the enemy germans my mother foreigner swiss. in panic my grandparents put their children in panic their own foreign children only children on the children's train to southern france in panic.

i would not be if in panic my grandparents in panic had not sent their children panic to the south. i would not be if my mother not my mother. if she daughter sister niece not sent freighted transported panic to southern france to her uncle to the farmer i would not be.
my mother does the matur teaches refugee children earns her own money draws paints makes music swims in the sea happy the young woman in southern france at her uncle's. but but i would not be if my mother had not had to ought to be go back to switzerland to reunite the family back as a swiss woman has to as daughter sister has to as swiss woman abroad from france back to switzerland so-called native land suddenly. living in basle as refugees or something similar or what or something as swiss refugees in switzerland in basle in wartime little money. my mother daughter sister has to work so that the only son can ought to must study in switzerland. my mother becomes a secretary in my father's business.
i would not be.

i would not be if my grandmother mother of my father had not said in 1933:
- either hitler or me! -
and has to flee fly with her sons from germany to switzerland not to the usa my father son much prefer to flee to the usa want to much much prefer to the usa but no affidavit of support therefore switzerland therefore flee have to ought to to switzerland and transfer the firm in minute pieces etc or somehow or however to switzerland. in switzerland as stateless german with J passport have to ought to be allocated by swiss confederation to that town which has no art trade in antiques. basle therefore here in basle here found friends of my father friends a plc so that my grandmother + her sons here in basle fled here can stay here with their firm during the war here in basle precarious because of refugee status precarious but at least something. very precarious above all in 1941 but nevertheless here can be here in basle can live even can do a little business modest but at least something.

i would not be if my father firm boss had not employed my mother i would not be. i would not be if my father, boss, married, had not fallen in love with my mother, secretary. a very long very very long long time he courted her. she had another man, he was married, she my mother was not a jew, he my father jew had a jewish wife. she my mother young woman wanted to become an artist musician, he wanted to found a family children imperatively i would not be i would not be.

after the war my grandparents back to paris my mother daughter artist perhaps musician in paris want to be but but but my mother my father now love now want to have now want to marry.
i would not be if my father not divorce want to ought to and marry loved one my father my mother both now want to family found have children by nature naturally am i i too i and again not i because if.

Palü 2015

Letter to Jochen Gerz[98] **basle, 11 december 1997**

dear jochen,
have read your interview in the NZZ[99] and am not only not at all in agreement, but consider it appalling. your sentence, "time alone is the knife that leaves the wound open etc." shows me at last the thinking at the heart of your works for commemorative sites, which always left me uneasy (with the exception of the "dachau project", which I continue to find magnificent in its full acuity and acrimony). your sentence shows me the German enjoyment of forever "rummaging in old wounds", instead of letting the wounds heal, bearing the scars, and through this natural course of time – what a wonderful saying: "time heals all wounds" – viewing the past with more composure, more interest, more variety and viewing it as "over".
I consider this holocaust commemorative site mania in Germany especially abhorrent, and the pseudo-atonement of my generation intellectually woolly and masochistic. This generation of Germans, after all, was not personally involved. That is not a "grace": but it is a fact.
You too manifestly enjoy your status as a specialist for commemoration in the form of contemporary art – but anyway:
In conclusion here is a conversation I had with my father which made us both laugh heartily:
miriam: and then this utterly cringeworthy business about the holocaust memorial … and what gets on my nerves above all is the perpetual emphasis on a "place of quietness", "place of rest" as if something like that ought somehow to be "restful" in the middle of a great city – "place of quietness" – I could work myself up into a real rage about this.
father: "place of rest"? actually, it should be called a "restroom" …
miriam: absolutely, they should build a public convenience there.
father: precisely, and certified holocaust victims can pee there for free …
miriam: … whereas the others have to pay, and the proceeds go into a holocaust fund.
warm regards, miriam

my jews in germany
my jews in switzerland
my jews in japan
ATOMIC BOMBS

I always thought I prefer to show my jews in germany it would be nice very nice today to show my jews in germany today in todays germany germany not of that time but to show my jews in todays germany. today my jews in germany. to maintain the difference between jews and the others, to be forced to maintain a visible difference through these pictures and to do the statements of that visible difference, what, hopefully, is not visible in the paintings isn't realized and hopefully not there in the pictures not to be seen in the paintings but maybe, and also maybe not through the main title my jews, and the history, and my information, my storytelling, and my statements to the single paintings of the installation.
the house would be not only building, the animal not only animal, the men, the women, the children not only what you see, but also what I maintain and how I name the pictures: my jews in germany require a different reaction than in switzerland. in germany always and still today is this heavy oppressive past through the naming: my jews.

in switzerland there is rather a naïve astonishment or full ignorance, a lack of interest, my jews in switzerland could be also in general my strangers or in switzerland I could change my storytelling from my jews into my muslims, the building wouldn't be funeral but a mosque, the headgear would be adjusted to the islam and the animals I don't know.

my jews in japan jews in japan are the strangers/the foreign/the unknown, and – if I may suppose while writing – maybe there are no jews in japan japan without jewish refugees/emigrants in the time of that time japan in alliance with nazigermany, japan free of jews (judenfrei), my jews go to japan. HOW BEAUTIFUL! maybe it's possible japanese people could see something completely different in the work my jews HOW BEAUTIFUL! my statements at the same time simultaneous to a free interpretation or maybe no interpretation at all but only looking only seeing in japan to look without to know only to look/to see anyhow a unprejudiced look, to see without statement, to have this wild look onto my jews without my jews. the information later won't destroy but complete the first wild impression.

HOW BEAUTIFUL! everybody says so looking at my watercolors without information with a wild look at my watercolors how beautiful! like flowers or mandalas or or or. they are not flowers nor mandalas or or or, they are exclusively and only atomic bombs – after the wild look there comes the knowing/perception/realization (erkenntnis), after the wild the zivilisation, the statement, the naming, the storytelling, the history:
hitler   manhattan project   hiroshima-nagasaki   lucens   three mile island cernobyl   fukushima   or or or.[100]

HOW BEAUTIFUL! my jews, my atomic bombs in japan how beautiful!

2011 [artist-author's own English]

WAKO – Atom bomb discussion conducted by e-mail between Tokyo and Bregaglia 11 August 2011

Dear Miriam,
Hello. How are you? Thank you for waiting. My father has come out of hospital and now stays well. Thank you again for sending me the drawing images for the small room. I thought they are very charming, but I think it would be better to show more oil paintings because this will be your first exhibition in Tokyo. For example – this is only a suggestion – but it might be good to show some of the schlafen series,[101] as you will show them at the London show in October. Or we can show the series of works on Sarajevo or the Iraq war, though I do not know what kind of images they are. (I have read only the press release). I think so because it would be better and important to show these political works in Tokyo now. Even though they will be shown in the small room, it will be a very strong message. What do you think? By the way, I was going to London at the beginning of October. So I will try to reschedule to meet the opening of your show (29th). How long will you stay in London? Can I see you and discuss with you on the following Saturday or Sunday (Sep 30th or Oct 1st)? (Of course we can discuss the show before meeting in London by email). Looking forward to hearing from you!
Best wishes,
Kiyoshi Wako[102]

---

11 august 2011

Dear Kiyoshi,
good news about your father!
and first of all: I am looking forward to seeing you in London for my opening!
on the afternoon of the 30th I fly back to Basel … but we could of course meet before the opening or – not too early! in the morning of the 30.9. and: I think it's good you see this show, then you will also see there is no possibility to take "some" of 'schlafen' – it's one work = 1 room installation of 13 paintings which have to be hung in a certain way – you'll see! which surely doesn't fit in the small room …
and I won't combine the SARAJEVO series with 'meine juden', it's a wrong political issue.
but I have politically speaking very direct works of atomic bombs, watercolour on paper (sorry: no oil), here I send you examples, but examples only. if you find it interesting in the small room, I would go in search in my studio for ones which would fit. the atomic bombs for me at least look all quite the same, but are going from very small to very large (2.00 × 3.00 cm).
ok. but maybe this work is "too direct"? too much connected to history? but they fit from the content exactly and perfectly with 'meine juden'. and, of course and anyhow: if you don't want them, that's perfectly ok to me – I'll think of something else.
so: tell me what you think!
all the best,
miriam
(maybe you realize I am searching for a possibility NOT to have "only" painting …)

30 August 2011
Dear Miriam,
Sorry for my late reply. Thank you for sending me the atomic bomb series. Please send me other images if you find any. Yes, I think it's a good idea to show this series in the small room. Please let me know how this is related to 'meine juden'. I would like to read your text about this series in English. As for the whole exhibition plan, we can discuss more later on. My flight will arrive in London at 4PM then I will go to your opening if my flight is not delayed. Shall we meet before lunch, let's say 11AM–12AM, for a meeting before your leaving on 30th? We can have lunch after that. I look forward to seeing you and the exhibition!
Best wishes,
Kiyoshi Wako

---

12 september 2011
Dear Kiyoshi,
I am looking forward to the show in London and to seeing you there!
here I send you the text connected to my jews and the atomic bomb, it's a text directly done for your show.
I translated the German text myself into "my" English. I did so because my German is also very special in this case and not easy to translate for a translator – it's a little like translating Gertrude Stein ... so I preferred to do it in English like a sound or something similar, a soundpoem or so. of course it has a lot of mistakes in the writing of the single words and otherwise.
I send you also the German version, so if you want to use the text in your catalogue, it would be far better to translate it directly from German into Japanese.
and as soon I have chosen the atomic bombs in my studio in Basle, I'll send you photos.
all the best!
miriam

---

15 September 2011
Dear Miriam,
Thank you for the text. I have read it closely. It is a very poetic and strong text. Although I like it very much, the last sentence which starts with "HOW BEAUTIFUL! everybody ..." can be linked to the ongoing incident of Fukushima and also, the sentence with the word "beautiful" and "atomic bombs" might cause misunderstandings here in Japan. I feel I cannot put the whole text in the catalogue. Of course, we can show the works in the smaller space and we understand your thoughts about relationships between bombs and Jews. Is it possible for you to change the last part of the text? See you soon in London!
Sincerely,
Kiyoshi Wako
P.S. which hotel are you staying in?

---

16 september 2011
Dear Kiyoshi,
the "misunderstanding" is intentional: ...HOW BEAUTIFUL! Everybody ... and so on I can't leave out, it's also some kind of

similar in an old text connected to the time I did the atomic bombs. and: it's NOT an invention, people reacted in this time and do also today at the first look like this, which I think is very interesting: the difference between looking and knowing, between "a beautiful image/picture" and the so-called reality.
so: the text is only to be had with this part.
we can leave out the real information after the history: "hitler manhattan project etc" and end with: the history or or or. that would be ok to me.
but you really can't leave out the crucial point: the beauty of the image of the atomic bomb! because it doesn't mean the atomic bomb is beautiful, but: the image of the atomic bomb is beautiful. the bomb itself in reality is something of the very worst, which happened only twice, because as a weapon it was unbearable after Hiroshima and Nagasaki. and this was the core of the cold war: to have a sort of balance because of and WITH the horror of this weapon.
when I did these watercolours, it still was in the time of the cold war. I am a person who grew up in the cold war, in the 1950-60-70s the image of the atomic bomb was very important, as a kid I saw these "beautiful" photos of the test sites in the USA and the Bikinis, they were common and daily in the print media and the documentary movies. and there was a heavy discussion about whether Switzerland should have atomic weapons in their army or not. and: there were also these interesting movies like Kubrick's "dr. strangelove and how I learned to love the bomb" and (forgot who did it) "atomic cafe" and a lot of this atomic discussion and sign and using it as a symbol of the cold war also in literature and art, specially in pop art.
my atomic bombs are really "beautiful". when you see documentary on atomic bomb sites like Bikini, it's also "beautiful", and there is the interest of political art, as I see it: what means beauty …
so, no way of leaving out the sentence of the atomic bombs and their beauty.
you wanted something political, you got something political. that might be not nice or respectful: political art as I see it – and this was also in SARAJEVO pieces – has to be some kind of hurting and has to be uncomfortable, biting, burning, keen, sharp. and anyhow: how do you want to explain my atomic bombs in your small room without my text?
you wanted something political, so: act like this. no way to have my atomic bombs without my text on the atomic bombs, in this case connected to 'meine juden'.
so, it's in your hands: if you don't want me to be political, say so. I can't be only "a little" political. but let me know by Monday, if you want me to choose atomic bombs or not for your little room: Thomas Riegger wanted to take them with him on Thursday 22.9. – I won't do the work of choosing and so on if you don't want them …
all the best and looking forward to seeing you!
miriam

16 September 2011
Dear Miriam,
Thank you for your long and sincere letter. It made me think so much. At first I thought it is impossible to show the text here. I have been giving it good thoughts all day

today and also translated it into Japanese to have better understanding. I talked with my wife and my staff, who was born in Hiroshima. I am still thinking. Could you give me one more day? The matter is very important. Of course I want to show the watercolour works here, but as for the text I just need to think more. I would like to thank you for giving me an opportunity to think so deeply about such an important matter.
Sincerely,
Kiyoshi

17 september 2011
Dear Kiyoshi – of course!
I am so happy you are thinking about what I think is important! and my very best wishes to you!
miriam
(do you know the movie by Sophia Coppola "Lost in Translation"? I feel like being in this movie)

17 September 2011
Dear Miriam,
Thank you for waiting. I have spent another day thinking about the matter really deeply. I still feel it is very difficult for us Japanese to accept putting the word "beautiful" with the atomic bomb. I still want very much to show your watercolours in the little room. When Japanese people see the figures in your watercolours they would definitely understand the subject at once, even before reading the titles. I think simply showing your works with the titles is strong enough to make viewers think. I think there is no "wild look" at the image of the atomic bomb. I understand your intention but when all the people around the world are under the fear of nuclear threat, putting the word "beautiful" with the atomic bomb is never acceptable, especially for us Japanese. I don't know anyone in Japan who said or wrote "beautiful" about the atomic bomb ever since. It is very important to think about the atomic bomb or the idea of beauty, but I cannot relate the word "beautiful" with the atomic bomb in any context. And I think it is not about what beauty is. It is beautiful and wonderful to show 'my jews' in Japan for the first time. And your watercolours are very beautiful (and scary). But the atomic bomb itself is never beautiful. Showing your works in Japan when only one year has passed since the Fukushima incident occurred is already very political. I think we can be political without words. How do you think? I hope you will understand my thoughts.
Sincerely, Kiyoshi

17 september 2011
Dear Kiyoshi,
I think it's very interesting what you think – and how different we think. and I accept of course the impossibility for Japanese people to connect the word beautiful to the atomic bomb. so I agree in the principle to show the atomic bombs I choose for your little room. I like also very much how important the discussion about horror and beauty is, how existential: the looking on pictures versus "reality". so: I choose next week and give it to Thomas for transport. is this

ok. to you?
the other thing is my new text about 'meine juden' and the atomic bomb. I want really to leave it like it is. but nobody is forced to read texts. if you don't want it in your catalogue, that's ok to me. you have the text Jochen gave you already translated in English which belongs to 'meine juden', so let's use this one in your catalogue, if you agree.
but I would find it very good to print the new text and to have it in the show, so people who want to read it can do it. of course even if I am a guest in Japan, my point of view is not the Japanese: it's a mixture between a jewish and european afterwar thinking and living with the IMAGE of the bomb. and it is also the Swiss at the time of the seventies point of view on atomic bombs and the use of atomic power:
in the seventies the people of Basle and surroundings (Germans, French) engaged in the anti-atomic plant movement and occupied the site where an atomic powerplant not far from Basle was to have been constructed. it was a very funny and nice form of occupation with very varied people – young, old, bourgeois, new leftist, farmers and so on – and the hard core was living for weeks in tents. at the end the swiss government decided not to build the plant, and we were all very proud of this success.
back to the possibility of showing texts in your catalogue, how we – old European and Japanese of the time today, 2011 – differ in our looking at the image of the atomic bombs and the interpretation of it and the reality (maybe reality?). my suggestion: why not take our mail discussion in its integral form?
I would like that, it would show the difficulties on interpretation. it would show the cultural difference on looking at images. it would show the difficulties about interpretation of reality and history and how the flow of time changes also the interpretation – very interesting, don't you think?
and a little "correction": there might be no "wild look" at documentary photos of the atomic bomb in Japan (somewhere else for sure), but even in Japan there is a "wild look" at my watercolours. I am very anxious to know how it will be ...
and I am really looking forward to speaking about all this in London with you, already I like a lot how intellectually seen our show goes on!
all the best,
miriam

20 September 2011

Dear Miriam,
I feel very happy to know that you still want to show the works after our conversations. As for the text, maybe we can just put it on the wall in the small room. Let's narrow down the options little by little. However, I am sorry I can not put the word "beautiful" in the catalogue. I would like to decide whether to include the mail discussion in the catalogue or not when we make the whole plan and layouts for the catalogue. We want to include the text of "my jews" for sure. I still haven't received the text translated by Jochen which you mentioned in your mail. Please send it as soon as possible. As for the shipping of the works, we'd like to have them here whenever after Oct 25th. By the way which hotel will you be staying in?

I will visit your hotel on Sep 30th. Let's have a brunch and discuss more. Could you kindly send me an invitation for the show in London? See you soon at the opening!
Sincerely,
Kiyoshi
P.S. The story about the power plant in Switzerland was very interesting! I really think the Japanese should act the same way!

1991

i came home at night and as was my habit switched myself into the television: suddenly the gulf war broke out.
i sat in front of the set.
then i just didn't know whether i should go to bed or not. got up, walked around, sat down again, slept on the sofa in front of the television, only to crawl into bed in the early hours so that i could begin the day as always: get up late, coffee, newspaper, working.
defiantly i decided that to work at art was better than to work at war.
as soon as my work was over, i turned to the war: newspaper, radio, TV. sometimes i forced myself to go out in the evening so as not crawl completely into the set.
when, however, israel was shelled and female announcers with gas masks commented on the latest news – jews were threatened by gas – suddenly – again at night – in front of the television – i burst out sobbing in panic. from then on i looked at the set briefly in the morning before work.
i worked: at the table, in empty space, in watery space, in dusty space; with pencil, finger colours, watercolour and chalk. plants and ulcers with my eyes closed, women, animals, heads and nuclear bombs with my eyes open. i had firmly installed the camera in front of the television in order to catch aerial pictures, which i could later work on in oils: the most attractive picture was the fire disaster in bhopal, which was shown in an anniversary broadcast about the greatest environmental accidents of the past ten years.
i phoned my relatives in israel. they said: that every evening after work their daughter came back from tel aviv to sleep in the kibbutz, that when my uncle first tried on the gas mask he almost suffocated and therefore never used it, that when there was an alert the entire family stayed in a sealed room, that they could see the scuds from the kibbutz and were filming them with their new video camera.
i worked in rage: i was already getting used to this daily panic, to these telephone calls to israel, to these completely different discussions with parents, women friends and male friends to the embarrassing public announcements of german-speaking male intellectuals – when, suddenly, the war was over.
i gathered all my works from this period together under the title "KRIEGSRAUM" ["WAR SPACE"], a temporally ordered space, and put them away. i began again working at the table and from scratch: blocked up my ears, drew/painted EVERYTHING with closed and open eyes – no order – no laws, naturalistic and not, explanatory and not, illustrative and not, political and not, sentimental and not – and in addition: nuclear bombs, processing sites, ulcers palpated in finger paint and dancing men, women palpated and read in chalk, animals, landscapes and the air, or the possibility of plants.
i brought these works together in various temporarily ordered spaces: 'nachkrieg (was fehlt)' ['postwar (what is missing')], '1 weiblicher monat (nachkrieg)' ['1 female month (postwar)'], 'WAS FEHLT (nachkrieg)' ['WHAT IS MISSING (postwar)'] and so on.
my parents became older, my women and male friends became more foreign, more alien to me. to work at art was better than to work at war.

 18 August 1967 CONVERSATION WITH MIRIAM (noted down by my mother, found among her papers after her death)

- with art one shouldn't have the feeling that it has been created by a man or a woman. it should, it must be generally valid. -
- being married, enduring the husband and having the children in one's legs - that's not something I want. I want to be free and independent. otherwise I cannot devote myself to art. -
- I don't know yet whether I'll attend the school of graphic design. the preliminary course, yes. But actually, I want to be a "freelance artist". -
- working regularly from 7 a.m. to 6 p.m., as in an office – that's not free study. I draw best when I'm not tied to a daily programme. It was wonderful when I was at home alone. -
- I have the need to be always drawing. -
- being a man is much better than being a woman. a woman is so dependent on her feelings. she can't be "objective" like a man. proof: how many women have achieved great things in art? few – and mostly these women were unmarried, with no children, or divorced. -
- with P. Moderson[103] one does not notice that her art is feminine. -
- with stage designers, it is particularly striking how a woman is incapable of constructing architecturally. she loses herself in details, tiny nuances. the big lines, the structure are not her thing. by the way, in the theatre women have great difficulty in getting their own way. that's why I don't think I'll become a stage designer. -
- if I do marry, then properly and I'll have at least 5 children. -
- the Afflerbachs are both graphic artists. the wife is a much better drawer than the husband. and yet she is not such a good graphic artist as her husband. she is too subjective. and then she's a woman with a profession and children, a husband and the household as well – that's no good. she does both things only half. Just the same as with the Zickendrahts. -
- I don't know if I'm capable of loving a man. -
- I wouldn't want to be like you with dad, so devoted -
- I am not a sociable person at all. I'm very shy. -
- I don't want to have a husband and children and carry out my profession on the side. that's nonsense. -
- oh, Doris, that cow... when her boyfriend was in Israel, what a tragedy... she let everybody know how much she loves him and is fretting about him. I think that's awful. basically, nobody needs to know what one feels. -

dr köchlin concerning miriam, 17 August 67
- speak with a woman psychologist? no way! -
- with mrs Afflerbach? I've already spoken with her. but, you know, it embarrasses me. you can't bother other people with your own problems. -
- at the Girls' High School, it's terrible. dr Amstutz is super and she tries to stimulate discussion. but there are only 3 in the class who speak: the others just sit there listlessly ... and I can't always be speaking and thrusting my ideas on the rest. it's strange actually, precisely the three who were no good in the landdienst discuss with dr Amstutz. the others are well-behaved, goody-goody girls, boring and terribly passive. they haven't got any opinions of their own. -
- it really annoys me when someone stands in front of a work of art and says "how womanly its sentiment is". with a work of art, one shouldn't be able to sense whether it's been made by a man or a woman. -
- all in all, things are so complex. I can't make head or tail of it all. -

to Ingrid Wagner, Berlin **10 september 90**

dear ingrid and auliki,[104]
many thanks for the documents you sent – i have read everything, including reading the HDK booklet[105] again.
i am not interested in participating actually: the language, the approach is simply much too academic for my taste – to my mind hesitantly academic in the bad sense.
you are, of course, free in your project to write about texts that i have already published, but i would not like to give interviews. it is my belief that such things backfire: this pinning down of us women artists to our "life nexus" (horrible phrase) is simply reductive – haven't we manifested ourselves through our work, just as the interesting male artists? have i not, from the very outset, equated private + political as an aesthetic strategy and worked in line with it? is the concept of "quality" in art created by women or men not to be sought precisely at this intersection of politics, the personal, the public and the private? etc.
if work = life, then academics such as yourselves should really start from the work, from the public. for women today there is no excuse at all if they want to create art. that, once this decision is taken, their path is a different path to that of the men is beyond all doubt. as is the fact that it is extremely hard work.
many of the paths you list here on the way to taking up a life as a woman artist, on the way to the right form of work, have nothing to do with working at art in itself – and here you are, for my taste, far too psychological and sociological in your manner of questioning and far too little concerned with the nature of working at art. this boxes us in too much: in this way we again become – to exaggerate a little – "hardship cases". for goodness' sake, ingrid! this is precisely the attitude that makes a lot of women artists, above all the younger ones, react allergically to any form of female designation, to any form of "women's policy" and above all to women's exhibitions, which i too reject if they are organized with this wailing-and-whingeing attitude.
the only thing that interests me now is experimental work and politically radical and combative work – in the style of the "guerrilla girls". i am still waiting for women art historians who are not afraid of e.g. comparing – with feminist verve – bruce naumann and jenny holzer, gabriele münter and nolde, miriam cahn for example with disler … but for goodness' sake stop producing these minutely-researched demonstrations that women still do not have equal rights and are therefore only victims. we know that. everybody knows that. nothing happens. and it's our fault if we're content with such chicken-hearted stuff because that's where the money comes from – and the conditions as well, in your case those laid down by the senate.
it's just not on that we – the women artists – invent a new language and that you – the women academics – don't change the academic discourse. to answer my question, auliki, as to how you arrived at such an abstruse, uptight title by saying that that's how the senate likes it, is enough to turn me off such projects completely.
yes, absolutely, everything is tougher for women – but also more comprehensive. we live – necessarily – in a men's world AND in a women's world, which leads to double information. very few men are interested in the women's world – in a cultural sense, I mean – and are hence only semi-informed. this scared-rabbit approach,

as represented in your project, is thus a total mental underload – which I consider fundamentally wrong.
well, that's that.
nevertheless, many greetings,
miriam
P.S. our symposium[106] is already a "full house" – but if you are interested in getting tickets as non-speaking participants, you must tell me and I'll reserve you some. 3 days = sfr. 100.-

Markus Merz[107] **1984**

Dear Miriam,
I have spent the past three weeks in monastic seclusion – namely, in the Liestal barracks. Outside my window is a stonemason's store-yard, slabs of marble, farther back stand a few fir trees, then come hills. If I blink a little, the marble slabs and the firs are transformed into pines or cypresses and the unexciting Baselbiet hills become hills in Tuscany – and the military establishment becomes a monastery. But, as I say, only when I blink.
On Saturday we are travelling to Champfèr in the Engadine – together with the military monastic life this is the reason why I can't come to Zurich on Friday evening. I have not yet packed and must altogether find my way back into my civilian skin.
At present I'm thinking a lot about the extent to which dreams have a communicative character that reaches beyond the dreamer himself. After all, there is no denying that a dream is first and foremost a highly individual formation. If I interpret another person's dream, I am employing the emotional and intellectual impression that I have of his or her person in order to interpret the dream in a more or less tailor-made fashion. The question now is this: is there a dream stratum that is supra-individual? In other words, can I interpret the dream of person A to person B or to group C, D, E etc. in such a way that B or C, D and E feel that they are being addressed personally?
I can hear your objection: why interpret at all and not simply narrate? To what extent – I ask in turn – does an image need interpretation? The fact is that I have often stood uncomprehendingly in front of this or that picture and have been made aware of its content and meaning only by being given a few little hints. And of course it happens on a daily basis that people tell me a dream and understand the dream image or the dream events only with the help of my interpretation.
Looking at a dream, or even better: looking into a dream – without any attempt at explanation – is admittedly a really important prior activity. My approach is first of all to describe the dream very precisely and to push to one side any interpretation that tries to impose itself in my mind. The "precise describing", however, is not, as it were, a photographic copying, but itself already a certain process of enriching in that I also describe the mood or feeling that triggers a dream image. If we assume that I dream of a light-green snake, then I note down: the snake is light-green like birch leaves in springtime. I then frequently observe that precisely the "birch leaves in springtime" lead to an understanding of the dream image.
I now actually do suppose that a certain dream stratum creates images that are of interest not only for the dreamer but also for others. I am considering portraying this stratum in my own dreams. The art will consist in finding the correct balance between portrayal and

interpretation.
Do you remember our conversation about symbols? I entirely agree with you: firstly, we must definitely forget what a symbol is, that there are such things as symbols, and what others – especially the academic world – understand by a symbol. The image is an image, full stop. But then the image needs to be communicated, and suddenly, completely unsummoned, a thought is there, an understanding, an inkling of sense, which imposes itself so commandingly that you can no longer thrust it aside. The decisive question, which I am still unable to answer, is this: is what is imposing itself here communicative? Is the other person happy when I immediately supply him with it, or would he prefer to find it out for himself? Would he perhaps like to find out something else and am I disturbing him if I tell him my interpretation? Or is there also on the level of interpretation a kind of "truth" which is supra-individual and should thus also be communicated?
So, these are the questions that I am concerned with. Now the sun has just crept up over the hills and is shining into my cell. Now everything is even much more Italian than before.
What are my brothers, the wolves, doing? They howled for us, perhaps especially for me because I howl so badly. But naturally they sensed that I had to go away again and expressed my grief for me.
I wish you a wonderful evening in Zurich. If you like, please write to me – I'd like to take a few lessons from you again.
Fond wishes and a hug,
Markus

1988

Dear Miriam,
I'm sitting in Bardolino on the lakeside, the sun is shining warmly, the lake is smooth, light grey in colour, shading into the even lighter grey of the haze on the horizon.
Thank you for the Beuys. The man clearly had a grand, universal vision. Adults are children, the real utopia of brother and sister states in a united Europe, the combination of freedom and self-determination on the one hand and spirituality on the other hand, the opportunity for Christianity to at last become Christian – he saw everything.
A white boat is passing. Where the water was churned up it is green.
I sometimes have a form of communication with animals, which my mind tells me is just an illusion. But my mind has told me quite a few stupid things in the past, and as a precaution I have adopted the habit of not taking any notice of it in certain situations. I prefer to be thankful when a bird begins to clamour in such agitation that I'm made to wonder when on a hike and then notice that I've just taken the wrong path. And when the birds quite clearly laugh out loud at me when

I, for example, think myself clever, then they're right too. He who has ears to hear, let him hear.
Just now three flew past and chirped something to me. Perhaps it's something to do with writing. After all, I haven't written for years – no letters, no short essays, no "academic" articles, no book. It seems I'm waiting until the writing flows out of me as easily as birds' chirping. And here I have a question to you: where among total non-exertion, non-intention, non-volition is the place for exertion and volition? I, at least, do not begin wanting until it emerges like a blossom or fruit from non-volition.
The birds are laughing out loud at me again. It hurts how they're laughing at me. The lake is even more immersed in haze. The horizon is a disappearing line that can just barely be sensed. Now the birds want something to eat. I'll order a brioche and throw crumbs to them. They're picking at them with their beaks. Meanwhile a pair of ducks have come swimming along and are also enjoying the meal.
This afternoon I'll go walking up into the hilly hinterland again. Olive groves, cypresses, fig trees, vines, and right on the hilltop an old castle, no longer inhabited, and any amount of light. Peccorino al pepe and prosciutto crudo.
Fond greetings and a kiss,
Markus

soldiers (men)
cars and carts
suitcases
water canisters
wood
sarajevo
women crying
picasso
WHAT LOOKS AT ME

for years i have been seeing soldiers soldiers look out at me from the television first in the gulf war much earlier before i had a television i saw fewer soldiers i saw soldiers above all in the newspaper but above all since i have had a television set soldiers have been looking at me out of the television and the most striking were the soldiers in the falklands war warriors whom one hardly ever saw even more striking were the soldiers in the gulf war warriors whom one hardly ever saw as in a promotional film because there was a ban a ban on showing soldiers at work or only at work when they did this work on machines on electronic machines that did not show them doing the killing work but pressing a button steering huge machines but one did not see the result although the camera was mounted on the projectile one saw the result actually only from the perspective of the projectile that is actually only from the perspective of the machine not from the perspective of the person of the soldier who naturally blew up not only buildings with this projectile but also people.

actually I first consciously saw soldiers or soldiers looked at me out of the television when that yugoslavian war broke out when young rambos soldiers who look like silvester stallone from the film proudly declared that they received a reward when they shoot at people in sarajevo from the surrounding area from the hills around sarajevo the mountains around sarajevo and that the reward is higher the higher the higher the smaller the target to be hit a child a dog a cat even brings a bigger reward than an adult person.

these rambos looked out at me from my television set exactly like a rambo or a schwarzenegger or a terminator in a film not only the expression on these young faces was interesting but they were after all men they were after all men they were after all men but the insignias that is the clothing that distinguishes this rambo type the sweatband the jauntily knotted kerchief around the head this head with a bandeau which for me distinguishes the head of a soldier today a white soldier a western soldier or central european soldier a soldier a man who is becoming completely brutalized.

For me these soldiers are at present now today one of the images of a man one of the images that look at me and look at me and which i as a female artist look at me as a female artist which i as a female artist which i try to depict which i try which i try to depict.

these soldiers looked at me when i was looking at gazing at guernica which had been transferred transposed transported to madrid protected behind armoured glass framed by soldiers two to the right and two to the left of guernica probably they were policemen guardia civil but they had on i think the same gear as the fascist militia picasso hated so much i gazed at guernica the horse the electric light the light bulb and the screaming women the grey of the picture the black-and-white of the picture and these two soldiers stared back into the room space in their guardian function stared at the male public and the female public who in turn stared at the picture that essentially had a political purpose inasmuch as picasso had painted it because the town of guernica had been bombed to rubble by fascists with the help of the national socialists but the two soldiers who were guarding this picture for which picasso had made it a condition that it should come back only when fascism in spain was over and the picture came back to spain after his death i think at least after francos death and so these two young soldiers were staring at me the two men still in the old uniform of the guardia civil and that amounted to an absurd situation.

i had seen guernica when it was still in the museum of modern art there it simply hung there it hung there just as it was a picture that i actually it was a picture in which i the light bulb and the horse the horse reminded me of the fact that as a young teenager i had always liked most of all to draw only horses it was a picture that showed something that i think cannot be shown that is women crying it was a picture that reminded me that the horse was my favourite animal as a young teenager as for very many girls the horse which i really rode as very many teenage girls the horse which i preferred to stroke touch brush down more than ride and above all looked at actually i loved above all looking at the horse the horse was a mystery to me the horse was eerie and when i see this light bulb with this horse in the picture guernica it is even eerier.

as a child i planned an entire motorcar i planned it entirely in my head and the next day made it in cardboard it was more a little car or cart made of cardboard and sellotape it was actually completed which was rare since even as a child i was very quick and impatient this little car was my invention it was my own invention because the previous night before going to sleep i thought through in detail how one would have to build a little car like that so that it really looks like a car on television during this yugoslavian war looking out at me from the television from the television set i see on television little cars and carts vehicles of all kinds carrying water canisters wood suitcases bags and necessities of life in general that the people of sarajevo or other occupied towns and villages have to lug along because there are no means of transport usable there anymore because there is almost nothing there anymore i look at it often every evening every evening i see these carts and have to think of that little car i invented and which actually is not invented at all but is a little car a thing with wheels a vehicle is an object of survival just as the water canister is an object of survival is a modern object of survival made of plastic which when i see it in a shop i think rather ugly and at the same time i have developed a love for it it is an object of survival just as strangely wood is an object of survival although i know of course that wood is used for heating i have never connected with this the idea that an entire town saws down its trees because there is no other means of heating available because the means of heating the wood is just wood now not a tree in the garden tree in the avenue i lived on an avenue every time i left the house there were these trees at the back the gardens sounds more idyllic than it was when i came back from berlin in january february in this over-early spring these trees these trees made basle more southerly than berlin in this early spring these trees led me to draw plants with my eyes closed always plants in spring spring plants in summer summer plants in autumn autumn plants in winter winter plants kneeling squatting on the floor blind putting it better with my eyes closed i felt related to these plants and drew these plants in chalk with my eyes closed.

during this time the "picasso - braque" exhibition took place in basle the period of collaboration between these two painters braque painted drew very many trees plants picasso almost none it seems perhaps that is true perhaps not he seems to know few plants he knows few plants no connection with plants or little and yet and yet the few plants the few trees in this exhibition overwhelmed me the few plants the few trees were the essence of the plant were plant-essential were tree-essential were thanks to his way of painting far more plantal than in braques more intellectual way of painting soon bored picasso stopped painting plants for me picasso was always someone who drew painted or whatever above all animals and people the animals and the persons animals and the women animals and the women and the men the animals the children the women the men and perhaps the animals the women the men the children in surroundings from bed via the studio arena to the sea and since as a child i naturally tended logically like many children to like animals best i liked picassos animals best too although to me they were eerie but they matched my observations in the zoo alongside which we lived and where if one looked closely at them the animals looked back the animals actually were very eerie above all the hyena whose smell sometimes got through right to our house the hyena had this lopsided gait when it walked the owl the white owl the snowy owl that lived in a little old house the owl in front of which i used to stand for a long time waiting until it at last turned its head opened its big eyes and looked at me as if it knew more than i myself the owl frightened me likewise.

when i think of sarajevo i think of the luggage of the suitcases not only of the little cart but i think of these streams of refugees of these streams of people whom i saw especially at the beginning on television or photographed strangely enough lugging old suitcases with them bundles as if they were from the second world war or i saw the second world war people who actually although they are people like us here in basle or in zurich or vienna remarkably rarely carried these new rucksacks that after all we all have who live close to mountains and sarajevo too in the mountains but they had again as if there was no other possibility when one is fleeing bundles old suitcases if they were lucky pull-carts sledges bicycles onto which they could pack everything if not then they carry the strangest sacks then they carry sacks things tied up into a bundle and what they have on their heads too the clothing they are wearing is strange insofar as its wool so-called old materials as if there had never been any companies there like "patagonia" or "jack wolfskin" or "the north face" as if there had never been these companies who produce these nasa materials which we all use in the mountains or when doing sport and which were certainly used by the people in sarajevo tuzla and so on when they were doing sport but perhaps these refugees were above all small farmers and poorer people who dont have these clothes that keep you warm in a practical way and are above all light light for flight strange also the old rucksacks and in general it seemed as if the term refugee people who suddenly have to flee look the same all over the world be it in africa be it in india be it in china in tibet be it in vietnam be it in south america and now i suppose again in europe refugees all over the world look the same bent over they drag themselves along the camera looks into their eyes their faces and the faces look back in an empty exhausted way and look into my room at me.

sarajevo is for me the same sarajevo is for me a different quality has a different quality from the wars before i have always concerned myself with wars naturally jewish perhaps also female and although born completely in switzerland i have grown up in the awareness that there is this possibility that people trigger off wars that people human beings persons men above all suddenly out of nothing trigger off wars start shooting at others laying into others and the others perhaps in that case us must flee the yugoslav war and the token sarajevo has this quality has a new a new quality for me something new because it has to do with people who are like us it is not so far away it is very close it is nevertheless very close although i have never been there it is very close it is too close although it seems cynical if things farther away wars farther away are less important but it is dishonest to believe untruthful that there are no differences inexact it is a major difference whether a war takes place in europe or somewhere else despite the so-called global village it is just not the case that all images that look out at me from the television become equal it is just not the case i am aware that images from somalia of these thin completely starved people dark-skinned people that these images despite everything despite their horror despite those dying are farther away from me although they are electronically just as close as the images from sarajevo.

i can imagine the similar effect when the so-called civil war in spain broke out although there was no television there yet no electronic things although there was still no so-called global village there yet it must have had a similar effect on intellectuals as on us intellectuals and politically thinking people it must have a similar effect must have had as for us today this yugoslavian war must have especially sarajevo as a token exactly like guernica as a token of absolute horror of guilt of failure hence the will to want to do something about it as every man and every woman has it in his or her power to do personally picasso was not a political a politically agitating artist in the sense that he took over illustrated pilloried things in an ideological way but he is a political artist in my sense because he is a completely simple artist because he sees the things that are happening around him and paints so simply it is precisely so simple and at the same time of course what one sees around oneself is so utterly overwhelming down to the last detail so utterly much that one also gets that rapidness that picasso had he went every day into his studio and painted like mad in a rapid tempo and drew that is the nature of drawing he painted madly rapidly at a mad tempo made sculptures at a mad tempo this has to do with the fact that he simply wanted to depict what he saw around himself and that was so utterly overwhelming every day part of it was the information from his spain about atrocities in the so-called civil war not a civil war but a trial run for fascist thinking for fascist thinking and military action of fascists a trial run in which the non-fascist the part of europe that was not fascist miserably failed because it dismissed this trial run as a civil war i can imagine that for many people this war was a shock hence many people saw themselves compelled to act to act inasmuch as they went there and joined the brigades and fought against the fascists others who remained at home because they saw themselves as incapable of fighting as i would be for example but stayed at home but sought forms of commenting on or portraying this horror this war for me guernica belongs to this sphere as a commentary on this war no more no less.

a remarkable thing about guernica and not only about guernica is picassos attempt to paint women weeping women wailing screaming weeping more likely weeping women these are the women who look at me today out of the television set the women who are weeping today however are differently dressed they have scarves over their heads when they weep when they are carrying their son their husband their brother their relatives to the grave wearing scarves over their heads but the gesture of these women is precisely the same as with picassos weeping women only picassos weepers have elegant little hats that kind of mantilla those spanish headscarves interwoven with lace light scarves lace cloths lace handkerchiefs that they crumple with their fingers in terms of outfit therefore they are very elegant which you cannot say of the women looking at me today out of the television set they are wrapped in humble cloths wrapped in a peasant muslim way or simply impoverished whereas these spanish women are very elegant the little hat is of equal value as the weeping and that baffled me it is weeping in itself that picasso wanted to portray i think and nevertheless the little hats are equally important it was important to picasso that the little hat was equally important as the hand and the little cloth and the eyes and the tears a passionate picture for weeping women of women weeping.

i saw these weeping women in the exhibition "picasso after guernica" in berlin during one of the worst phases of the war in yugoslavia every day images were shown me were commented on looked at me out of the television torture concentration camps raping of women and girls women who were carrying their relatives to the grave whose faces had this expression of picassos weeping women actually on the one hand these images looked at out of the television set on the other hand i saw photographs in the newspapers that haunted me and from which i then tried to make series by copying these photographs directly partly also from memory and part of these works was that i copied a postcard of those weeping women of picasso because i was sure that it matched this situation spot on this european situation this shameful disgrace again.

as a child i was always looking at books my parents had this book "the face of fame" with photographs of famous men and women there were a few women but predominantly men of course especially artists and picasso there was a picture of picasso in which he is wearing a hat and has his coat collar turned up one can see only his eyes of course i wanted to become like all these people it is absolutely clear i wanted to become an artist from a very early age naturally i didnt in my wildest dreams think that there was a difference between female artists and male artists i wanted to be an artist i wanted to be like picasso i thought that was the most wonderful thing the greatest thing this life forever going into the studio every day to do something to paint to build just as i had planned the little car the night before and afterwards i built the little car and was very satisfied with my little car my mother was very satisfied with my little car everybody was always very satisfied when i did something in this direction and so very early on i wanted to become an artist like picasso also because he looked so good with his striped t-shirts moreover he lived in the south by the beach by the sea.

i got this information from photographs not from pictures from photographs which i greedily devoured i thought that as an artist one had to live like that picasso the primordial figure these photographs which emanate a very joyous aura because there are always women children animals involved a southern a wonderful life that i wanted to live as an adult even if at that time my models changed daily these three remained over a longish period picasso giacometti munch my model in puberty this bleak sombreness these youthful women this inexpressibly flowing dramatic mood and the shadows above all behind the figures sick people dead people lying in bed people screaming looking at me dissolving on the lsd trip giacometti the region bregaglia the mayor of the village in which we were every winter who had gone to school with giacometti i knew all the details and here too the appearance of this handsome man almost more handsome than picasso i wanted to become like giacometti because he lived beside his studio in the mountains in the big city and every day always went across into his studio and all this information was again confirmed via photographs these photographs looked at me through this looking i wanted to become like these men for a very long time i did not see any difference between woman and man i wished for every child that it would not have to make this distinction only around 23 did i really and truly see that i cannot become like picasso like giacometti like munch at all i will lead a different life i will live a different life just as up to now i have already lived differently because i am a woman and because women live different lives from men.

this recognition was a shock which however did not handicap me on the contrary this anger became my driving force my machine a new world opened up i was lucky in the seventies many women of my age thought that way somewhat older women artists thought that way and acted worked in young media video performance thought worked similarly to me with their bodies out of rage anger female body unknown as an implement never used before as an implement active seismograph as an absolute novelty working directly with the body as implement new insights my new territory that mixes with my old childs knowledge combines commingles into my own brew that was what i wanted to do i wanted to work with my entire body with space with time move in space in time and at the same time not forget all that i had already done all that i had already wanted all that i had already wanted to become who i had already wanted to be i wanted to become picasso and me myself i wanted to be as good as picasso i wanted like picasso to go every day into my studio to paint draw build and yet knew that this old image of the artist is over bound by its time classically with house wife children café discussions going to the brothel life circumstances that i would never have nor wanted any wife any whore any house any children but something new where the woman the artist the woman working and acting is the focal point i myself i myself working acting a woman artist then i had to put this artist myth that i had loved so much behind me assign it to my past and to history yet what i have seen i have seen what looked at me i have seen.

jan./feb. 1994

this text was part of the performance for the exhibition "picasso" in the haus der kunst des 20. jahrhunderts in vienna in 1994: the text which i read in a rush and as fast as possible was interrupted after every paragraph by the "short pieces".

lecture delivered to the symposium "the exhibition medium" during the Wiener Festwochen[108]

ANGER MY MACHINE 1990

chaos, exaggeration, unreliability, liquid and volatile thinking, work driven by love or hatred, multi-cultural living, neurotic, abnormal, ugly, working to physical excess, giggling hysterically, roaring with laughter – now the one thing, now the other – and many things besides: attributes that are ascribed to the image of the artist (and hence to myself) – and also to women in general.
while in politics quota systems are being – slowly – introduced, and in the business world women are being given advancement in line with the cost-benefit principle, and in the academic world – very slowly – the different, networked form of thinking and working is coming to be understood as a novelty and an enrichment, the art world indulges in whingeing and whimpering postmodern theories, whose pre-eminent insight is the absence of any avant-garde; and in megalomaniac exhibition and museum projects, whose pre-eminent features are ostentatious content, titles and buildings – and the almost complete absence of women architects, women curators and women artists.
perhaps you should approach the works of women artists with more exactitude, get closer to them instead of putting them away in fright under the flippant headword 'post-feminism'. – perhaps you should refrain from using such well-worn remarks as "good art always comes out on top" and "art is gender-neutral" – foolish sayings that I have heard ad nauseam as an argument explaining the fact that women artists are so under-represented. "But you have been included," they then say, in the belief that I ought to be flattered by my alibi function (as here and now for example), and, innocently and in a gentle voice, they say "tell me a few names", which I of course do, in the full knowledge that the gentlemen are no longer paying any attention.
3 weeks ago, we – a few women artists, women academics and women who work in many other fields – ran an international public symposium in basle: 'SCIENCE, THE ARTS + EVERYTHING ELSE'. the idea was mine; the joint work of planning and organization lasted about one-and-a-half years.
I wanted to see if the procedures I used in my own work could be extended to other areas – to see whether there was a relationship between my working at art and working in the academic world, in politics, in industry and commerce, sport, nature etc., if I presented them in public side by side and all on an equal footing. is it possible for me to organize such a symposium with women academics, women politicians, women mediators, women farmers, women social workers etc. while using my procedure of the too personal, the too close, the rejection of distance, of the assertion that the private is public and that everything is of equal importance, of equal value.
my anger is not only personal when I see that exhibitions, art historical comparisons, collections, interdisciplinary discussions etc., when all these wonderful public things still – still – take place almost without the participation of women. my anger is also the anger of the woman academic who, after years of work, still does not receive the professorial chair or the leadership of the research institute, the anger of the woman manager who is denied the highest position, the anger of the woman politician who loses her

post although – or precisely because – she pursues a witty, less power-oriented form of politics, the anger of the woman art mediator who will always remain just an assistant or deputy director – has any woman ever been in charge of the documenta? – the quite general anger about the fact that I (i.e. all women) am still, in 1990, judged by my hair, my higher voice, my breasts, my hole, and my legs – that is, by the fact that I am a woman.
"SCIENCE, THE ARTS + EVERYTHING ELSE" was a great success. why?
our starting point was the people we wanted to invite to take part, was our personal point of view, was the knowledge and the personal contacts that each individual organizer had from her work, was the likeability, the impression that these women made during their public appearances on radio, in the print media and on television. each organizer issued invitations and was then responsible for those she had invited. parallel to this we worked out the programme as a group – a variable blueprint that took the invitees as its starting point and whose manner of proceeding was the assertion that everything was of equal status – the natural sciences and sport, the humanities and politics, social work and research, working at art and running a farm, working as a television announcer and running a publishing house, woman manager and model, computer language and musical performance. and the arranging of the lecture theatres or exhibition rooms and the technology involved throughout, the design of the tickets, posters, programme and labels ...the real events and their parallel transmission ...and so on and so forth.
the essential thing was that we ourselves did EVERYTHING, from the technology to the public relations and the secretariat – the museum placed only the empty husk of the building at our disposal. yes, WE were totally independent.
I am certain that with this symposium we invented a new form of thinking, of co-operation and of public sphere: for this symposium was a CONSCIOUS reflection of us women organizers in contrast to the UNCONSCIOUS reflection evident in similar public events where a male-oriented, targeted planning, thinking, acting and feeling is communicated as a general good ("this is how it's done") and receives corresponding attention from the media and the art world.
the audience at "SCIENCE, THE ARTS + EVERYTHING ELSE" (it was always full) were women and men – men in the minority, which mostly intimidated them. their feeling of fright is my everyday experience: being perpetually in the minority, like here and now, for example. BUT: my (i.e. every woman's) mind, my feeling and my actions are sharpened when I live in two cultures. in a male-dominated culture, I (i.e. every woman) have to and want to concern myself with this culture: I too love men, love their work and their art; their everyday world surrounds me, gives me food for thought, exerts influence on me and enters into competition with my work. BUT: I am a woman artist, working from out of my day-to-day life, out of my female history and biography, working with my body in anger against disregard and violence, working with the discord and disjointedness that I experience daily because I live in 2 cultures – BUT: is not living in two or more cultures the best prerequisite for working at art?!
art is never neutral, neither gender-neutral nor whatnot neutral. the

art that I love is always committed, engagé – made by women and men alike. that is why I find it wholly incomprehensible and hugely insulting that you male curators, you male art historians, you male journalists take so little interest in our work and foist everything on your women colleagues. you don't want to sharpen your minds, your thinking, your feeling. you still want your fireside conversations and your reserved table coteries to be considered universally valid and you quite evidently have no desire to cast a curious eye beyond the comfort zone of your cosy power.

I am not only talking of the fact that a certain, always diminishing percentage of women artists actually is represented in exhibitions, collections and museums. I am talking about our way of living, of loving, of working, of thinking, which points to new possibilities because it comes from the empty "half of heaven", from nothingness, from what is ascribed as the private, the personal, the non-public, from the place of giggling observation and hysterical laughter = from powerlessness. we work precisely, we don't take ourselves so dead seriously, because we have nothing to lose in contrast to many a male artist who believes he must carry the whole weight of the world on his shoulders, all of history, art history, the power of the public realm, the responsibility for the here and now – they're not to be envied, the gentlemen!

but: THEY do gain public attention, especially those artists who work with the male clichés of possessing worldwide portent. the art world leaps eagerly at any mirroring of its self. it's so easy after all: this suffering in and from the world, however lachrymose it may be, the posture of the artist or sculptor as man of genius, however banal it may be, every gag, however corny, enters into a public domain in which it is immediately processed in both practical and theoretical terms.

nothing against this male world: it is the mirror image of itself. but I refuse to accept that this mirroring gives any exclusive rights in theory and praxis and above all in codification and language regulation – refuse to accept that the art of male artists comprises the entire truth, has a general, worldwide claim to truth, that museums are the central buildings of the art world, that exhibiting in them and the makers of these exhibitions are the central, focal point of art! on the principle the bigger, the more expensive, the more significance-laden the title, the more important = the better. most new museum buildings are useless, spatially and technologically, even for displaying their own collections. for some 10 years, large-scale exhibitions have been uninteresting because always the same male curators bring along always the same ideas with always the same works of always the same male artists – and a few women artists as garnish on the side.

what is an exhibition?

every man, every woman looks at everything from the vantage points of differing lives and places. to arrange an exhibition is to show our differing works precisely in differing places and spaces, in line with their differing characters and manners. from a certain size upwards, precision is no longer possible because it can no longer be personal. the central, focal point of an exhibition is the activity of working at art: our working at art with its forms and content, and your work of mediating these diverse forms and content. at the central, focal point are people: we, you and the art-going public.

your work is to publicly display our working at art in such a way that every man and every woman can see, hear, read and physically encounter it from the vantage points of their personally differing lives.
to curate an exhibition is no more than that.

Jocelyn Wolff
merci!
mail **le 15 novembre 2016**

cher Jocelyn,[109]
ici tu vois une photo en 1991 pendant notre symposium inventé par moi, où nous avons invité à peu près 90 femmes de tout le monde. les Guerilla Girls étaient la première fois en Europe. ici mon père qui reçoit une banane, parce qu'il avait posé une question intelligente … derrière moi Diamanda Galás,[110] une performancer avec une voix extra-super.
amitiés
miriam

Diamanda Galás
24 King Street
NYC New York 10014
Miriam Cahn
Strassburgerallee 68
CH-4055 Basle
Switzerland **7 September 1991**

Darling girl!
Thank you for sending me your catalogue and the photos of us. Matthias said he thought it was perfect that the two of us strange women got a chance to work on the same festival. I thank you for your patience with the idiots whom I recently fired. (I fired them last year right after your concert.)
I am giving your catalogue to Fiction/Nonfiction gallery in SOHO, who, I believe will be interested very much in your work.
I am actually writing you at this moment to ask you about the fellow who has organized AIDS exhibition work – the man came to our concert in Basle, remember? Was his name Wolfgang?
My current agent is the manager of Philip Glass, and we are touring the updated Plague Mass in Europe – focusing at the moment on spring and summer. We have been all to the ROYAL FESTIVAL HALL in LONDON, to Athens, Greece (I just performed there at the Athens Festival), to Paris (to Grande HALLE de la Villette), to Matthias, others – so expenses would be shared by different organisations.
Obviously, dear girl, you are an ARTIST, NOT my agent, but if you have any suggestion, even churches, etc. will you write or FAX me?
My FAX and phone no. are the SAME number: 212-255-***
I am working with a WOMAN named Linda Greenberg at IPA (she works with Ged Wheeler, who is the president – she is the vice-president). And the FAX is: 212-925-***
How you are doing this year? What are you up to? Since Basle, I still keep in touch by writing with the Guerilla Girls, who are TRULY GREAT! That was a great meeting. Will you give my regards to the wonderful women I met after the show – I can't remember all the names, but they were great!
I am sorry we missed each other when you came to N.Y.!
LOVE, Diamanda Galás

Movement of trees (and other plants)

spring:
1. water
2. earth
3. seeds
4. roots
5. trunk
6. branches
7. buds

summer:
1. earth
2. seeds
3. roots
4. trunk
5. branches
6. leaves + blossom
7. water, "skin", "glow"

autumn:
1. earth, hills, roots
2. trunk
3. energy from outside
4. branches
5. energy from outside

winter:
don't know yet

WITH EYES CLOSED (W.E.C.)

i can see the movement of plants only when i draw with my eyes closed: i close my eyes and imitate the movement of plants. as i do so, i lose my way on the paper. when I open my eyes, the work is finished.
in the landscapes i walk the paths that i know with my eyes closed. when i open my eyes the work is finished.

READING IN DUST (R.I.D.) glow

reading in the chalk dust, my hands feel their way towards the animals and women. Thus every day the animals and women glow differently. "glow" is related to "radiate", "irradiated".

reading colour (processing)

yellow = toxic, deadly, death, destruction
magenta (red) = to preserve, to store, a storehouse
cyan (blue)= plants, shadow, shade
mixture = paths, roads, car-parks, indeterminate terrain

movement of colour (nuclear bombs)

i hurl the water with the colours/paints – yellow, magenta, cyan – up the paper (like a nuclear explosion), they flow down again (like fallout), escape my control and mix together (contamination).

various ways of seeing

with my hands in the hills of dust I see animals, women, children and other things (R.I.D.).
while drawing I close my eyes and see the landscapes, buildings, trees and other plants with photographic exactitude. (W.E.C.)
while I am painting pictures in oils, I look for hours on end at photographs of: pantex, savannah river plant, hanford, gorleben, stade, auschwitz. ciba-geigy and sandoz (processing).
with my film camera I follow animals for 3 minutes (only animals).
placed on the ground, the film camera looks for 3 minutes at the movement of the landscapes, animals, plants, water and weather (movement of nature).
when painting watercolours, I look at the movement of the water flowing down (atom bombs).
the movement of hurling white plasticine into the black dust determines the form of objects (weapons + leaves).
listening to the sounds as I scrape with the knife determines the shape of the chalk (R.I.D.). the video camera watches and listens to my work (monitoring and recording).

La Fete des quatre cultures
700 years/ans/anni/onns
La Festa delle quattro culture
Confoederatio Helvetica
La Festa de las quatter culturas
The Festival of the Four Cultures
Beaux-arts
EXTRA MUROS art suisse contemporain

8 April 1990

Dear Ms Cahn,
You have made an indirect response to our invitation to participate in the EXTRA MUROS exhibition by sending us the signatures of artists who refuse to take part in any events related to the 700th-anniversary celebrations on account of the fiches affair. We would be pleased to discuss this issue with you and would like to ask therefore whether we might pay you a visit in Basle on Friday, 4 May? I would suggest an appointment in the late morning.
We would be pleased to hear from you.
Yours Sincerely
Dieter Schwarz[111]

---

basle, 17 may 90
dear dieter schwarz,
many thanks for your letter. of course, my response was a refusal, but perhaps my closing words "until later" were open to misunderstanding – they referred to the subsequent political course of this entire fiches affair.
I would have declined anyway because I want to have nothing to do with such tenuously justified events born out of nationalist considerations. this whole fiches affair just magnifies the absurdity of a situation where we so-called culture-creators on the one hand don't fit in politically but on the other hand have to do our bit for prestige events.
does it have to be like this – that every time mediators sniff money in the wind, a maximally "innovative" exhibition HAS to be set up, without any thought being given on your part to the context in which such exhibitions are to take place and what they are supposed to be for?
for me, actually, there is nothing more to be said about this "issue" – if this situation is not a problem for you, then there is not much left to be discussed either.
well, now you know my attitude. if you are nevertheless keen to visit me, I've got nothing against it.
I just ask you to please not come with the objective of intending to talk me round.
warm greetings,
miriam cahn

Invitation …
With warm regards,
the student body, Art History, Munich
Reinhard Spieler

to: reinhard spieler **basle, 10 march 91**

dear mr spieler,
since your letter is written in an exaggeratedly male-oriented manner that I haven't encountered for a good long time (making no use of the appropriate dual-gender German forms for 'art historian', 'artist', 'art mediator', 'agent', 'participants', 'students'…), I assume that you do not know any women students, women professors, women art mediators, women artists, women art historians etc.
in order to remedy this – somewhat one-sided – condition of yours, I now make the following proposal:
2 events:
1. a public lecture from me on my work + ensuing discussion
2. a panel discussion with the title "ART/women artists – perception and mediation + MONEY". on the panel are: a woman student of art history, a woman professor of art history, a woman gallerist, a woman active in museum work, a woman art critic, a woman art student, myself and a woman moderator (woman active in the media).
it is now up to you to take your first steps in this – for you – totally new field and to find these seven rare examples of female humanity who would be prepared to take the stage with me for a public discussion of this topic.
concerning the details, we would need to have a telephone conversation. with my oeuvre I think that it makes little sense to speak in front of original works, since in munich there are examples only in the galerie van de loo and in addition speaking in this manner is interesting only when it takes place in the artist's studio or in a spatial installation. individual works yield nothing in such a context.
hoping to hear from you soon – with warm regards,
your m. cahn

jürg wildberger
10vor10 editorial office
schweizer fernsehen
fernsehstrasse 1–4
8052 zurich **basle, 18 january 92**

dear herr wildberger, dear editorial team,
I am very grateful to you for having shown these extracts from a hardcore porn film, because for the first time I have now SEEN where the difference between hardcore and other pornographic productions lies. in the long-running porNO debate there has been for some time an unchanging confusion between the portrayal of images and acted scenes and the "documentation" of real events. as an artist, I am against censorship and a prohibition of images, even if these violate my dignity as a woman.
hardcore videos that are involuntary documentations of torture inflicted on women up to and including their death are, however, something different – I do not mean acted presentations of whatever kind that simulate images in order to get people aroused, but these women are being tortured in front of the camera. even if this is not what the producers intend, their products have the value of proof of crimes committed – and that, in combination with the idea that men find this a turn-on, is naturally unbearable to watch. of course, such producers should receive severe punishment and such videos should be banned – and should have been for a long time now – but to make people aware of this it is precisely necessary to watch such products and to compare them with the other, simulated, acted variety so that there is no wrong censorship imposed.
when starting her porNO campaign alice schwarzer unfortunately did not acknowledge this distinction – so turning all women artists and women film-makers against her, even the well-inclined ones. your women's representative is making the same mistake, instead of demanding one or two programmes about this very delicate issue in which the matter is PRECISELY analysed with the help of examples that SHOW when and where the demands of the porNO campaign are justified.
in this instance you are the bearers of bad news who get given a beating – hence I wish you continuing courage and good luck in future.
your miriam cahn

Fernsehen der deutschen und
rätoromanischen Schweiz
Frau Miriam Cahn
Strassburgerallee 68
4055 Basle **Zurich, 17 February 1992**

Dear Ms Cahn,
Many thanks for your letter concerning our Brutalo broadcast. It was a great pleasure to receive your words of encouragement.
We received a very large number of letters from viewers. Some 60 viewers criticized the broadcasting of this item, 160 were in favour. The images, they wrote, had admittedly shocked them, but they had opened their eyes and provided information about conditions in society which they had hitherto thought inconceivable. The letters, which I have read very closely, taught me a

good deal about the profound concern felt by many viewers. Most of them had thought at length about violence and videos portraying violence and, in individual cases, had also changed their own behaviour patterns.
As you have perhaps read or heard, the broadcast had a major impact. Firstly, there was a discussion among journalists as to whether such images should be broadcast at all. And secondly, a debate on sexual violence is at last getting under way. On this latter topic 10vor10 is planning a variety of contributions.
As I have stated in various places, we made certain mistakes concerning the above broadcast. In future, we will announce such topics more clearly in advance and will follow on with a discussion session so that viewers can cope better with the emotions aroused.
I trust that we can continue to count you among our alert and critical viewers.
With kind regards,
SCHWEIZER FERNSEHEN DRS
10vor10 Editorial Offices
Jürg Wildberger
Editor-in-chief

Adolf H. Kerkhoff
Gerberstrasse 5
W - 4250 Bottrop 2
Miriam Cahn
Strassburgeralle 68
CH-4055 Basle
Switzerland **29 September 1992**

Dear Ms Cahn,
When I phoned you last week in an attempt to gain your support for the campaign to re-designate the poster "For Oskar"[112] into "For Article 16(2) of the German Constitution", your reaction was very reticent. I fully understand your position!
For an artist it is difficult to become involved again in politics if one thinks, indeed knows, that last time one was wrong. But it is important, very important even, because it is no longer a matter of day-to-day politics: what is at stake here is the Federal German Constitution, whose Article 16(2) is to be altered in its very essence – the personal and actionable right to political asylum is to be replaced by a legal formula which, it is becoming clear, amounts to political asylum becoming an act of grace which is granted in individual cases and to which there is no longer a legal claim. All citizens are called on to resist (Article 20[4]) this fundamental alteration of a basic right – but on the streets people are fighting not for but against the right to asylum, indeed against all foreign elements in our country. And in the Bundestag, this struggle serves the CDU/CSU as a means to exert additional pressure on the opposition to comply with their wish for a change to the constitution and to play its part in achieving the necessary two-thirds majority.
And the SPD? Instead of defending basic rights, it is setting about becoming the government's accomplice and – thrusting 60 years of German history aside – assisting in the evisceration of Article 16(2). And in the van is Oskar Lafontaine, two years ago still the great white hope for a new wave of democratization, but now, it seems, having taken leave of his senses! In order to show that we are not in agreement with this politics of capitulation, we must put down markers where we can – I by initiating this campaign and you by participating in the re-designation process, we together thus making clear that the constitution is more important to us than persons, which is precisely the point of this appeal and this campaign. If, as I very much hope, you wish to support the appeal, then please return one of the copies enclosed. I would then send you your poster, you re-designate it – from "For Oskar" into "For Article 16(2) of the German Constitution" – and send it back to me. In the meantime, I will be getting in contact with all the other artists involved in the "For Oskar" portfolio: if more than half of them join in, which I fully expect after the conversations I have had to date, then the re-designated posters will be put on display shortly before the decisive

SPD Party Conference in Düsseldorf or Bonn on 16/17 November – I will take care of this myself.
Hoping to hear from you soon, I remain
With warm regards,
Adolf Kerkhoff

basle, 3 october 92

dear adolf h. kerkhoff,
many thanks for your letter. I would like to explain once more why I consider this campaign to re-designate the posters wrong.
I don't consider it so bad at all – indeed, I don't even consider that I was wrong to be in favour of Lafontaine. essentially, it would still have been better if the SPD had managed it – with him. in politics, I don't make absolute demands on individuals or parties at all – for me, the SPD is simply the lesser evil.
but don't misunderstand me: the fact that Germany intends to change its constitution in this way I consider terrible. I would unhesitatingly be in favour of campaigns that condemn it – but not if they petty-mindedly single out individual persons and parties as your campaign does. that reminds me increasingly of the old "who were the betraying rats – the social democrats"... and already back then it was wrong to boost the party image by contrasting it with the spiritless SPD instead of forming a broad front to fight against the nazis.
if (as you write) the constitution is more important to you than individuals, then just leave the persons alone, stop this bashing of individual politicians.
why so complicated? nobody will understand "for article 16(2)" – any benetton poster is more explicit. why not "for our foreigners", "for our foreign cousins", "for our refugees" "for our turks, italians, bosnians, tamils"... and the same stressing the female side: "for our turkish, italian, bosnian, tamil women". of course, better formulated than that.
with campaigns such as yours I always get the creeping, unpleasant feeling that it's not only about the issue at hand but also about putting oneself in the right moral light as a 'left-winger'. and yet it's no longer a question of left-or-right but from-case-to-case and with the issue always in view – I am sure there are also people in the centrist parties who are against this change to the constitution.
the severity with which you justify your campaign reveals to my mind self-pity born of disappointment...then I was for oskar and now this...now I must quickly (mea culpa) clarify that I am no longer on oskar's side...what a critically-minded contemporary I am! – thus making not only lafontaine's person much too important but also your own. and in the process forgetting the personal and private that really can become the political and can thus be made visible as political energy.
when I created that poster, it had plants and ulcers on it. what they have in common is their energy for growth – oskar, I'm afraid, chose not the plants but the ulcers.
cordial regards, m. cahn

how stupid of me
how witless of me
to believe
again and again cyclically routinely
that i have to act public-spiritedly
that i have to be just
to help
to teach
phoney work
a confusion with what i
consider to be human.
that was what i had forgotten.

SARAJEVO 1995 (all FAXes)
PRO HELVETIA
to: victor durschei **basle, 8 september 95**

dear victor durschei,
even in the most peaceful peacetime, it is quite impossible for me to travel from split to sarajevo by jeep – so we must find a different solution. having consulted the film-maker edith jud, who has contacts with sarajevo, i now recognize that it is fully possible to fly to sarajevo with the unprofor as long as the airstrip is open, and that this can be organized relatively short-term. the journalists do this, artists such as marcel ophüls do it, so why not a woman artist such as miriam cahn. as regards the date we can be a little more flexible, after all – can also be a week later, perhaps in november …
could we please discuss this by phone in the near future, perhaps – get your brain gyri dancing – something will come to your mind – edith, at any rate, will make inquiries with her people in sarajevo.
warm regards
your miriam cahn

Obala Art Centar
Sarajevo
to: Izeta Gradevic **Basle, 11 September 95**

Dear Izeta,
It was very nice to meet you at my studio and speak with you, and I hope you got back home to Sarajevo alright. Now to our show:[113] unfortunately because of my stupid back it is not possible for me to come on the Split-Sarajevo road. I didn't realize it was such a long way when we spoke together. So we have to plan the show with the possibility of flying to Sarajevo, when the airport opens again. I spoke to Victor Durschei about it and we think this will not be possible until the first of October, or what do you think? Anyhow: I could possibly come between the 5th and 26th of November, but the dates are not clear yet, as then the production of the catalogue for the show in mid-February in Bonn starts, but if the war situation allows, I could come. If not, the next date would be spring about the beginning of March 1996, what do you think about it?
for the transportation of the works as we spoke about it – small box and so on – there will be no problem, I know a very nice man with a good transportation staff and a lot of imagination, he always does everything for Harry Szeemann, so no problems.
I really hope we can do our show in spite of the stupid war – and back-problems …
sincerely yours,
miriam cahn

OBALA ART CENTER SARAJEVO
to: Miriam Cahn
from: Izeta Gradevic **14 September 1995**

Dear Miriam Cahn,
I recieived your fax but was not able to answer the same day. I get stuck with too many jobs that I should finish fast here.
After my trip over Mount Igman on our way back home I agree with you regarding the idea to wait for your trip to Sarajevo for a while.
In the meantime, we can work on the catalogue. If you can send us some texts in English we can start

translating into Bosnian.
The meeting with you was one of the most exciting moments on my trip so I am really looking forward to start preparing your exhibition here in Sarajevo.
In the next few days we can see which date would seem reasonable for your trip to Sarajevo.
Warm regards,
Izeta Gradjevic

Obala Art Centar
Sarajevo
to: Izeta Gradevic **Basle, 27 September 95**

Dear Izeta,
Thank you for the faxes. Soon I shall send you the texts in English – some have to be translated here first from German into English. It would be nice if you could do the texts both in English and Bosnian.
Somehow I remember you speaking about being on the Internet in Sarajevo. I myself don't understand anything about the Internet, but I have a friend who does, and also we have here an Internet café. so maybe I could send you some photos for the catalogue by Internet, if this works. could you fax me your number (or code or whatever?)
Then I spoke to Victor about the dates, and we thought if the situation goes on like now I could come in November between the 5th and 26th. So let us know soon which date would suit you, if you also think it's ok.
for the transportation: we would send the box with Swissair to Zagreb, and then it would be good if somebody would take it from there to Sarajevo.
So I hope you are well and sincerely yours,
m. cahn

Obala Art Centar
Sarajevo
to: Izeta Gradevic **Basle 3 October 95**

Dear Izeta,
Here I send you the texts I have in English. 2 are texts about my work, 3 written by myself. The one of 1995 is connected to the work I would like to do at Obala – if I ever get there, which I hope. This text I did simultaneously in German and English, so the German has to stay connected. The text "1991" belongs to the work 'KRIEGSRAUM', a big room-installation, which I never showed. 'Relatedness …' is connected to several room-installations I did between 1989 and 1991 (blue catalogue[114] pp. 52/53, and 64/65).
The text of Sabine Gebhard I like, but I don't like the one of Jean-Christophe Ammann, even if I like him a lot and like very much to work with him. But I send it to you for your information.
Tonight in the news I saw there is some fighting near Sarajevo. So I hope you and your people are ok!
with best regards,
miriam cahn

obala art centar
sarajevo
to: Izeta gradevic **Basle, 16 October 95**

Dear Izeta,
I am looking forward to the 8th of November – I realized it is in

about 3 weeks! So I would like to know if a box with about the measurements 110 × 060 × 075 cm would be possible for you to get from the plane – in Zagreb? Please let me know soon, they have to build it.
Then I heard and read and saw in TV Sarajevo has electricity – you must be glad. If you want and are interested and it would be technically possible, I could bring some super-8 movies I made. They are very simple, without sound, "dilettante" movies. The shortest 3 min. where you see only a tree moving, the longer ones up to 45 min. approx., with mountains, clouds, flowers and so on. The hardest one is a storm with lightning, but you see only black and this short lightning (approx. 12 min.). We could show them during my stay in Sarajevo. It needs only a rather dark room and a super-8 projector and something like a white wall.
so, that's it until the next fax or so … sincerely yours,
miriam cahn

OBALA ART CENTAR SARAJEVO 17 October1995

Dear Miriam,
We started organizing your coming here and we are all looking forward to seeing you and your works in Sarajevo. I really like your idea of showing super-8 films. So far we have no projector for that format but we will try to find one. We can run the films in the gallery in some late hours in order to avoid daylight. The gallery itself is very light. It has huge windows on one side, but after 6 p.m. there is enough dark to show the films.
Today I sent all the important information regarding your trip to Ms Corinne Rochat in Pro Helvetia so she will be able to organize it properly. I am sending you the copy of the fax I have sent to her.
The measurements of the gallery are 10.36 × 10.73 × 7 m. I believe that you made the best choice of the works for our gallery but I would like to suggest you to take one big size drawing in case you suddenly feel that the space is too big or so.
My suggestion is to send the crate by land because the personnel of UNPROFOR airport is not very kind, and it is very likely that once you are in their space you have to take care of the crate yourself. It is a military airport so they have no cart for luggage …
So this is all now.
Please don't hesitate to ask whatever you need to know!
Warm regards,
Izeta Gradevic

Obala Art Centar
Sarajevo
to: Izeta Gradevic Basle, 18 October 95

Dear Izeta,
Thank you for your fax – I am very glad Mrs Dostal comes and gets me in Zagreb and helps a little with the blue card.
For the shipment of the crate this will work: Fryday Josy Kraft will get my works, then they build the crate and I think following next week it will be sent. So: if you want something you need in Sarajevo and I could also put it in this crate, please let me know soon.
For the installation in the gallery I have the idea of combining the small works you saw with works which are only a little bigger with

plants on them which I did with closed eyes, some kind like in the catalogue page 52. The very big ones are too overwhelming to combine in one room with the small ones. But anyhow I shall take more works than the measurements of the space, so we can try – no problem.
Now I am putting all the works together for the show and I like very much doing this work and especially for your situation even more.
warm regards,
miriam cahn

Obala Art Centar
Sarajevo
to: Izeta Gradevic **Basle, 23 October 95**
Dear Izeta,
Now I have the ticket for the Flight to Zagreb, 5th November:
Zurich 12.20 SR452 arr. Zagreb 13.45
Then Josy Kraft built the crate and the measurements are: 116 × 102 × 025 cm – looks like nothing, but in it are 58 works, quite enough, even I think too many to hang them all. So I am looking forward to working with you in your space.
Josy is now sending the crate over the connection you sent me in Split, so I think everything will be ok on my side and I hope on the destiny side (war and so on) also.
Of course I am a little afraid, but more I am really a lot curious.
Anyhow: is it cold in November?
warm regards,
miriam cahn

Basle, 29 November 95
Dear Obalas,
At the moment I am listening to "Cranberrys" and think a lot of you and this so-called peace – at least hopefully no shooting anymore. I see a lot of Sarajevo in TV and thank you I know it now better, so, if people here think Grbavica and Ilidža[115] is half the town, I can explain to them.
In the moment I am packing for a little intellectual "carepacket". So, if you need something from here please let me know over the next few days (floppy disks? whatever?)
Surely you are all in full work for the Ljubliana festival – so I wish you good luck and big kisses for everyone.
yours,
miriam

OBALA ART CENTAR SARAJEVO **1 December 95**
Dear Miriam,
We have finished the Slovenian project – NSK state Sarajevo, and it was very successful, at the moment OBALA is quite empty. Izeta, Lela and Mujke are on the trip to Budapest and they are coming back on Sunday. It is much better now in Sarajevo, because of the results of the peace negotiations. Thank you for all your faxes. Tiki is also fine, but I think you don't know that she was lost for a couple of days. Right after you left maybe a day or two after, she got lost. We tried to find her, but we couldn't. We were all very worried and we even gave an ad on the radio that we are looking for our dog ... She came back alone five days after. Now, she is all the time at OBALA. I hope I am not tiring you with this story, but I know you like Tiki a lot.

The exhibition is closing on Sunday 3.12. Everything was alright.
Thank you for asking us if we need everything. What we always need is the floppy disks and VHS cassettes. It would be wonderful if you could send us some of those.
Warmest regards from OBALA,
Elma Hadziredzepoviv

OBALA ART CENTAR SARAJEVO 7 December 1995

Dear Miriam,
We have just come back from our trip to Budapest where we did a great job. Unfortunately we didn't have time for rest.
The situation here is still the same. We are very suspicious about the continuation of peace conference in Paris (14 of this month).
Your exhibition is still on. The Swiss Ambassador wanted to see it (he arrived in town yesterday) so we prolonged it for two days. Tomorrow we are going to take it off after taking photos. The exhibition was really successful. These days we are going to start to work on the catalogue.
I was in Berlin ten days ago in order to visit Lettre International ... I saw your contribution and I really like the works you have sent. I brought with me the draft print of one colour page with few of your things. Everybody here likes it ...
I had dinner with Rebecca Horn there. We had a very good conversation about Sarajevo and the war in Bosnia. I invited her to come to us and do something ... She accepted.
I am worried about this issue of Lettre International[116] because there are a lot of misunderstandings between Maruša[117] and Frank Berberich,[118] whom you met here. He wants to involve more contributors from former Yugoslavia and Europe and some texts that are too old and less interesting for Sarajevo readers. And Maruša is trying to convince him to use more texts from Sarajevo. The biggest problem is that they (Frank and his co.) don't have enough time to do things properly. The two weeks they give us for such a serious job is not enough. But we will see ...
We will stay in touch.
Lots of love from all of us!
Izeta

To: izeta gradevic Basle, 10 December 95

Dear Izeta,
Thank you very much for your fax – time is really flying, I didn't realize the exhibition is already over ...
In some days I shall get LETTRE and see how it is. Of course the "Berlin boys" are a little old-fashioned and at the same time do everything at the last minute – but all of these LETTRE issues have some interesting contributions, so I hope this time also there will be some interesting things to read. Of course also I would have been more interested in texts from Sarajevo written now, not some time ago.
So let's see. It's very nice Rebecca Horn is doing a show at Obala.

Let's hope this so-called peace is at least an end of shooting, I understand very much you being suspicious. Here the information at the moment about all this is quite good, but people are more interested in the big strikes in France – it's closer around the corner. So when there are some discussions between friends here about Sarajevo and they say: oh but the Serbs have half the town and that's why they demonstrate against a Muslim state, I always get the map of Sarajevo and the frontline Mike showed me and show them what Grbavica is and there is not a "Muslim" government and there are not "the Serbs" and so on … the moment there is officially a so-called peace, nobody is interested any more. makes me angry sometimes.
At the moment I have a lot of work with the catalogue[119] for the show I have mid-February in Bonn, but I like this sort of work. As soon as I have it I send it to you, it's a book combined with a reprint of the blue one you already have and an English translation of all together – so finally for English-speaking people!
I sent you a little parcel, but I don't know if it will arrive this year.
So, many kind regards and kisses to every one of you and I am looking forward to your catalogue …
miriam

OBALA ART CENTAR SARAJEVO **16 Dec. 1995**

Dear Miriam Cahn,
We received your package! Thank you very much! It is really great. I like the catalogue you sent us. And the little book too! The photos you did are also very very good.
Now I have to tell you that your works are all in Split and you can expect them soon in Basle. I put the films together with the rest of the materials.
Aida has finished her interview with you. We will translate it and send it to you as soon as possible.
Lots of love and thank you again!
On behalf of OBALA,
Izeta

to: Izeta gradevic **Basle, 20 December 95**

Dear Izeta,
Now I have read LETTRE on my way to Bonn for my next exhibition, and I think it's really good – of course not everything, but this is never possible when you have so much text. Of course it would have been even better if there were more "young" texts like Lasarevska, Kebo, Vesovic and so on – this "cynical" writing is my favoured type – but the whole is very informative for people here who know really too little or don't want to know. I think the Berlin boys did a good job and they seem to have a strange and very chaotic way to do their LETTRE, but it works. Also the printing looks very good – so: I think everything went better than I personally thought
When I sat in the train to Bonn reading these different texts, and the train went through the Rhine valley where it gets narrow near the Loreley, I had a very plastic and strong sensation of the geographical view of Sarajevo and Miljacka[120] and for a while I had a very strong feeling of being there – every detail is now in my head and feet and somehow I couldn't look to the hills surrounding the Rhine without thinking of Chetniks. It was nice to sit there in the train with LETTRE and have these feelings and thoughts and also

reading these go-between texts of Maruša and Susan Sontag.
Also there was now in the ZEIT, which is the biggest German-speaking more culturally-oriented weekly paper, a nice critique of the LETTRE.
When does the Bosnian LETTRE come? Even if I don't understand a word except pivo, I would like to have one if possible. Also I send you a sound-cassette from a radio-interview I did here where we speak very much about art, OBALA and so on, and there is – I think – the music from the CD "rock under siege". Unfortunately everything in German.
So I hope everybody and the dog is ok in OBALA and you especially and I look forward to everything I hear from you.
+ nice NEW YEAR 1996 (with water, electricity, heating and so on)
+ kind regards to MARIA,
miriam

26 December 96
dear Izeta,
thank you for the fax – but pages 1, 3, and 4 didn't come well – so try again please. I shall read it soon and fax you back.
for the photos: unfortunately mine are not very good also of the show at Obala. you can look yourself at the little ones I sent you with the first package – they are all too grey.
maybe it is possible to manipulate them, but for this I have to do it myself, and this I would do, but later. I am in full preparation of the big show I have on13 February in Kunstverein Bonn, and it is really a huge space.
unfortunately I forgot also to do a photo of the whole of Obala space. but maybe – as I have some photos I think from some of the works, we can manage somehow.
well I hope all of you are nice and well and in a good shape (how is Miro's back?) and after the 13 February we can plan this photo thing (maybe we could try with originals and so on …)
kiss for everybody,
miriam

Basle, 26.1.96
dear Izeta,
Aida Kalender is really a hit of an interviewer – it's very nice and ok!
only 2 small things: the name of the artist is Pipilotti Rist, and generally I would speak less about painting and to paint except with oil-painting, I would speak more about drawing and to draw, or to work or works or the work, especially when I am speaking.
So. That's nice.
kiss,
miriam

Obala Centar
to: Lejla **basle, 20 february 96**
dear Lejla,
uff! complicated: most of the works I had in your show are now in Bonn. so I suggest to you: as I go to Bonn the 6th March to do a performance, I could try to do some kind of proper black and white photos myself of most of the works for Obala and scan it to you (or by e-mail) or send it – but sending is so long …
so maybe we get something.
what do you think?
give all my kind regards,
miriam

to: Lejla **basle, 13 march 96**

Dear Lejla,
unfortunately, kurt didn't get your message. we phoned and he gave me his number: kurt@nethos.net
he will try again, but if you could try also and send him the right format? tomorrow he is in the internet café.
I thought of you yesterday when I saw on TV the people going to ilidža – that's a great thing you have still your house!
lot of love,
miriam

OBALA@ZAMIR-SA
to: kurt brauchli **Weds, 13 March 1996**

Please, do not send any binary files to ZaMir-SA. We are transferring files by telephone and you are causing too much expense with this.

basle, 21 march 96

Dear Lejla,
How are you + your house? I thought a lot of you lately because of ilidža + grbavica on TV …
I fax you the reason why the e-mailing finally with so much pictures doesn't seem to work as I understand – shall I still keep it? Maybe you have another possibility? The scanning was some sort of expensive, that's why I still don't give up, and somehow I like very much the idea too of this sort of sending even if I really don't understand.
Anyhow I sent the photos with the new catalogue last Friday over Soros Split, so you have everything. As the whole thing is already scanned, I could also let it load on something like 12 diskettes and send it to you over Soros Split (the photos I sent you are slightly different than the scanned ones).
so let me know soon.
and a lot of love to everyone,
miriam

to: Lejla **basle, 26 march 96**

Dear Lejla,
I am very happy everything arrived to you – and some kind of fast. I think it's good you scan the photos – here it would take a while, and the photos I sent you are better.
So I am looking forward to the catalogue.
Here it is complete spring – and in Sarajevo?
love to everybody and kiss,
miriam

8 June 96

Dear Izeta, Lejla, Mike etc.,
Here I send a catalogue of Pipilotti Rist and Matthew Barney and a video of my performance I did in Kunstverein Bonn.
Pipilotti Rist I think in the moment is the most interesting Swiss artist for video and she is doing a lot, and a lot different works. Matthew Barney I saw a show in the Kunsthalle Bern and for me the biggest difference between him and Rist is his absolute coolness, this clinical coolness which makes his work less interesting than Rist's one. First in the whole show I liked it, then – the more and more I saw it seemed to me all the same perfect installations something in between a condom-thinking and the TV series "enterprise" and some kind of retro-sentimentality of the 50s in the USA, but it's all done so perfectly that it may be the actual

thinking. anyhow he is the shooting star at the moment.
I myself have a lot to do: end of August the opening in Saarbrücken, then I go to London for half a year, and on 21 September I have a room-installation in a group-show in Castello di Rivara in Piemont, Italy, the first time I do something in Italy. So I have a lot to do and I even wanted to go to the mountains, which is the best I can do for back and soul …
And you all? How is the political situation, if there is one? Here the media are all very negative on the voting in September because of Karadžić[121] and co. and put them to Den Haag, which does the whole moralistic stuff again completely untrustworthy which is told by our politics. anyhow: I hope you are all very well and travel a lot and do nice things.
kisses for all (and does Tiki still exist?),
miriam

Dear Izeta,
here my address in London:
miriam cahn 3 Smithy Street, Jubilee Terrace
Stepney LONDON El OHF GBR
from 4 September on –
and I wish you the best
kiss,
miriam
and thank you VERY much for your fax.

5 × beautiful

beautiful whispered the woman exhibition-goer standing in front of huge watercolours gleaming in vivid multi-chrome: mandalas! flowers…
i laughed: nuclear bombs!

the series of men and women making love, which I love to draw, are classical in appearance. women and men find them beautiful because they are horny.

i find it beautiful to get black all over while drawing women / animals / plants / landscapes on the floor and rolling in the black chalk dust.

beautifully painted! in the exhibition they go up really close to the small many-coloured oil paintings, which show aerial views of production sites copied from photos. you want to know the precise names of these factories? savannah river plant, hanford, pantex, ciba-geigy/sandoz, schweizerhalle, chernobyl, stade, auschwitz, rabta, gorleben, pentagon, johnston atoll, rhode island test site, bikini island, CNN/gulf war.

we stand, sheepishly and undecidedly, in the fully set-up room showing my work 'sarajevo' with its predominantly thin-line drawings of people lying on the ground. stampa: beautiful dead bodies! gilli: it's almost an embarrassment to make up a price list. me: who on earth wants to buy this? at which we break out into hysterical laughter.

monuments **Basle, 21 February 97**

Dear Ms Cahn,

In the context of the public debate on Switzerland's wartime past and the country's controversial policy towards those fleeing from the Shoah, the proposal has been made that Switzerland might use the money collected in a fund for a monument recalling this Swiss past.

What interests me now is to discover whether there are artists whom this debate has prompted to take up the topic of the wartime past in their artistic work or even to elaborate a proposal for such a monument.

Probably, you have not witnessed the debate of the past few months at such close range as we have in Switzerland. Nevertheless, on the advice of Theodora Vischer, I venture to inquire whether the topic has occupied you as an artist over the past weeks and months. Should this be the case, a project sketch for such a monument for example could serve to trigger further discussions on the issue in the BAZ.

You can reach me with any response you may have under 0041 61 *** (tel.) or 0041 61 *** (fax).

With many thanks in advance I remain with

Warm Regards,

Benedikt Vogel

Basler Zeitung, Dept. Home Affairs

to: benedikt vogel **london, 21 february 97**

dear benedikt vogel,

if there is one thing I hate, it is monuments, and in the context of the annihilation of the jews I find them hateful per se. I (and others) have always been well-informed about the role switzerland played, partly because my father emigrated from frankfurt to basle; and here in london via the NZZ, which is reporting on the issue in an admittedly most comprehensive way, but in an unbearable tone. in addition, whenever I was in basle I was always able to catch the general mood.

good artists are never illustrators of specific issues, and if you are familiar with my work then you know that I NEVER make working sketches. during the competition for that unspeakable "sorrow-stricken" monument in berlin, the schulthess architectural offices wanted me to "decorate" part of the interior of their "project" – which led to heated discussions on art, jews etc. …

the issue and the content-matter are of burning interest to me: I would immediately declare myself prepared to take part in a public discussion on the sense and non-sense of such a monument. in this context I am always of the opinion that a publicly accessible archive would be far better, far more meaningful, of far more use. precisely in basle it would be possible to work together with the jewish museum: the ideal thing would be a building – even better, a newly constructed building – that would house both the museum and this archive. because, the "woeful situation" of Switzerland at present has to do with the fact that KNOWLEDGE was suppressed, in part wilfully suppressed, and then there is only one counter-possibility: a place of public attention and information.

and quite definitely not a monument that just stands around, has cost a great deal of money and is absolutely and utterly useless …

so, if you want something intelligent from me I can offer you anything that has to do with language: a discussion, a panel discussion, an interview, a text of mine …
the cliché "paint, artist, paint, don't talk" has long been a thing of the past …
from next week on, I will definitely be back in basle.
warm regards,
your miriam cahn

i hate the men friends who love me i hate the woman friend i love why did A make that remark what has she got against me why is she lecturing me what does she want from me why doesn't she tell me anything why doesn't she love me why does she love others and why doesn't she love only me + every day + always + daily + phone every day + see one another every day + every day eat together every day.

i always have to think in circles everything in my head turns around and around so much that i have to think the beginning then the thoughts turn around + because i somehow forget again everything that I think everything begins again from go at the same point as before. certain music goes around and around in my head for days on end certain rooms and spaces my own and other peoples' turn around and around in my head m2 × m2, air × air, edge × edge, light × light.

i hate my appearance. my face, my breasts, my unused sexual parts my bad feet my knees my skin is tighter than me myself i'd like to get out of this skin my back oppresses me my shoulders restrict me.

why don't they fax why don't they phone why don't they get in contact why do i hate everything that loves me + and why do i hate everything that i love why am i forever questioning why this circular movement in my mind i think of auschwitz every day i think of dying every day i think of wars every day i think of the nuclear bomb every day i think of A every day i think of B every day of C of D i think of my parents every day i think of myself every day + and of the sense i think every day senselessness.

how long have i not touched anybody how long have i not been touched my skin is becoming too tight for me my skin is becoming flabby my skin = my self what have i got breasts, sexual parts, armpits, ear lobes, knee-pits, stomach, uterus for what have i got a body for for whom. what do they all mean by life. they are not addicted they don't have to run up debts they don't have to think of auschwitz they don't have to think of the nuclear bomb they don't have to think of death they are like the others they know how to live.

show me the right way. show me what i'm doing wrong show me how i should live show me the right way tell me the right way of behaving tell me what i should do tell me whether i'm a woman or a man tell me how i should love.

i'm always dropping things i'm always bumping into things words get turned around in my mouth + gush out in an uncontrolled way.

poison = openings where i stand there + know nobody. if i show/write/say/convey that i'm feeling down they all back away. the more i think that way the more they back away if i impose myself they back away + i lament all the more + they back ever farther away + i become more and more lonely + the more i say so the more they back away.

they don't phone any longer, fax any longer, write any longer.

all wrong: i spread my loving over my friendships – too much for them too little for me. i watch myself doing the wrong thing i watch myself doing everything wrong watch myself pestering others watch myself saying the wrong words they gush out of my mouth out of the rapid circling in my brain out of this junk that is slowly poisoning me. why do you never have time why are you so busy why do you have a private life on saturday/sunday why should i still talk with you why should i be with you i always have to postpone my feelings my thoughts till later when you do have time but for you that comes under the heading relaxation + so i do the wrong thing again because everything got bottled up and i could not get rid of it through activity. 2 hours working per day makes the rest of the day seem as dull as it is long who on earth has gone through this in the evenings i sit all night long in front of the television – the first night is good, the second so-so the third night drives me to despair.

 for the empty rest of the day i bore myself to death the rest of the day bores me to death every minute lasts hours if only i wasn't so fast at everything if only i could extend the length of my concentration if only i was like A, like B, like C, like all the other women artists + male artists who leave their private life/house/apartment and go to work in their studio/laboratory etc. go to work with a walk or journey to work, there they then work + have problems to be solved of an intellectual + above all technical nature how agreeable for them here are problems to solve + and to overcome then towards evening they can proudly go back into their private lives + have worked or solved problems or not but in any case work is done things are solved material is produced whatever in the evening with the work done they are tired like all those around them too.

i know i'm treating them unjustly but i envy them envy this balanced life probably also just seemingly balanced but it is a possibility. – i too pretend satisfaction because i am panic-stricken about not belonging.

i hate women they are too close to me too similar or i would like them to be too close too similar to me + and to want to know more about me but they don't want to they act coyly + and if need be they always have a man on whom they can lean in some form or other if things get dangerous. i hate women because they pretend to be nice understanding public-spirited as expected of them i too am nice, giggle, listen, reason patiently. at the same time i am watching myself + and hating myself in my endeavour to belong, be one of the crowd.

if i'm feeling low they all back away whether i've made an effort or not. they get afraid or they don't know what to do with me + i know it is unjust to think like this about one's own women friends + the more i think like this the more they draw back + the more they draw back the more i think like this. there are those circling thoughts again that are gradually poisoning me + and on days like these everything tumbles out of my hands i cut myself my feet my knees and my pelvis aches + and i want most to kill myself but since that's not allowed i hide.

HATRED my destruction.

again and again for decades "classic loving" my personal porn films only male hunks turn me on always the same always these sexy violent images – surrogate – unchanging yearning – made by myself – drawn by myself – a meagre image of men the image of the handsome only-fucker – the fuck-machine the compulsion today to show lovers hornily horny-making turns me around and around in circles. WHAT'S MISSING? sleep badly thoughts circling inner emptiness inner hate-emptiness circling around only my friends they think only of their work – of their leisure time saturday/sunday they are there for me only when their partner/dearest happens not to be there am surrogate, fifth wheel, entertainer, in times of tension buffer state: above all they never have time i have too much time. my own procedures are slowly dragging me on a downward spiral, 20 hours each day i find horribly boring + if i don't see anybody after a few days i flip out. if i do see someone after a few days i find it hard to talk. i've forgotten the words, they turn sluggishly in my mouth there is a pressure it presses against my throat my tongue from behind on my eyes booms in my ears.

my procedures were not intended to bring me abandonment but concentration. much however is damn loneliness even in dreams my ears multiply plugged with several layers of ohropax which I laboriously wiggle out of my ears while a woman friend watches + is horrified and accuses me of being filthy dirty.

vivian suter[122] **Panajachel, December1991**

Dear Miriam,
Your letter was such a pleasure and I really liked the Stampas postcard. Along with your letter came also a letter from Susan Wyss;[123] she is moored in Grenada harbour. Claude was here for a fortnight over Christmas; when he arrived, he was in a bad way, but when he left he was fully recovered. At present I have several visitors: Both's mother, sister and child, i.e. Panchito's cousin and my mother. The first three move on today to Miami. My mother is staying on for another month. Hans did not come on account of the risk of cholera – pretty bonkers because there is almost none. The reports in European newspapers are exaggerated and he confused Lake Amatitlán and Atitlán. Have not heard anything of the submission to the "Werkjahr". But whatever comes up, I will try to come back to Switzerland, even if only to try things out. I will rent out the place here. Now it's the dry season – cold in the morning and in the evenings, hot during the day. The avocados from the garden are good: we compete for them with the squirrels. There are also bananas and the coffee is drying. We also have telex here, only I have never used it. In my next letter I'll send you the no.
Perhaps you could come to visit me before you go back to Switzerland. Since you are now, after all, in the same hemisphere. I can send you precise details. There is a courier service that is very cheap. Or TACACostaRicaAirlines $ 500 to $ 600 normal rate.
I wish you a really great time in N.Y. I'd be pleased to hear from you how you are getting on.
I send you a big hug – take care,
Vivian

jewishness

miriam cahn
giessliweg 81
ch-4057 basle **basle, 16 september 98**

dear mr newman,
many thanks for your letter; I am pleased that you like my text.[124]
now to your question concerning swiss jewish literature: all of a sudden I realize that I don't know of anything like that here – there's not a single person who comes to my mind, in contrast to, say, austria and germany (schindel, broder[125] etc.). it's not at all clear to me how important this is here – in fact, it's not clear to me myself how important this definition 'swiss jewish' is to me (please not: "of jewish EXTRACTION" – horrible ...).
through the REACTIONS to my works and also to my texts, however, I can see increasingly that my jewishness does become more evident than I ever wished or intended – which moves and pleases me, because I consider my work to be ALWAYS better than myself, and hence you can read the picasso text as jewish – women tend to read it as feminist – art aficionados as art-historical – etc. ...
for sure, you can use the text for your series – but ONLY if it is printed as an integral whole WITH the opening description of the performance – and with the correct title "WAS MICH ANSCHAUT" ["WHAT LOOKS AT ME"] – the title used in "DU"[126] was an 'attention-grabbing' compromise.
I am sending you 3 additional texts that perhaps also have this jewishness about them – I myself see it that way after the REACTION of a swiss friend who, on reading the letter to jochen gerz,[127] restricted himself to the dry comment: "different culture" – perhaps he's right actually, but it is a comment that has become unbearably trendy here among those who do not want to concern themselves with awkward matters. I read the "I am a refugee" text[128] out loud on swiss television before that unspeakable ballot and at the end even croaked out schubert's "fremd bin ich etc." ["a stranger I came ..."], which, however, they cut out ...
these are, therefore, APPLIED texts and quite definitely not 'literary' ones – in the end, I hope, it is art in the best sense.
warm regards,
your miriam cahn

my jews in germany
my jews in switzerland
my jews in japan
ATOMIC BOMBS

i always thought that i would like most of all to show my jews in germany most of all today most of all my jews in germany today germany not of that time show my jews in today's germany. today my jews in germany. to assert that there is a difference between jews and others, to have to assert a visible distinguishing with these pictures an assertion of visible distinguishing, which, however, however, is i hope not visible, not perceptible, not there, not to be seen in the pictures, but in the ascription through the overall title my jews and the history, my information/narratives/assertions on the individual pictures. the building is not only a building, the animal not only an animal, the men, the women, the children not only what can be seen, but also what i ascribe to them. by naming pictures by naming them my jews different reactions are aroused in germany from in switzerland. in germany still today there is this heavy oppressive past summoned up by the naming and asking of questions: my jews.

in switzerland there tends to be naïve astonishment or utter ignorance, a total lack of interest, my jews in switzerland could also be my strangers absolutely in general or in switzerland i could change my narrative from my jews into my muslims, the building wouldn't be a place of burial but a mosque, the headgear would be ascribed to islam and the animals i don't know.

my jews in japan jews in japan are the strangers/the foreign/the unknown as such, and – if i may suppose while writing – there are perhaps no jews in japan japan without jewish refugees/emigrants at that time japan at that time in alliance with nazi germany, japan free of jews (judenfrei), my jews go to japan. HOW WONDERFUL! that japanese people maybe possibly might see something completely different in the work my jews HOW WONDERFUL! that simultaneous to my ascription there might be a completely free interpretation or maybe possibly even no interpretation at all in japan only looking without knowing only contemplating beholding at any event an unprejudiced looking, looking without ascription, the first wild look at my jews without my jews. the information later will not destroy the first wild look but complement it, since the information "my jews" is narrative.

HOW BEAUTIFUL! they all say looking at my watercolours at first without information with a wild gaze how beautiful! like flowers or mandalas or or or. they are not flowers nor mandalas or or or, they are exclusively and only atomic bombs – after the wild gaze there comes the realization (erkenntnis), after the wild comes civilisation, the ascription, the naming, the narrative, the history:
hitler manhattan project hiroshima-nagasaki lucens three mile island chernobyl fukushima or or or.

HOW WONDERFUL AND BEAUTIFUL! my jews, my atomic bombs in japan how wonderful and beautiful!

august 2011

Iwan Wirth[129]
miriam cahn
giessliweg 81
CH-4057 basle **basle, 8 august 99**

dear herr Wirth,
a swift and utterly and entirely undiplomatic reaction to your interview in the SonntagsZeitung: I feel insulted. your claim that it is only since the appearance of Iwan Wirth that artists living in switzerland have been appropriately "placed" on the international stage (whatever "placed" is supposed to mean: it means nothing to ME), is quite simply false and a corruption of historical fact to suit your argument. since, according to the interview, you wish to make a modest contribution to the history of art and culture, here are a couple of pointers: diter rot, oppenheim[130] etc. certainly lived entirely or partly in switzerland and definitely exhibited their work more abroad than in this country, as has also my own generation. and now, not having died yet, I'll talk about myself: over the last twenty years I have held so many exhibitions and sold so many works outside switzerland and overseas, while switzerland and especially zurich tend to be barren soil … perhaps because I still decide for myself when, where and with whom I exhibit and don't just let myself be "placed".
sure, if you divide up the world into a "real" world = wages, performance and value added here, and define the world of art over there as a "spiritual" one, in which "imagination" reigns (whatever that is supposed to mean: it means nothing to ME), then artists are in your logic creatures who can and should move around in the "real" world only with YOUR assistance – fantastic – welcome to the 19th century.
then there's something else: this perpetual dishonesty about money, which really gets one's goat. only galleries with large financial reserves are able to pre-finance major projects – I've nothing at all against that. but your programme, the artists you represent, all that depends to an overwhelming extent on your financial possibilities and has little to do with any "obsession" (whatever that's supposed to mean etc. …).
many greetings,
your miriam cahn

in N.Y. i couldn't work because the apartment i had rented was cluttered up with extremely heavy furniture. so i went to the N.Y. library and looked for aerial photographs of production sites which i could paint in replica. things became hectic: opening hours, search – not find etc. = full-time activity. as soon as i started painting the material proved recalcitrant, picture unrealizable, end of the series 'VERARBEITUNG' [PROCESSING]. with great effort and input of time had paper sent from N.Y. to basle that i needed to produce nuclear bombs. was of course the wrong paper, watercolour unrealizable, "A- + H-bomb tests"-production ended. too targeted, too material-complex, too hectic and too professional: the entire procedure put an end to a piece of work which was already ended earlier, and i reacted with hectic, time-consuming activity and panic-buying and was thus like you and thought that I was now one of you.
i thought that i was one of you because i had things to do, because i was perpetually busy instead of doing nothing. since this nadir i have come to recognize that in working at art, as i understand it, there is nothing to go in search of, nothing to be implemented, to be organized, to be tried out, and above all no tasks to be accomplished.
our conversations degenerate into reporting on heroic acts: you heroically overcome immense difficulties in record time. you love the war report on the exhibition managed at the last minute, and, topping everything, the catalogue! an enterprise rescued on the brink of disaster, the invitation cards sent with the very last post etc., etc.... that's what you understand by creativity or reality respectively. to act = reality. i am downright gleefully frustrated/ delighted when, in such situations, the material proves recalcitrant. like the weather that pays no regards to your fixed vacation times: the humour you so often like to prescribe to others is then suddenly gone if it pours with rain for a week or if there are blizzards.

i clearly play no part in your private life. i thought i was a friend, but i am/was only a partner/colleague. the distinction you make, this separation into work and private life is a total mystery to me. when you tell your tales of compensation: "I need the daily stroll as compensation, I have to be able to withdraw to our house as compensation", is it leisure time or work when you choose to meet me? i have to book an appointment days or weeks in advance just for an evening meal, with improvisation on my part unwelcome but last-minute cancellations on your part frequent: "something important has cropped up". if there is a misunderstanding/a problem/trouble, out comes your pavlovian reflex: "we can discuss that later" – which means never. feelings – please postpone them to the next session. unpredictability you want to have nothing to do with unless it gives rise to "art": "turn it into something", you say when i tell you a dream – and, believe me, it's the last dream i'll ever tell you. dim-witted me, i've swallowed this hurtful rubbish much too long, far too long because dim-witted me thought that we were friends. i confused friendship with conformity, conformity with friendship. i had comfortable explanations for what i saw: "that's just the way they are". what i see today are people, contemporaries, who cannot cope – cannot cope because of what? people who can only react, only respond – to what? everything is too much for you: your work, your living conditions, noise, people, weather, the city, everything, and, of course, me too. "you know i never ring". because, dim-witted me, i believed this self-portrayal far too long, this self-portrayal of people who can no longer cope, i did not see the convenient/

 practical side of it for you, i conformed, dim-witted me, i conformed because i loved you.

you men i can assess correctly: i can talk with you, plan with you, argue, debate, assert my positions and get things done. i know when/how you are domineering and accustomed to giving orders, and then i go. you women lack distance, with your so-called closeness you swamp me with things in which i am often not interested. your continual appeal to "likeness", this continual "just try to understand me, just believe me" and thus a refusal of all explanation, speculation, assertion, of intellectuality, of the enjoyment of playing with words, which take on beauty through being distant, apart, faraway.
can't you, don't you want to distance yourselves from yourselves? the private = public – this originally self-assertive battle cry has now degenerated into a convenient tactic for housewives. you "know better", but act in the background, don't you, because otherwise – god forbid – you're considered to be masculine. what am I supposed to do with you? at first, i find you super: we mock, joke, giggle, make common cause, stand by one another, are friends – and there precisely comes my misunderstanding: for me, a few friendly/nice gestures are love. just can't get it. just can't find the right balance, the right proportions. while i move away from the hail of bullets fired by men, i don't recognize your "soft" warfare and am engulfed.

re-encounter with my former "best" woman friend: they are still her eyes, which i completely love. otherwise a shift in style right in the middle of her face: her mouth and nose distorted in an embarrassed laugh, a horrible business laugh, gestures of justification with ugly hands, body language à la monroe – breasts out, stomach pulled in, so-called sexy walk in combination with so-called feminist comfort clothing in inconspicuous colours. the meeting point/low point a high-class vegetarian self-service restaurant with a woman's name, in which predominantly critically-minded, socially-established businesswomen from my generation eat – and i put up with all this garbage because on the invitation to her fiftieth birthday party, which i refused in sheer hatred, there were photographs of her head from childhood to today, and those eyes of hers shone out above all else and enabled me to survive this entire culture crap for 2 hours.

you have chosen mediocrity. your thinking is dominated by the day-to-day routine: husbands, partners, children, customers, clients, buyers – what they do/say/think/feel determines your thought patterns. thus everything becomes a reaction to, a response to, becomes responding, only reacting, the others are to blame/are the cause, predominantly determining your lives. the personal, the unique disappears in this tangled mass of requests; efficiency is professional routine; mediocrity due to shortage of time is a question of survival. forgotten now any dilettante, time-consuming beauty. you think it is sufficient to cope, to deal with/execute/fulfil assignments that others have commissioned; you think, therefore, that this is life, you explain this to me as life – brazenly even as THE life.
realistic life: "just be realistic". and yet it is simply your life, no more, and you are forever telling the same stuff, the same everyday stories, the discarded and junked belief in humanity and in the future/utopia/salvation of art as an avant-garde, as the new, the different, as what you lack, as a compensation for your day-to-day life, just as you need nature as a compensation for your non-physical work. this, therefore, is the so-called life that i will never understand: over here work, over there recuperation – from what? leisure

time, vacation, family, social commitment and the compensation, "time for oneself". over here the "serious business of life", over there nonsense, play, flippancy, superfluity, possibly even art. could never understand that. i work always or never.

again and again you say that there are more important things than work. relationships, you say, are more important, loving is more important, living is more important. what interests you first and foremost, however, are yourselves. your family, your business, your shop. so this "more-important than-work living/loving" propaganda is just not true. all conversations, really all talk centres around your bastions of family/business, and everybody else has to toe the line. i will always be the weaker party, a female knight riding against the windmills of these sturdy strongholds. i telephone/fax/get in touch in order to remind people that i exist. if i don't do so, then as far as you're concerned i'm absent. oh, yes, sure, sometimes you do think of me – this "i've just been thinking of you" white lie when i call …
i've had enough. i now take your perpetual "got no time" personally. i've been conforming to your ways too long; for too long i've gritted my teeth and submissively shown understanding. no longer will i come running after you; no longer will i come begging for friendship.

me – the non-lover, non-wife, non-girlfriend, non-customer, at most partner/colleague with no lobby. me as a human being working always or never. my system of conformity doesn't work and never has worked, was a world of friendship in my mind. i am my work and less and less you. i watch you: you forget everything that is not immediately applicable/utilizable. everything has to be immediately understood or implemented – IMPLEMENT – how i hate this word, which has been hounding me throughout my entire life! and this perpetual having-to/want-to-understand as a form of morality! and if there is no immediate ability to understand then the compulsion to file it away in that socio-psycho-mysto-cultural drawer! all cut and dried! task accomplished! good doggy! and you womenfolk! rear the men you need. a belated revenge. now you've got them at home, and they do everything for you: household chores, sex, kids, money – the guilt-laden successors to the patriarchs become so-called motherly creatures, and in your so-called partnerships equality is negotiated down to the minutest detail until it becomes ingrained habit. you womenfolk want everything: job, kids, family, nest, sex, EVERYTHING. goal: perfect, unmitigated happiness. terrible, unmitigated happiness, the opposite of the wonderful, grand, short-lived happy moments, unmitigated happiness as an immobile condition. i imagine/think up/live out my people: man, woman, mother, father, child, gender-neutral being, tri-gender, animal, soldier, female warrior, woman offender, victim etc., etc.: that is EVERYTHING, and not, as you mean, HAVING everything, but being everything.
"i can't imagine that", or worse: "i don't want to imagine that". so you don't want to imagine either murder or manslaughter, nor war, hatred, starvation, destitution, poverty, because you haven't "experienced" it. you poor swine can thus only imagine what you have experienced. if what you have "experienced" prevents you from imagining things you haven't experienced, then you haven't experienced anything but just defended your meagre property. you would never murder, hate, rape, commit manslaughter, never, out of the question, those are things others do, foreigners. you refuse to think about your potential for the negative: you can't "imagine" it and therefore think that you have overcome it. you think that HAVING EVERYTHING protects you. barricade yourselves away in this protective custody, refuse to think about the possibilities of your own brutality. imagination called for and

 refused. "you're interested in the Balkan war and war in general because you're a jewess. not even a question but immediate pigeonholing, an unchallengeable assertion that cannot even be bombed out of your brains. so we've got the hots for suffering/victims/wars and above all we are auschwitz experts. in former times we were allowed to finance your Christian wars and run your money-lending businesses so that you didn't get your hands dirty. today we are not only considered to be money-grubbing but are also your specialists in suffering so that you don't have to sully your minds with questions/analyses/taking sides/speculation. you don't want to see your reverse side. you don't want to imagine anything. the Balkans were "always that way".

i owe these insights to the shoulder pads in one of those career-woman jackets worn by my equals. one evening, I put on my green jacket and looked, suddenly bathed in sweat, into the mirror: this wasn't me, this was a person who needed broad shoulders to survive. looking out at me was the cliché image of the successful woman with her shoulder-padded jacket who was meeting up with you broad-shouldered successful types in order to be one of the in-crowd.
at last, therefore i take it personally that you don't phone, don't ring back, don't call "just because, for no real reason". i take it personally that i must be visible, must call you (up) audibly to come into contact with you at all, to touch you. who are you then? any instrument is more interesting than you, every note produced by touching the strings of my violin. every line drawn on paper, every movement of my hand over my canvases has more surprise in it than you.

and then a nice fax, a gentle phone-call, little questions, brief pleasure, calm until the next time, and my mind is clear and at peace. may this loving and hating finally cease.
may this perpetual turning and turning in my head never come back again. may my brain never again revolve around and around.

i don't want this system any more – i'm quitting this system, dropping out.
my former "best" woman friend came to visit and talked about job/family/dog. she loved the daily evening walk with her dog. her fantastic eyes gleamed as she lovingly described her dog; this dog was her one-and-all. then came the old "when-i've-got-so-much-to-do-i-need-these-walks-as-compensation" crap. don't want to hear this any longer. and especially don't want to understand it any longer at all.
because i non-comprehending dimwit woman simply didn't get it, she patiently explained her system to me, in the hope of teaching me something so as to make me wiser. suddenly, decades of life fell away from me: that's how it had always been – "best" friends had always tried to teach me something, to lecture me, and had given me lectures. i was their pupil, their vessel, their whatever, and i willingly offered myself up to them as a dimwit. your commandments were my commands. i fell into line with you. i adopted your language right down to its sentence structures, i adopted your men friends, women friends, colleagues and with them their morality. your words, your sentences and your behaviours seeped through me.
so i sat opposite my former "best" friend and spoke with myself: finished, all over, and with the other so-called clever/intelligent/competent "best" friends – system change.
you don't interest me anymore with your output targets and your compensations. i'm turning a deaf ear to your affluence lamentations. and to sufferings inflicted by men – to them too. womanness as myth – to that

most of all. i'll live with my own mind, not with yours any longer.
what's the point of my being here. you're not really interested in what i think, what i do, who i am: i saw more than was there, an error on my part, silly imagination. i like you, love you even, but listening to you and watching you really drags me down. i want nothing to do with this perpetual, wearisome only-reacting to the so-called external world, which you call life. are we really living in a perpetual catastrophe?

2000/2001

36 WOMEN APES
performance with woman ape mask

zaha armajani
fiona artschwager
marlene bacon
jenny baumgarten
miriam beuys
barbara blum

hanne kavara
elvira lichtenstein
marisa merz
rebecca mucha
ulrike naumann
niki oldenburg

muda fischli/pipilotti weiss
helen foerg
kiki gober
mona hamak
maria jones
tracy kabakov

rosemarie boetti
annette boltanski
nancy borofsky
valie chamberlain
rachel de maria
roni flinzer

charlot paik
isa richter
katharina ruthenbeck
gisele ruscha
silvia schnabel
sarah slominski

meret stella
dorothee turell
marie-jo viola
nan wall
louise warhol
cindy watts

and one male ape: johannes darboven

by a coincidence I was invited by jean-christophe ammann to take part in a question-and-answer game before an audience made up of the "friends of the MMK" while at the same time the MMK was presenting the exhibition "a european view of american art". this led to the following spontaneous ideas: yet another exhibition of the boys for the boys. bring on the guerilla girls with their gorilla masks! up there on the podium I'm only monkeying around anyway!

so I thought up the names of "36 women apes": wearing an ape mask I had made myself (a kind of cardboard box) I would whisper these names. after every bunch I would emit an ape-like noise which would rise at the end into a crescendo of screeching. shortly before setting out I decided not to carry this performance through. I had had enough of monkeying around.

Letters to the editor: weltwoche[131]
miriam cahn
giessliweg 81
4057 basle **basle, 11 january 99**

let herr fasel[132] found an "against the future party" with herr blocher![133]
edgar fasel has still not got over the fact that the "event" (fasel's chosen designation for the sandoz disaster of 1986) led to a cultural uprising against this kind of "leadership", which he now – puffing away at his pipe – paternally recommends to the expo management in his interview. what he, back then and again today, disparagingly calls "self-appointed avant-gardist élites, freaks for various stylistic directions" etc., etc. was the population of basle, which in 1986 had escaped death by the skin of its teeth and which portrayed this existential experience through the means offered by art, creative events, dramatic performances and others – among the many people involved being also pipilotti rist with a film …
woman artists such as her are not just people "who cut a competent figure in their particular territorial area", as fasel so dazzlingly puts it. the beauty of pipilotti rist's work is loved (or hated) by the "people" because her art treats their day-to-day life, using existential, banal, comical, abstruse and virtual means and much else besides …
miriam cahn

fax

dear miriam,
with great dispatch
i reply to your fax:
this new gadget is fine
quite sublime
after a week of frustration
’twould be a great delectation
to try saddle of venison or hare
would you find that luscious fare?

 NOVEL SCULPTURE (having to eat)

the woman stands in the darkness outside the restaurant and looks down the street and across the extensive roadworks. she is crying. the woman is crying. she looks down into the dark town into the dark town centre she looks down at the main square of her town late at night. she looks down at the main square and sees nobody the woman sees nobody. she sees no human being. the woman cries looks at the roadworks and at the town centre and sees no human being. there is no-one there no man there no woman. they are all gone disappeared there is no-one. crying the woman sees no human being. crying she stands outside the restaurant looks into the dark town and sees no human being. she stands and cries. the woman stands there crying. in the darkness late at night the woman stands outside the restaurant looks across the building site at the central square in her town and cries. there is no-one, no man no woman no-one. late at night the woman stands outside the restaurant looks down at the roadworks at the main square of her town and cries. here there is no-one any more. she thinks of her friends now no longer her friends recognizes her lack of friends recognition all of a sudden: me just me. there is no man no woman no man they are all gone there is nobody no man no woman nobody. the woman walks. she walks past the roadworks down to the main square and walks, strides, thinking. she walks in the direction of her part of town. she walks she thinks and walks. under shock she walks thinking. she walks through the town over the bridge over the towns dark river into her part of town the woman walks. she walks with her characteristic step with her characteristic large steps the woman walks and thinks. she walks into her part of town and arrives at her workshop. the woman enters her workshop. her part of town and her workshop consolingly form a shell around her. her workshop is consoling: here this large empty quiet room space here the tables here the lamps here the bed the little kitchen toilet shower here her pictures here her storeroom here the dark room the telephone the notebook here the file card system of her works and her curved desk. here her shell her workshop here. she goes to bed. she thinks of this evening. she the woman the artist thinks back.

she is at this opening. the woman sees herself the woman at this opening. she will always have to bring herself to go to openings. but the woman artist from britain the meal after the opening and the prospect of meeting her friends and gallerists. so the woman will go there will go. she is always punctual and always stands around at these events much too long. she stands around then always. the woman goes first to her local pub and reads the newspaper and drinks a beer. she stretches her time out and will not be over-punctual. as always the woman is on edge and tense as always when she has to be among her own kind she is on edge, panicky when she has to be among people. especially when she has to be among her own kind.

for the woman it is bothersome each time bothersome to prepare herself for encounters for meetings with her own kind she the woman is on edge when she has to be among her own kind on edge. she thinks she shouldnt be over-punctual and stand around and drinks her beer and reads her newspaper. she is agitated while reading she reads inattentively she skims she drinks her beer too fast she cant be unpunctual she hates unpunctuality in herself and in other people unpunctuality in those around her unpunctuality in others and in herself the woman hates. the woman hates unpunctuality, she knows that its imbecile, idiotic, stupid to hate unpunctuality at openings. the beer and the newspaper are the womans adjustment strategy. she acknowledges through reflection that she should has to have to adjust to a custom. at last she can take the tram at last its the adjusted time the time has been to some extent stretched out. in the tram she sees that she still has overmuch time. she will have to stand around too long. she walks and thinks around she walks strolls and looks around walking. she walks and thinks. thinking the woman walks. she trots to the museum. outside the entrance to the museum the woman adopts a different posture. imperceptibly almost she walks differently looks around differently. the woman is only half-conscious of it. assuming a different hardly different body posture among people of her kind is for her what flipping open their pocket mirrors combing painting over their lips is for other women and clothing clothing to go out in outfit. the woman enters the museum through the revolving door. her strategy of arriving later has the effect that she has missed the official speeches. so the woman can stand around like the others like all the others and she the woman standing around among all the others can do what she likes best: observe and watch and look and see. the woman sees her friends. she thinks that she wont rush over to her friends now most of all the woman would like to run over to her friends to run all around her friends like a young dog. most of all she would like to run around her friends embrace them impetuously kiss them noisily leap around them leap up at them like a puppy like a young dog leap up at them like a puppy puppy-like like a frisky young dog not only not only to mark out that these people are her friends but also her family her chosen family. whom she loves whom she the woman has chosen to love in contrast to her physical family. these her people her loved spiritual family soul family whom she loves, the people whom she loves.

but the woman stands around. she doesnt rush she doesnt leap. she stands. she watches. she sees herself the woman from above, she sees herself standing in the room, she sees the others from above, she hovers and stands at the same time, a possible strategy that stops her from rushing forward, running all around, embracing like a young dog. a strategy of years of work. she stands around. finally the woman walks strolls slowly to the group where her gallerists and friends are standing. the closer the woman comes the more slowly she walks. she is afraid is in panic is panicky she arms herself she puts on her battle gear she becomes a warrior. she arms herself against her gallerists and friends she is on her guard against people of her kind she really must take care. she must take care. she must be wary here is the jungle. she the woman is a jungle warrior. she arms herself against being ignored foolish remarks false kisses small-talk and so on. the woman knows or has learned or believes she knows or knows because she has learned has had to learn should have learned must have learned has had to knows. she knows that people of her kind mean no offense dont do it deliberately. she the woman has had to learn to have to ought to know this. this knowledge is her armour her survival strategy among her kind. if the woman did not arm herself and if she stood there without armour unarmed and stood alongside stood by unarmed she would frisk around her friends and throw herself around their necks and call them show them mark them out out them as her family her protection against her surroundings as her herd against these surroundings. her friends would totally not understand certainly absolutely at this moment absolutely not understand. they wouldnt understand the woman at all certainly not not even after thirty years. so the woman goes to join them, kiss-kiss, how are you. fine here, nice and full too, are you going to the restaurant afterwards too. she continues to stand around waiting. she waits and stands she waits and strolls and walks and stands waiting. at last a move is made. she goes with her people to the tram. she waits for the tram with the others. they all go together to the restaurant they go as a group all together.

the woman wants to go into the reserved area with an artist from her gallery, the woman and the artist are not allowed in, they are not on the list, they have not accepted in writing, the acceptance in writing should have been sent weeks ago. the woman tries once more to get in she tries once again she cant believe cant grasp whats happening to her here. she cant get in. she cant get past these two women with the lists of names her name is not on the list. the woman sees friends and acquaintances go in. the female museum director shrugs her shoulders. the woman has known the director for decades for thirty years. for three hundred three thousand years. the gallerists man and wife go in. they are accompanied by an artist the woman knows, an artist who is working assiduously at getting an exhibition in their gallery. of course his name is on the list. he accepted in writing months ago of course his name is there after all working assiduously at his career after all. after all assiduously after all slickly assiduously. his name is on the list. he walks past the woman and shrugs his shoulders. she the woman stands at the entrance she stands there with the other artist who is also not on the list. they both expect their gallery to do something. the male gallerist speaks briefly to the woman museum director and shrugs his shoulders. the female gallery director does nothing and goes to her table. all go single-mindedly to their tables all go hungrily and single-mindedly directly swiftly to their tables directly swiftly and hungrily they take their seats at their tables on their chairs hungrily they sit down they sit. they sit they feel hungry they are hungry they sit they sit they sit and wait for their meal. inwardly the woman is almost beside herself. she wants to go home straightaway. at first she actually really wants to go home straightaway now home now immediately straightaway back home go home. not because she considers herself to be tactically inept, not because of this unspeakably bureaucratic organization of the culturniks in her town, nor because now, in this way, at all costs she wanted to be included. she is beside herself the woman is beside herself beside herself the woman the artist is beside herself at the lack of regard shown by her people her gallery her gallerists her gallerist couple these two people her people whom she believed to be her friends. over these decades for long years she the woman thought that she with her the woman people on friendly terms for decades her gallerists too. she is beside herself the woman is beside herself that she has to witness the boorishness the boorishness of her gallerist this dullard hungry urge to get to his table in order at last to be able to have to want to take his meal. the woman is really beside herself for the first time really beside herself. it is not the first time she is beside herself because of lack of regard from her gallerists and friends folk, but it is the first time the woman is so utterly beside herself that she suddenly sees clearly. the woman sees suddenly in her cold fury and icy anger. she sees the complete lack of friendship she sees the complete absence of friendly action. she the woman the artist recognizes and sees. she stands there with the other artist from the gallery and is not admitted. they stand at the entrance and are not admitted. the woman and the artist see their gallerist shrug his shoulders and see him sitting down with the others at his table, hungrily. they watch their hungry and shoulder-shrugging male gallerist they watch their female gallerist who goes runs races single-mindedly hungrily to her table. the woman and the artist watch their female gallerist single-mindedly hungrily being hungry having to wanting to go to her table and sit down. she didnt even bother to shrug her shoulders. eyeing her two people the woman thinks that she would not be so beside herself if her gallerists and friends had come and sat with them in the public part at the restaurant bar and taken a brief apéritif if they had at least taken that time the time to show their artists to show them over an apéritif that they stand by them that they somehow belong together briefly belong together the time briefly this little time their two people their gallerists should have taken wanted to take ought to have at all events this time brief time that they belong with them belong to their set belong together. professional at least at all events. their hunger should have had to wait that long the time for an apéritif with their artists at the bar that long that short time at least nonchalantly and elegantly their gallerists ought to have ignored their hunger. it would have been good style stylish of their gallerists nonchalant and elegant to share their powerlessness for a brief time at the bar with their artists and to ignore things. an elegant gesture as the woman and artist considers and thinks while observing her people from the entrance a handsome gesture it would have been to their successful artists. elegant humorous at least for the length of a brief apéritif at the bar to share this time with their artists. the male artist angry thinks further more coolly than the woman the artist. he comes from berlin and thinks considers that they both the female artist for ages internationally and in her town and he already internationally and from berlin that their gallery must without fail take care to see to it without fail and always is responsible for seeing that both of them their artists the artists of the gallery have admission to such events as this evening. a gallery their gallery should take care to see to it that its artists do not have to do everything themselves a gallery must see to it that its artists do not stand around as if they didnt belong among those of their kind. a gallery should take care of not love but take care of.

the insight that the male artist could be right, the insight that the woman the female artist had already had these thoughts at other similarly structured events, the insight that she the woman had already had the same thoughts but had not wanted to embrace them, had had this insight but not embraced it this recognition makes the woman very angry. she feels this anger against herself against her own person the artist herself against herself dimwit against herself a dimwit believing thinking dimwit believing friendship with her gallerists her people would protect her the artist against such a gallerist/artist/relationship. blindly she the woman the artist believed thought dumbly for decades that she was protected by her friendship with these two people against this galleristartistrelationship. she the woman the artist had blindly believed dumbly to be able to wish to have to protect herself through this friendship against these clichés between gallery and artists blindly. the woman the artist wanted blindly to protect herself through friendship. she now has the feeling, however, she sees now, however, however, now, at the present moment, that her balancing system over the last while at least but also for a longer period for some time now for a good while for a longish time has, however, no longer worked. the friendship has become too weak in fact perhaps even perhaps possibly in part or even possibly perhaps has completely disappeared. perhaps possibly thinks the woman even always from the very start for her part been more love. for her two people she was perhaps possibly from the very start perhaps one among many as a person. she thinks that as a person she is silly. she sees herself as a stupid person. she the woman sees herself as an intelligent artist and a stupid human being. she has always known that her art is more intelligent than she herself her work the signs and language of her existence. they are direct signs and pointers of her existence and to her life more intelligent than she the woman herself more intelligent than she woman human being artist than she human being herself alone. she herself reads her art aright reads her art as true. yet as soon as the woman needs to apply what she has read aright she becomes stupid. as soon as she the woman needs to apply what she reads apply aright needs to read her signs and apply them she becomes stupid she becomes a stupid woman a stupid person. the others read her signs her language the

 womans work differently/wrongly the others read the signs and language as art and only as art. they do not read they look. the others look at the pictures and do not read the signs as language. they look at these surfaces at these attractive surface areas the attractive objects pictures drawings. the others dont see the womans speaking. they the others could not see it. some see the womans speaking when she the artist sets up her exhibitions herself and presents entire room spaces she the woman can must show her signs and her language in entire room spaces. then the woman is the artist intelligently she shows the others her life, intelligently, she makes the others an offer: showing her existence. years ago the title of an exhibition in her gallery was I AS A HUMAN BEING. at that time she didnt actually know what this her own title actually maybe meant. but as she stands with the artist at the entrance to the private function reserved seating area she thinks however of precisely this title I AS A HUMAN BEING thinks standing there of this exhibition whose title she chooses at that time out of an uneasy presentiment. an uneasy feeling also when setting things up. the language of this exhibition that she set up in her gallery among her people this exhibition I AS A HUMAN BEING shows her very clearly her the woman very clearly too clearly that she actually she the woman herself here in this gallery is probably possibly almost certainly not on friendly terms here with the gallerist couple her people, not or no longer, or that she the woman as a human being had never been on friendly terms. she the woman the artist wants the others to read this. she wants above all her friends her gallerists her people to read it.
nothing happens. its art nothing else.
even she the woman doesnt really understand the title and the exhibition even the woman doesnt read her own work or doesnt want really to read it doesnt want really probably certainly to read her own work. she doesnt want to countenance what the fact signifies what it means that the friends her people do not read the offer I AS A HUMAN BEING. at that time she was stupid at that time the woman was stupid very really stupid …standing around at the entrance to the private function area the woman thinks the woman thinks that she doesnt want to be cant be stupid really not stupid certainly no longer stupid. it is later not earlier. she the woman thinks in cold anger thinks icily: she the woman she will no longer allow herself to be driven away she will no longer allow herself to be humiliated allow herself to be pushed away no more shrugging of the shoulders to her. now immediately the woman no longer stands around. she goes and takes with her the artist who is standing around. they take seats in the public part of the restaurant. they are both still very incensed. they place their orders. they eat and drink and try to talk about other things. at the same time they both know that in their minds a two-part dialogue is going on: an internal basso continuo to the external rhythmic talking of their conversation an internal angry basso continuo an internal hum an internal sound angersound furysound. they eat they drink they talk. very late on they can at last go and sit with the others. very late everybody already wants to leave everybody is already tired they have another drink get up and make a move and walk to the restaurant entrance. the woman tells the gallerist that she is just making a quick trip to the cloakroom. when shortly after very shortly after she comes out of the restaurant there is nobody there any longer. no man has waited for the woman no woman. they are all gone. in the dark the woman looks across the roadworks down to the main square of her town and cries. crying the woman looks down the street to her towns main square. the woman stands crying outside the restaurant and looks down at the main square of her town.
then she walks. she walks strides walks with large steps with the swift walk characteristic of her through the town over the bridge over the dark river

walks to her part of town home walks and thinks and walks home to her workshop to her shell her real true shell her protection her workshop her shell her place of work her workshop she walks and thinks. she walks at even pace with her rhythmic stride thinks and walks and feels. the woman thinks of the accumulation of similar situations to this evening, of this increased forgetting of her the woman in recent times in recent times this accumulation accumulating several times one after the other recently forgetting her simply forgetting her the woman. she thinks of her probably no longer friends who in recent times frequently forget her the woman, ditch, forget, fail to see, overlook, forget, make invisible.

she the woman will talk with her people the woman will have to talk to ought to talk to them. she will talk with her perhaps still friends she wants to talk with them she will want to have to talk with them. the woman will want to talk the woman wants to want to talk she will talk. she phones she picks up the receiver she dials the number of her gallery and phones. she speaks with her gallerist and no longer knows whether this person is a friend whether this person was a friend. the woman phones and talks she wants to talk and show and talk about the evening yesterday and the dismissive gestures of her people towards her the woman. she talks directly about it about the situation about the mental picture about the course of events which she the woman feels brutal to be brutal brutal forgetting her brutal. she still believes that among ones own kind among friends such things such mental pictures such words and situations disappear among her own kind disappear when she the woman talks with her friends, disappear, no longer occur, will no longer occur, disappear. the woman talks she talks she speaks on the phone she talks and talking speaking describing on the phone talking she notices the woman sees that on the phone in portraying the brutality towards her the woman sees a test she sees the test situation the test. a test situation is taking place talking on the phone is a test friendship test. she the woman observes herself talk on the phone. talking she considers this perhaps still friendship. the gallerist doesnt understand anything and thinks the woman oversensitive. the gallerist doesnt understand the woman, he considers her socially awkward, he doesnt understand he doesnt understand the woman, he justifies his actions, the woman the artist sees on the phone that he has flunked not passed the friendship test, he not only does not understand the woman it seems thats how the woman sees it thats how she considers it when listening to his justifications when listening that she doesnt matter to him either is a matter of indifference. he is he has he believes that he is behaving correctly did behave correctly had had behaved. presumably thinks the woman listening she and her gallerist were only a little bit friendly or perhaps never. perhaps only at the very beginning of their acquaintanceship possibly and later less and less friendly up to now today now actually no longer friendly at all the woman thinks while speaking on the phone. the woman thinks while speaking she thinks while speaking on the phone that needing to speak is in this case the right action that her act of having to want to talk is the really really right thing the true thing. right because true. the womans recognition is a shock. shocked pummeled taken aback she ascertains a lack of friendship. shocked pummeled wounded she sees no friendship any longer. the woman is shocked at herself wounded in herself had not wanted to see the moment the moments of the disappearing of friendship. the woman herself was the only person who failed to see the dissolution of this friendship. the woman could not did not want to could not believe see notice she the woman alone was absolutely unable to see and to notice and to believe that this friendship had at some point dissolved itself without her. the woman alone she remained on friendly terms. she remained on friendly terms with her people. she is on friendly terms with her people

 without her people being on friendly terms with her. her people that is the shock she feels when phoning with her gallerist her people are no longer on friendly terms with her. her people are not her people. the womans shock and the recognition of truth real truth for the woman the artist for her herself alone only for the woman the shock and the recognition is this: that she the woman just like that she dimwit is on friendly terms just like that with people who at best are colleagues partners business partners and work colleagues at best at most atmostatbest.
the woman is suffering from a shock. what she has long suspected becomes a certainty. what she never could want to believe blindly becomes a certainty. the certainty of a lack which she the woman now wants to believe must be able to believe undeferrably must see must want to. she ends the phone call and leaves her workshop she walks the woman walks beside her river towards the town she walks along the river bank the woman walks. piz palü chugchugs past lai da tuma, lunghin, the maria turns and ties up on the bank alongside the wharf. the woman thinks under shock again and again under shock still the woman thinks back.

she thinks while walking thinking of the re-opening of the museum in another town. she meets her gallerists at the railway station they travel as a group with others the group travels. in the exhibition her work has been hung wrongly. the woman is annoyed, she feels annoyed, she will not stand around here for long. she stands around, she walks around, she sits around, she stands around, she the woman doesnt want to stand around any longer. shes happy to see that her gallerists are making a move. shes happy to think that her friends feel the same way as her. shes happy to travel back with them her people. the woman travels back with them. they travel with the others the group travels and during the journey they discuss the exhibition the new museum extension the architecture. they get out at their towns station and go towards the exit. the woman goes to the exit. the others go to the foodstore. they go as a group en bloc to the shops entrance. they all want to go into the store to shop. the woman stands there and looks at the group of people making a beeline for the store. no-one, male or female, sees the woman. just before the entrance to the store the woman gallerist hesitates and shouts to her that they are buying food something to eat during the match during the match later on. then they all disappear into the shop. the woman stands there. she stands and doesnt understand. the woman hasnt heard anything about a match the woman hasnt got a clue about football the woman is not a fan. the woman stands and thinks that she thought she would be going off with a few to a bar or something, to drink an apéritif or something, the woman thinks she was thinking of an unpredetermined evening with drinks and at most eating out and such stuff or something. the woman stands and thinks that she has thought amiss unthinkingly thought wrong. the woman stands at the exit to the station she thinks and now is sure: the football was the reason for the early departure en bloc of her perhaps probably no longer friends. of course she then goes along with them of course she the woman can go along with them amble along trot along. of course she can join them as they travel and walk there and can join in their discussions sure of course she can join them of course. yet she the woman can just as well not go with them not go along not trot along stand around with them join in their discussions.
only just barely and then only a shouted explanatory sentence is what the woman is worth to her more likely than not probably no longer friend the woman gallerist. she the woman can equally not join them. its all the same whether she joins them or not. its a matter of indifference. its all the same. the woman is as if not there or as if there. the woman stands and looks at the

group. the woman reflects on this group of people. this herd these swarm people this herd this grouping this herd like a swarm of course all like a swarm swarmingly informed knowing in their herd instinct of course going single-mindedly to the store en bloc more a herd than a swarm. more an incarnate informed group than a loose assembly of human beings a group informed about the reason in general absolutely of course rushing walking running knowingly into the store. a pigsty-like urge towards the trough. only for informed group members only for football fan members of this herd. informed. arranged long ago. of course. a herd consensus not needing to be voiced.

this image of the group of people disappearing into the store will always be in the womans memory. she the woman goes home to her workshop her shell her existence. she must go back to her existence. she goes back to her workshop. this burn wound is summonable for the woman at any time, this image will have to become have to be visible at any time have to be want to be usable for her. this image of the burning should become usable, this image of the herd this the womans image of herself standing there and looking at her people. standing around as a condition of image production. standing around and watching contemplating seeing looking seeing among other things that this herd this group of people is branding her and watching her own branding. standing around and watching contemplating seeing contemplating these people long too long friendshippeople for the woman. standing around and seeing this friendshipherd and recognizing that these people are not friends any more probably almost certainly. probably for some time already. standing around recognizing seeing contemplating seeing. the woman sees this branded wound. this burned wound of recognition will always be working material for the woman the artist always. this image of recognition will want to be turned into work straightaway will have to become work survival work. the womans chance needs to be a coming to terms. the gift and the skill of the woman the artist enable the work of coming to terms work the gift the skill the life of the woman consists in the work of coming to terms work working away at her contemplating gazing seeing. the chance the gift and the skill consist in the contemplation of and coming to terms with such existential images situations in her immediate surroundings. when the woman feels low, when her spirits flag, when the woman is off-colour her mind thinks in circles her brain circles around her thoughts the sentences forever land up in the same place they go in circles. the words, the single words the situations the images the spaces the sounds circle and start up all over again and again from the same place forever the same sound the same verbal tune the same circling tune the same circling composition one-dimensional on one level and in its tonal movement similar to old gramophone records whose scratches on their black surface make them forever fall scratch into the same groove the scratches on the black surface making the pick-up arm forever fall scratchingly into the same groove and so play only one rotation one rotation of forever the same tune unfinished through the duration of the rotation brutally unfinished and becoming unbearable through the continuing repetition even if the sounds are lovely. if the woman however if the woman however however is strong she thinks in loops. if however however she thinks back in loops if she can think back in a loop-like way if she thinks back in loops if however the woman the artist can can think back in a loop-like way and her brain thinks in a loop-like and interwoven way powerfully interweaving the loops however then the woman is fine. if the woman is fine she thinks perspectivally archaeologically on several levels in interwoven loops. she thinks the words the individual words the sentences situations images sounds backwards and forwards up and down in a loop-like way. spaces are formed by the interwoven loops they form spaces chains of series that resemble one another and are not identical. repeat themselves each time different interweave with one another and repeat themselves spatially similar to steve reich and phil glass. if the woman is fine she lays down these lovely thought loops interwoven spatially serially if the woman the artist is fine she can determine them she herself the woman she the artist determines them herself and by herself. she files everything away by custom. her whole life long she the artist has by custom filed this loop thinking away interwoven and spatially. so she the woman the artist can summon up at any time what she has filed away can at any time re-activate everything that she has filed away in her life loop-like spatially interwoven. her brain is her archaeology and geology. in the course of her life her brain consists of ever more strata in the course of her life strata she has experienced have become interwoven spatially and in loops have formed deposits in her body, thought, seen, heard, felt, experienced. loop layers image layers interwoven spatially stored by the woman the artist layer by layer. this material stored in her body can be summoned up any time and waits to be worked on worked over come to terms with in work at any time. a vast store of materials to be used all the time at any time. the personal geology and archaeology of the woman the artist is layered material the layer and material store of thinking her thinking. layered thinking to order her feelings the womans feelings to guide the womans overflowing effusive feelings and yet and yet the feelings that often overflow the woman the overflowing of her feelings into visible form through her skill and her gift to use her feelings the womans feelings to think the womans feeling to reflect and direct the feeling of the woman the artist into a method. the woman practises her life her whole life long. the woman the artist practises her whole life long a method of portrayal a method of portrayal a method of portraying and displaying her life.

the woman draws her lips apart the woman grimaces smilingly the woman bares her teeth she smiles she shows her teeth her face contorted into a smile actually however in reality she is baring her teeth like a helpless beast of prey like a she-wolf who sees that she is the weaker member of the pack. like a she-wolf subordinate in the pack. a she-wolf subordinate to the pack a she-wolf subordinated to the rules of the pack. a she-wolf subordinating itself with bared teeth with a smiling face. she the woman she bares her teeth contorted into a smile because she has to watch her gallerist and maybe friend. she observes her gallerist the woman watches her human being as he she doesnt believe what she sees the woman sees how with his hand she sees his hand his hand with thumb and middle finger she sees the woman sees how her gallerist maybe even a little bit friend rubs thumb and middle finger together he rubs thumb and middle finger together obscenely together he rubs thumb and middle finger together and speaks of jews. he rubs his fingers together and speaks of the forever money-grubbing jews. automatically animally the woman bares her teeth as she observes this hand of this friend this gallerist as he rubs his fingers together the woman bares her teeth and smiles at him automatically. of course she belonged here until this gesture belonged here to him to the others felt she belonged for years on end until this gesture this obscene gesture. how can one of her people make this gesture. how should she fight back against such gestures and words as these coming from one of her people. how can the woman how can the woman then the obscenity of this gesture even more obscene when people of her kind use it as a matter of course in connection with jews. if someone around her acts like her gallerist. the woman cant. then the woman cant. against pack behaviour she is helpless helplessly she observes this gesture and automatically bares her teeth smiles submissively at the leader of the pack thus subordinating herself showing her teeth the smile on her face the constrained smile that paralyses her in all her reactions that paralyses her smilingly immobile paralyses paralyses and rigidifies. the womans face rigidifies. with a rigid smile and a friendly farewell kiss-kiss she goes she the woman goes she goes she walks she goes with her swift steps out of the gallery through the town over the bridge through the town back home to her workshop and home only in her workshop at home does her rigid smile dissolve and do her bared teeth relax. with bared teeth and bristling hair she has trotted attentively through her town. at home in her workshop there back there here in her house in her building the woman becomes herself again. she herself she alone herself at last and she is utterly ashamed of herself. she is ashamed of herself she is ashamed of herself. she is ashamed of herself for not having defended her jews. she did not protect her jews not give any protection for her jews against this obscene gesture this obscene remark. she the woman didnt protect didnt offer any protection for herself. she is ashamed of herself she is ashamed of herself. in panic by baring her teeth to the leader of the pack the woman had preferred to flag up that she wanted to had to should belong to the pack whatever the cost. that she wants to belong whatever the cost makes her ashamed of herself. the woman is ashamed of herself before her jews and before herself she is ashamed of herself.

she is ashamed of herself and doesnt want to be ashamed of herself. her name should become battlename may her name be battlename: when people of her kind rub their fingers together, obscenely, and at the same time speak of the money-grubbing of the jews her name will be battlename. her body the womans body automatically reacts animally. the womans body is more intelligent than she herself. baring the teeth and bristling hair are a survival reaction in the moment of absolute helplessness. the womans body and art are more intelligent than she herself her work is more intelligent than she herself. no longer will she bare her teeth. no longer will she smile. may her name be battlename. she will defend her jews she the woman the artist will defend herself and her jews unconditionally. if through the baring of teeth and bristling hair her body reveals her subordinate position in the pack among her kind she will have to want to leave her kind. may her name be battlename.

the woman walks. the woman walks and treks and thinks and walks. she treks through the hills in the surroundings of her town she walks in her mountain shoes walks she treks she walks treks shouldering her rucksack thinking she walks through arlesheim, gempen, nuglar, sankt pantaleon, seeven, arboldswil, titterten, oberdorf, waldenburg, schönthal this springtime the woman walks treks walks thinking. the cherry trees shortly before breaking into blossom the fruit trees in glorious flower. she walks and thinks. thinking the woman the artist the woman herself walks alone walks and thinks as she walks thoughts think themselves inside her as she walks her thoughts wander. she thinks back over loops and loops she thinks of herself of her herself the woman thinks herself thinking. she sees herself in her workshop in the mountains walking trekking through the hills around her town trekking through the hills she thinks walking in her mountain shoes she thinks of her workshop in the mountains. contemplating the hills around her town she thinks of the mountainscape that surrounds her workshop in the mountains of her mountain workshop her mountain studio her mountain house in which she spends half of her lifetime. her mountain house her workshop.
she watches herself the woman on the phone sees herself in her mountain workshop on the phone sees herself on the phone as she treks through the hills around her town. she sees herself in the mountains in the alps on the

phone. she is phoning her gallery. she the woman the artist phones without any professional reason she phones just like that. she phones because she would like to talk a little with her friend her woman gallerist just like that without any reason. to know what shes up to whats going on in her town to chat a bit to gossip. later when trekking through the hills around her town the woman sees herself phoning in her mountain workshop. so she phones. her woman gallerist has no time she has customers. the woman the artist understands. she has always known even as a child that customers are crucial vital always even as a child from childhood she has known that customers bring money lifemoney the money to live to survive even as a child and now as an adult as an artist. for the woman it is really a matter of course really absolutely clear automatic that the woman the artist says some other time that is says over the phone some other time will ring back soon till later. for a long time much too long much too long for a long time much too long for decades on end much too long always the woman then phoned back herself she alone she herself always much too long always always. phoning an act that was too long far too long one-sided always always one-sidedly performed by her the woman. she the woman phones she the woman has to phone back if the others cant talk at the moment. while walking and trekking through the hills around her town the woman sees herself not only phoning from her mountain studio in her workshop surrounded by mountains. she sees herself in her mountain workshop thinking after these phone-calls. the woman sees herself in her mountain studio standing beside the phone and thinking of a situation an image earlier much earlier a film still that reminds her of her standing beside the phone. the woman the artist is in N.Y. in an apartment unsuited to her way of working but precisely but but N.Y. she is working in the knowledge that unsuited is suited to overdue shifts and changes in her work that unsuited breaks through shakes up routine and leads to new procedures. the woman the artist works and walks through the city walks goes through N.Y. which she doesnt actually like. walks and doesn’t actually like it much probably predominantly because the woman has difficulty finding her bearings in right-angled cities.

after weeks months she longs to talk to a female friend. she phones her woman gallerist back home. the woman gallerist says shes cooking at the moment and cant talk now. she hangs up. the woman stands beside the phone and is at first surprised that her friend picks up the phone and then cant talk. then the woman thinks she thinks then that the woman gallerist will of course phone back after cooking or later. yes actually then the woman the artist thinks if the female gallerist is a friend then she will phone back then the friend will surely want to know what the friend is up to how things are with her and so on. just as the woman wants to know about her friend decidedly actually lovingly actually after weeks and months. yet the woman gallerist doesnt phone. the woman despairs. she doesnt want to phone call up call like this any more. shes not begging for friendship although shes stunned. she the woman cant really grasp that probably possibly her female gallerist is no longer her friend. she the woman at the moment in N.Y. is incapable of grasping this loss of friendship. she is incapable of grasping, of comprehending, the possibility of thinking that possibly perhaps no friendship is possible here any more. it is absolutely impossible for her here in N.Y. just now to grasp to see something like that. when trekking through the hills around her town the woman knows as she sees this image of herself phoning from her apartment in N.Y. thinking of that walking trekking she the woman the artist knows this: that decades ago donkeys years ago there in N.Y. a truth took place that she was incapable of seeing there in her apartment in N.Y.

there in N.Y. the woman the artist writes a text. after this phone-call a text writes material written stunned material collects writes walking collects writing walks and writes in 3 notebooks. the notebooks are red, yellow, blue: red for feelings, yellow for hatred and poison, blue for procedure and method. later much later the yellow notebook becomes the foundation basis for the text POISON/YELLOW published in the womans the artists blue catalogue WHAT LOOKS AT ME. a truth which the woman the artist doesnt want to see even when publishing it although she knows that her work is more intelligent than herself. even the woman she herself is incapable of reading her work! even she the woman the artist is incapable of doing what she reproaches the others the beholders of her work for! even she the artist doesnt read her work! cannot! doesnt want to! doesnt want to cannot have to want to! so she continues to phone continues to keep in touch continues to drop by and for years on end much too long again and again and again and again allows herself to be fobbed off! allows people to say that she should please some other time and so on and so forth! she the woman the artist should understand that her friend the woman gallerist has so much to do so much her woman gallerist maybe friend has so much to do too much to do so much so much too much to do later even more to do too much to do lets talk later. gradually the woman notices gradually much too late the woman notices the artist notices much too late too late she sees herself standing by the phone in her mountain house and thinking and standing and saying to herself out loud: why is it always me who keeps in touch actually! why is it always me who asks! why is it always always me who phones! and the woman sends a fax a fax from her mountain workshop with these questions to her woman gallerist maybe still friend. with the fax the written character of the fax the binding character of the fax the woman tests the friendship value of this maybe still friendship. she stands the woman stands in her mountain workshop surrounded by mountains and lets her fax run through sends the fax. she the woman wants an answer without fail the woman wants an answer the woman wants an answer without fail categorically she wants an answer. it is a test of friendship she wants to end this one-sidedness. she she the woman has subjected herself much too long to this friendship routine smilingly with bared teeth smilingly subjected herself. trekking walking through the hills around her town the woman sees herself standing in her mountain studio and at last at last no longer wanting to play along. now at last the woman really no longer wants to now at last at last the woman no longer wants to not like that any longer not like that once again not like that at last really at last not any longer and sends her fax. the woman sends her fax from the mountain studio. she expects an answer without fail a reaction a sign of life a drawing a speaking an answer without fail. for the woman the artist it would be a token a token of friendship. she waits. waiting she the artist works waiting she walks she treks through her mountains she walks she treks. as she treks walks waits her anger grows. waiting too her angry thoughts her feelings of anger towards this supposed friendship. she the woman waits waits. the longer she waits the clearer it becomes to her as she works waits walks thinks feels: that this friendship with her female gallerist no longer stands. there is no friendship here anymore. now here at this point in time with no answer answerless with no reaction answer to this fax the longer the clearer no friendship anymore. perhaps it was never a friendship anyway in the way the woman believed it to be. a friendship for the woman essential for the woman for her herself alone even familially essential in essence family for the woman an essential friendship for the woman gallerist one among many perhaps in accordance with its nature perhaps possibly only one friendship among many or perhaps possibly even perhaps not a friendship a partnership friendshipless. a friendly business relationship a business partnership for decades not a friendship a confidential partnership maybe not a friendship conceivably possibly. with an effort the woman calms herself down a little the woman the artist lays aside her recognitions lays aside her rage her anger her sadness she works she lays aside her feelings she works her anger away lays aside works and forgets. doesnt really forget doesnt really calm down but slows down and looks after her feelings. the woman the artist works. she lives regularly and works she works in her town workshop and in her mountain studio. she the woman works and walks in the hills around her town walks and thinks walks and strides and treks and works in her mountains.

for the reopening of the season of the art season in her town she the woman the artist has an exhibition in her gallery. the looked-after feelings the postponed anger cascade out. she the woman has an uneasy feeling about it an ominous sense of foreboding at the idea of setting the exhibition up with her gallerists. she is sure and sure without reason perhaps sure with reason that she the artist can make a good exhibition in this case only by using a strategy of avoidance by employing a strategy of avoidance. to her way of thinking and feeling an intelligent exhibition can be achieved only through avoidance with a strategy of avoiding her gallerists probably no longer friends. an avoidance of contact during the setting-up avoidance of contacts of any kind an avoidance. in line with her idea the gallerists set up two rooms alone by themselves with material from their archive and the artist sets up the third room alone by herself with her latest works on a cluster principle. the exhibition is a success. the opening being the re-opening of the towns art season lasts an eternity. the woman the artist stands around stands and talks and stands around and stands around stands around cheerfully and happily in her room. the room is a success her strategy of avoidance was right the room is true. these are works that exactly in essence exactly match her existence moodwise exactly intellectually as a feeling feelingwise match her being. the room is true at this moment in time. the others stand around and contemplate and see and consider the room and recognize truth maybe possibly maybe possibly not. the woman the artist will never really really be able to know that her whole life through never.

after her opening the woman goes after this closing at last after several hours of standing around talking around she can go. she the woman the artist goes at last to the re-openings opening meal. opening meal of all her towns galleries. she goes and knows goes and knows that events like this goes and thinks and knows. she arrives and jostles her way through to the bar. the woman very thirsty drinks a beer at the bar thirsty from the long standing around a beer handed across friendlily to her the woman by a friendly acquaintance of hers friendlily. she drinks the woman drinks. then she goes to the event part to the outside event opening meal re-opening opening meal out into the mild september evening into this outside area event opening re-opening outside space with long tables under the viaduct in the mild september evening the woman sees the table she sees this long table with her gallerists and probably no longer friends and friends of the no longer friends. she the woman sees them all together at this long table she walks over to join them and sits down at the still free place at one end the woman joins them and sits down opposite her male gallerist. her gallerist is shovelling his food into himself. he is eating boorishly concentrating on eating. her gallerist is eating. everybody else at the table is eating everybody eating. everybody eating everybody else eating. the woman the artist asks her gallerist how it works here and how she the woman herself alone could get a plate a full plate of food she the woman actually she could now get her meal how she the woman now here sitting at this table now here could get something to eat here now like everybody else evidently eating she too wanted a meal needed a meal. her gallerist concentrates on his eating. he lifts his head a little and points to the queue where she the woman the artist could get hold of her meal. her gallerist continues to eat boorishly concentrating on his food. she the woman gets up and goes to the queue food queue to get hold of her meal army fashion. strategically she realizes standing in the queue that she wont be getting any food for an eternity. she will have to queue here for a very long time she the woman will have to queue here for an eternity she the artist today successfully opened her exhibition will have to queue here for an eternity an eternity to get her meal today. in front of her an acquaintance is standing who says – didnt your gallerist look after you – the woman immediately breaks out in tears and immediately she dries her tears immediately and stomps walks strides flamingly angry to her table immediately to the table of the gallerists and their friends. they are eating they are drinking. the woman sits down and lashes into her gallerist. he shrugs the gallerist shrugs his shoulders goes on eating boorishly. mumbles boorishly and mumbles a few excuses. the woman the artist observes the long table: her gallerists, the woman architect, the star male architect and their friends are eating. the entire long table is occupied by eating and drinking creatures. these people are eating and drinking. they have organized their eating and drinking in an efficient manner. they these people have organized themselves and know how its done know how to act know so that they can all eat and drink together. the table this table. the table and the people who are eating and drinking together here. the reason for their eating and drinking together believes the woman the artist thinks the woman is the opening of the womans the artists exhibition. the reason for the eating and drinking together she the woman thinks is her opening. she considers these people she contemplates these persons who, as she, the woman, thinks are here, present, eating, drinking, because of her opening, her celebration, the opening celebration of her work. she the woman the artist has opened her exhibition today. she considers the table she contemplates the entire outside space under the viaduct of her town in the mild september evening lovely. she considers her table which is not her table never was her table possibly or is no longer her table since she the woman the artist has realized this: that these people have forgotten her that these no longer friends in their efficiency have not thought for one moment of organizing the meal for her the woman the artist organizing for her too efficiently. she sits at the end of the table contemplates these people. she contemplates them she gets up and is about to go. by chance and at this moment her brother comes and sees the situation. he sees and understands. he sees and understands and acts. he organizes his sister her meal. he sees. he sees her the sister his sister exhausted sad angry still standing at the end of her exhibition opening table and having to be about to go. he the brother sees his sister taking her rucksack and being about to go unfed and unnourished at her own opening. the brother he sees and grasps this total lack of style and acts. immediately. acts. she the woman the sister is at this precise moment infinitely grateful to her brother. she loves him for this moment of seeing and acting. in this situation she is infinitely glad about him her brother glad about a man who acts about her brother. this brother whom she rarely sees and whose life she doesnt understand. better a brother who acts than this utterly uncouth silence eating drinking. better a brother acting with savoir faire a brother with whom the woman the artist the sister often quarrels than this utterly uncouth boorish mumbling nothing. this utterly uncouth group this herd of utterly uncouth people. better a difficult savvy brother whom she the woman the sister rarely sees than these no longer friends who declare themselves savvy cultured act the intellectuals consider themselves to be easy to get on with and stylish and grade degrade the woman the artist as difficult. better this brother with his innate style who immediately grasps uncouth situations and acts. better to quarrel than uncouthly shrug ones shoulders and eat and drink avoiding conflict concentratedly boorish provincial sluggish. the woman eats. she eats alone since all the others at the table have already eaten. having eaten his fill the gallerist attempts reconciliatory gestures with good wine with which he plies the woman the artist. the woman calms herself down. the eating and drinking play their part the woman calms herself down and calms down. she the woman the artist will not forget this scene. the woman calms herself down by not forgetting and by storing up. she calms herself down by storing the image of this event this evening this image the table and its people. the woman calms herself down. that will be her strategy. these images of situations concerning her the woman affecting her inflicting wounds on her the woman hurting wounding the woman. deposit these images and store them away and later employ and make use of them. later. she calms herself down. she is wounded and calms herself down the woman the artist deposits her material. she deposits her latest layer on the other already deposited layers. the woman calms down and deposits her material.

the woman stands at the counter in the gallery and makes an appointment with her woman gallerist makes a meal appointment an appointment when they intend to go out for a meal together before the woman the artist departs. they make an appointment. they look at the gallery diary together. they make the appointment. on the day of the appointment they will phone again to arrange where they want to eat out she the woman and her gallerists. she the woman and her gallerists perhaps friends make an appointment for an evening meal to go out for a meal in the evening. when on the afternoon of the appointed day the woman the artist has still heard nothing from her gallerists she phones up. her male gallerist knows nothing about an agreement to have a meal he has not heard of any appointment there is nothing he says in the diary. already somewhat angry the woman insists on the evening meal appointment he the gallerist she says should cancel what he intended to do that evening. the gallerist makes his wife the woman gallerist responsible for this error and refuses to change his plans. already very angry the woman lashes into him. they argue. she lashes into him she grows more and more angry. she the woman is in panic and angry she is in panic and now no longer bares her teeth now at this moment really no longer smiles submissively and as they say understandingly really no longer contorts her face in this rigidified even understanding smile now really no longer shows her teeth as a gesture of submission. rather she the woman the artist is angry the woman is so angry the woman is in such a rage the woman is in such a rage. she the woman the artist is existentially angry as a human being and in a rage and in panic and angry. the male gallerist does not apologize, and says that such things, well, you know, happen. through the phone the woman sees his shrug of the shoulders his shrug of the shoulders towards her. she sees this shrug of the shoulders this lifting of his shoulders. after this phone call she the woman stands beside her phone and thinks. she thinks enraged angrily but no longer in a panic but angrily she thinks even no longer in a panic at all but coolly. the woman thinks in a cool fury. the woman thinks furiously in a cool cold rage. life-rage. her life-rage her driving force the cool furious cold enraged thinking: she thinks. the woman the artist thinks and knows that enough is enough now simply enough is enough things have simply gone far enough. she the woman no longer wants to have anything to do with such people. she thinks in her cold rage that she the woman the artist has smiled far too long and has bared her teeth submissively even understandingly far far too long. far too long for too long a time she has adapted herself to this group this herd far too long she has wanted à tout prix to belong to be one of them come what may come what will. far far far too long thinks the woman the artist in her cold fury. now she will not let her anger her rage her thoughts sink down into her geology and archaeology not in this case. today she the woman will not deposit her thoughts and feelings in her layers of materials. she the woman the artist will at last act she the woman think and act in cold fury in cool anger and put an end to these situations at last. put an end to them at last. she the woman will at any event à tout prix and with all means at her disposal now put an end to these actions situations moments scenes that humiliate her the woman the artist. the woman writes a fax:

in recent times you have "just happened" to forget me a few times too often. this shows me that i mean nothing at all to you as a human being. you are not aware of your brutality: you are not even sorry. to hell with you.

as she sends the fax that same day the woman knows that her cold anger is condensed unrefracted in such a text the woman the artist knows that her cold fury is condensing into such a text. it is condensed anger compressed fury that drives her in this text that drives this text. condensed condensation of several years. condensed fury and year-long anger. the woman considers and sees her text her sentences as an exact description. exact describing writing condensed writing of the situation now at this moment now just as she writes the fax now now just writing an exact precise formulation now here at this very moment she the woman the artist is writing exactly and precisely and truly: a condensed describing of how she the woman sees her people acting now towards her acting indifferently and brutally without noticing it. after the woman gallerist sends back an outraged fax full of rebuttal rebuts the idea that they the two people gallerists friends are brutal people they are she says not brutal people she the woman the artist is she says totally off-beam to dismiss them the two gallerists as brutal people rejects the idea that they are brutal people denies naturally that they are brutal people the woman thinks in cold anger that it is at any event pointless to write such texts. in cold anger the woman the artist thinks that it is obviously hopeless to write precisely and condensedly if the addressees only skim the text en passant and then misunderstand it. such texts are read wrong. its pointless. they are read wrong. even by her gallerists even after 30 years her texts are read wrong or not read at all or read too fast but at any event read wrong and misunderstood thinks the woman coldly reading the outraged reply from her female gallerist standing beside her fax. she the woman the artist wants however thinks however she really at any event ought to talk ought to want to talk face to face with her two people before she leaves at any event nevertheless talk over as much as possible clear up clarify talk as much person to person face to face she the woman the artist alone herself talk with the female gallerist and male gallerist the maybe still probably no longer friends she the woman wants to sit down with this couple at a table and have to talk want to talk once more the woman will talk wants to talk speak talk with the two people her two people.

they meet in the restaurant in the restaurant where they have all been going for a hundred thousand years again and again and know everybody and so on the woman reluctantly even puts up with this place puts up with the compromise puts up in order to talk with her two people she alone herself she the woman the artist. she is punctual. in the dining area on the first floor she leaves her things and goes to the cloakroom. as she comes out again in the corridor in the stairwell near the stairs down in the corridor she hears her male gallerist saying to the bistro-owner old friend for donkeys years of course bistro-owner that he, the gallerist, he, won't, today, be staying, here, till the cows come home, and will, he hopes, soon, be able to go again, be able to go home. the female gallerist stands beside him and nods. a coincidence coincidence terrible coincidence that the woman the artist hears this hears this sentence sees and hears these three people all together in agreement standing together all together. she the woman stands upstairs beside the stairwell looks down at the three people and hears. she stands in the doorway and shrinks backwards mindlessly in panic she hides she didnt want to see to hear that now she doesnt want now to see her two people coming up the stairs she didnt want to overhear that now she the woman doesnt want to greet her people hardly friends any more after this overhearing on the stairs. she moves backwards. she goes back into the cloakroom. she waits. she tries straightaway to forget she would like to forget straightaway what she has seen and heard. the woman tries to forget. waiting she must forget straightaway at all costs now straightaway forget. she stays in the cloakroom until she assumes that her gallerists have got to their table and sat down. she tries straightaway to forget what she has just heard she the woman must forget straightaway what she has just heard she must forget straightaway coldly forget and make use of her cool head her cool thinking and use them usefully. she the woman in her cold anger must be able to think and speak coolly should be must be able to. because otherwise she the woman again automatically again again bares her teeth bares her teeth in an incessant subservient smile. she the woman the artist must must have to remain coolly angry. she leaves the washroom and goes to their table. the two people the couple are sitting as always at this table at their as always table as for always at this round table as always. the woman the artist greets them briefly and sits down without any kiss-kiss. her anger her strategy prevent physical contact. she sits. of course they have first to place orders. they order. of course the wine is discussed and ordered by the male gallerist and naturally as a matter of course tasted by the female gallerist as always and found to be in order. at last at last finally everything is ordered and the three of them are sitting over their food and drinking. at last really at last the woman talks the woman the artist tries to talk the woman talks and talks her flow of talk she talks unstoppably and she talks and her talking in cold fury and the cool thinking and talking flows on thither whither thither where it will of its own accord the talking talks sentences and connected words of its own logic the inner logic the archaeologic of the woman the layers of her inner archaeology intermingle and talk. earlier now later. she sits opposite this couple she the woman talks and sits opposite this couple. the woman tries to speak at one and the same time to the two people her two people who as individual people used to be friendpeople at least the woman thinks so and is certain that she the woman in the course of her life in different ways was on friendly terms with each individual person in this human couple used to be on different friendly terms with the individual person among these two. also the woman knows the woman believes she she at least she herself used to be on friendly terms with the couple. now she is sitting opposite the couple and thinking and talking talking. she is talking to the couple she is talking the woman the artist is talking to the individual people in the couple with her two people. she is talking towards them. she is feeling the woman is feeling her way towards her people while talking and while feeling her way while talking she notes in cool fury: this talking is no use talking is no use. nothing will get better these her two people no longer want to be felt towards in talking they are no longer the womans two people her two people. the man the gallerist justifies himself while eating he speaks in self-justification he speaks only in self-justification he doesnt make mistakes he. in self-justification he speaks to the woman the artist towards the woman in self-justification. the womans mind goes full storm at this self-justifying talk at this gush of self-justification storm in her mind brain. she interrupts him she blocks off this gush of self-justification by talking she interrupts she talks knowing knowing also through the mans the gallerists remark in the corridor which she the woman overheard although she the woman did not want to hear this sentence by coincidence terribly she the woman overheard knows that this man is now at this time not interested in her speaking in her way. the man the gallerist prefers to eat boorishly concentrating on his food. he eats and justifies himself while eating. thats that the woman thinks thats that she the woman thinks thinks thats that thats that. the woman pokes around at her food she cant eat now she talks talks interrupts the gush of self-justification from her eating gallerist. she talks and interrupts and talks talks until the female gallerist interrupts the talking woman the artist. the woman the female gallerist interrupts. like all couples like all women from couples couplewomen she first of all defends her territory her husband. she the female gallerist the woman speaks a psychologizing language she speaks psychologizingly and quietly persuasively to the woman the artist. she the female gallerist the woman uses a so-called soft female language a soft language water-language a very efficient weapon a weapon that reveals itself to the woman the artist as a weapon through the eyes lowered for attack and through the down-turned corners of the female gallerists mouth. the woman the female gallerist describes the woman the artist as difficult the woman the artist she says is difficult the woman the artist is a difficult person the woman is difficult hard to deal with and she the female gallerist the woman therefore describes dealings with the woman as difficult because the woman the artist she says is difficult the woman is difficult. the woman the artist however in her cold anger now wants to be difficult in her cold anger she really truly really prefers difficult really prefers truly difficult the artist she. the woman thinks that the woman the female gallerist in this roundtable constellation in this table setting and situation would never talk to a male artist to a man in this manner like this in this manner and style would never ever use this psychologizing so-called soft female language towards a man would never ever in front of her own coupleman spouse husband describe a male artist a man in this manner as difficult. looking at her female gallerist the woman the artist in her cold anger thinks that this woman her female gallerist would never ever use this pseudo-language if she the woman the artist were a man. in cool cold fury she the woman the artist immediately now from now on immediately thinks as a man. she the woman rebuffs this so-called female language this understanding-pretending female weapon immediately now rebuffs immediately. the woman the artist rebuffs this language she woman as man the woman despises this pseudo-language this i-for-my-part and you-for-your-part-talk language rebuffs immediately immediately now really immediately. the woman the artist ironically coldly points out that when she speaks nobody else but her is speaking. she the woman is always speaking she alone herself when she speaks. she points out now in fury she makes clear that she the woman will now not begin every sentence with i-for-my-part in order to make clear that it is she speaking. she the woman the artist will not descend to not accept this cheap psychological level never ever. the woman the artist will never again talk in this femalely soft so-called female language in this manner she will not have done it for some time now for a good while she remarks ironically furiously to her woman gallerist. she the woman the artist has long since changed her language with a gain in clarity gain in happiness for some time now for a long time. thats that thinks the woman thats that thats that thats that she thinks the woman the artist sitting at table with the human couple and talking. talking speaking the woman the woman sees this couple remain seated this couples routine their remaining seated the routine of wanting to be quickly over and done with this situation unpleasant for the two of them consuming their time unpleasant situation the woman the artist sees the routine the language of routine dealing with the woman and artist from the point of view of the gallerist couple difficult and hard to handle. for this seasoned gallerist couple the woman is a care case. the woman the artist sees herself becoming in the eyes of her gallerists a case now at this very moment immediately now here. becoming a difficult person a difficult care case. a case. she the woman sees herself becoming a case. thats that thinks the woman the artist thinks thats that thats that. she the woman gives up her cold thinking in anger and grieves. the woman gives up she gives up thats that. she will not fight because theres nothing left to fight for. thats that thats that thats that the woman thinks. she wont fight shes not fighting any more. she doesnt fight she grieves she cries she doesnt talk she doesnt fight she cries she the woman cries. she didnt want to cry. she doesnt want to fight any more she the woman cries water floods into her eyes from below she cries. water floods from below into her throat into her eyes through the tube of her throat into her eyes and out of her eyes. crying and thinking the woman the artist explains to her gallerists why she is crying. she talks and she cries. crying she talks she talks talks crying. crying she declares this nolongerfriendship to be over and puts a conscious end to it by talking crying talking. it is the end of this friendship which possibly never was one at any event has been over for some time the woman the artist cries the woman talks. the crying stops dries up and her angry thinking and cold feeling. she the woman thinks talks talks about it about her capital life mistake towards her two people. she the woman the artist was much too long on friendly terms as an attitude of life just like that without any return value much too long blind really truly blind. much too long she the woman has kept up this her own the womans the artists illusory world of friendship as a substitute for loving a substitute for family. blind much too long blind really much too long. hers the womans herself alone her life mistake. she alone herself only she the woman the artist the woman has made this life mistake she alone herself she the woman the artist. while she the woman says this she feels truly. it is true really really true. she is speaking right and truly. she the woman feels her speaking to be true. she is speaking right. she is true.

thats that thinks the woman. she gets up and goes home. thats that.

2007

From: Miriam Cahn
Sent: Sunday, 13 January 2008
To: Philipp Kaiser
Subject: mountainsides

dear Philipp,

actually, I really wanted to go to the Avner Ben-Gal[134] opening and of course to see you again. but in the meantime, I had so much to cope with: moving my entire storeroom from the STAMPA Gallery to my place (I now have my entire oeuvre here and it is a huge amount). and then also, my mother has died. afterwards I was so utterly exhausted that I've retreated back here to my Palü, where I see nothing but the mountainsides surrounding me – and the wonderful snow, of course.

so, I wish you a super exhibition and a fine opening night!

warm greetings, miriam

---

5 February 2008

Dear Miriam,

At last – and please excuse my not having got in contact before. Back from Switzerland, I found heaps of e-mails waiting and it was simply too much.

I am very sorry that your mother has died and that then everything happened at the same time. Shortly before flying to Basle I at last had a chance to read your text.[135] Perhaps I now also understand that you presumably had no desire to come to the opening night in Basle. It's a really fine text – the stuttering in face of the inconceivable, that things can change overnight. Silently, almost imperceptibly. The text is also unsparing, however, perhaps especially for me, since I was able to remember certain scenes. The meal in the Aqua, the Schaulager opening,[136] which I also attended – only witnessing the evening from a totally different narrative perspective. Nevertheless, I can understand you and think that is a good new beginning, a good new invention.

Is there any news concerning galleries? Let me know if I can help in any way, even from faraway California.

Hope you'll have an opportunity to see Avner Ben-Gal's exhibition and of course hope to see you again here. I have pretty good contacts with Lilian Lerch/Tanner[137] and we would, of course, all be pleased if you were to come round here.

Warm greetings, Philipp

Philipp Kaiser

Curator

MOCA THE MUSEUM OF CONTEMPORARY ART

From: Miriam Cahn
Sent: Thursday, 17 April 2008
To: Philipp Kaiser
Subject: news

dear Philipp,

I hope everything is fine with you in L.A.!

news from me: thanks to your intermediary role, Meyer Riegger[138] have paid me a visit – they are absolutely great and I will work with them from now on. likewise: Jocelyn Wolff, Paris. I was there yesterday to take a look – a small gallery in the heart of Belleville

and very good as a whole – I'm now joining them too. Schmela[139] I have discarded, because I think that actually one gallery per nation is sufficient. so, real and repeated thanks to you from all my heart! on other fronts, I'm in the final stages in Schönthal[140] and am looking forward to setting everything up, even if this church space is somehow not well designed and kitschy. I'll cover over as much as possible, partly using large old drawings. and here too a few pictures from my sculpture garage with part of my future work.
warmest greetings, miriam

22 April 2008

Dear Miriam,
Good to hear from you! And, of course, I'm delighted that things worked out with Meyer Riegger. I've known the two of them, especially Jochen, for a very long time and consider the gallery to be a very good one. Above all, of course, they are present at all the key art fairs and as gallerists they are also capable of talking about their artists. Wolff I also rate very highly, above all the fact that they have many video artists on their books, among others Clemens von Wedemeyer.[141] So, my hearty congratulations! What is fantastic above all is that this is a younger gallerist generation that is taking an interest in your work. In the medium and long term this will pay off on the institutional front, no question about it.
Hope to be able to see the Schoental exhibition, although I won't be in Basle again until the Art. Over here, things are fine with us. Pauline is growing and growing and I always have plenty to do. Last week was in Chris Burden's[142] studio in a wonderful canyon near the Pacific and have otherwise come to know many exciting artists. L.A. is a real blessing for mind and soul.
Hoping to see you soon, warm greetings, Philipp
Philipp Kaiser
Curator
MOCA THE MUSEUM OF CONTEMPORARY ART

From: Miriam Cahn
Sent: Monday, 13 April 2009
To: Philipp Kaiser
Subject: news

dear Philipp,
how are you? I know I haven't been in touch for a long time, but I've been very much on the move – first, a one-month's stay in Paris in a wonderful, huge studio in Belleville, and then setting up an exhibition and the opening night at Jocelyn Wolff's. it turned out very well and was really excellent, the opening too super and good. Many people of all types, young, middle-aged, old, and Catherine David[143] came and thought it was great …
then back for a bit into an absolutely snowed-under Bregaglia, from which I almost couldn't get back to Basle for all the snow: Maloja blocked, Sils + Julier too, had to go via Italy. in the pouring rain one could see absolutely nothing of Stendhal's beautiful landscape, just grey, then the Gotthard Tunnel to BS, and in the TV news a report that, shortly after I passed through, there had been a rockfall onto the Gotthard motorway! OOPS!
then I went to Berlin, lived there too in the same flat as two years

ago in Friedrichshain, setting up and opening with Jochen + Thomas, and there too it turned out really well: they have such wonderful exhibition spaces (do you know them?). in the rear room, all of my super-8 films and in the front a load of very large oil paintings and 1 nuclear bomb (this looks good!), 1 landscape, 1 W.E.C. tree,[144] 2 "old" series with women, children + animals + 1 soldier drawn in Berlin.
2 weeks later Meyer-Riegger again in Karlsruhe: there too, things turned out super, 3 completely different spaces ...
+ after all that I was jaded + run-down, worn out + tired and just keen on withdrawing to the Giessliweg + working. I'm sending you ex. of probable + space with the latest stuff – but precisely: can't judge it at all yet, perhaps it'll all be painted over later ...
yesterday, I was in an abysmally awful exhibition in the Schaulager.[145] the wonderful works from the Kunstmuseum simply don't fit these non-spaces with their unchanging lighting, and the exhibition is completely lacking in imagination. at times even irritating. on the other hand, I recently saw an absolute hit: Tracey Emin's[146] exhibition in Bern: super! such a good artist! top rate! (although you might think it's all over and done with: there just aren't so many good women artists at this level). afterwards, I went into a shop and the agreeable young sales assistant asked, 'äs mü mehr?' ['a wee little bit more?'] – so that I immediately had to think of you and send you this mail.
so, all the best to you and Liliane too
warm regards, miriam

16 April 2008

Dear Miriam,
Good to hear from you! A few days ago, I had a look at the Meyer Riegger website and was impressed! All of this looks like a good deal of work – Karlsruhe AND Berlin. Hope the exhibitions were a great success. Above all, I like these new, abstract works. Their colourfulness is very striking.
Here everything is going pretty well. A short time ago, I was on a long trip, three weeks, to New York, Boston and then Tel Aviv, where I set up an exhibition with Avner Ben-Gal in the Tel Aviv Art Museum. It was pretty exciting over there. Have you ever been to Tel Aviv? Lilian also came along, while her parents (who cannot drive) looked after Pauline here in L.A. Avner had won a renowned Israeli art award including exhibition and catalogue. That was the reason why he was able to invite me to be the curator. Tel Aviv is a fantastic city with almost exclusively young people, a lot of Bauhaus architecture and good food. Yet Israel – we were in Jerusalem for only one day – was somewhat scary. Too intense, too much history, too many conflicts.
And now I'll be flying off tomorrow to Austin, Texas, to Alexander Birchler and Teresa Hubbard,[147] and will also be delivering a lecture at the Uni there. Am greatly looking forward to it. Austin is a rather good city, the only democratic place in Texas ... and has a good music scene. At present I'm working on a large Land Art exhibition and a Jack Goldstein[148] retrospective and still give courses at the University of California for artists

and Art History. So there's quite a lot going on ... and soon we'll be flying to Venice for the Biennale opening and also to the Art Basle. I shall only be in Basle for a short time, but it would be very nice if we were able to meet for a beer/coffee/lunch or whatever.
Hope all is ok in Basle and van Gogh[149] hasn't become too rampant.
Will you be there during the Art?
Warm greetings,
Philipp
Philipp Kaiser

one must look to the future – quote stampa
every problem becomes insoluble if you look at it too long – quote pauli
no reaction is also a reaction – quote cahn. 2007

dear gilli + stampa,
this summer I have worked in the grounds of kloster schönthal, have sent you photo material by way of information and informed stampa at your last opening that I would be in basle for another fortnight to exhibit 'brutalitätenskulptur'. apart from stampa's inane remark ("so you've turned up again") no reaction, nothing. I sent you the relevant ROMANSKULPTUR text: nothing.
no, I'll no longer hang around at the STAMPA counter, or phone up myself, or in any other way again and again request that my gallerists look at my works or read my texts and comment on them. my reasons are there to be read in the text ROMANSKULPTUR. the fact that the two of you write me off as "difficult" is your business: the resultant cosy inaction and lack of all interest on your part, however, is mine.
and: for too long STAMPA has been using my still international potential far too little.
I will therefore be making changes to my co-operation with you. I have established contact with Hauser + Wirth, the only gallery in switzerland which I would consider. if that does not work out, then I will look farther afield outside switzerland.
at any event:
1. I will withdraw a large part of my works and also my file index.
2. no more co-operative agreements (schmela, wolff) – they make no sense for me.
3. 2007: settling of accounts with all outstanding items within the current calendar year.
4. works sold from my studio will no longer be charged off via STAMPA.
in the case of exhibitions in Switzerland I leave this open for the time being.
soon – not just sometime in the future – we must meet and discuss how we want/ought/are able to work together from now on.
greetings, miriam

From: Miriam Cahn
To: Jocelyn Wolff
Subject: antiminaret-suisse-shame **le 8 décembre 2009**

chers Sandrine, Jocelyn et autres,
après que 57% du peuple suisse[150] ne veut pas de minarets dans leurs villages paisibles sans aucun musulman (les villes comme Bâle, Genève, Zurich étaient contre cette initiative hideuse) j'étais vraiment politiquement écoeurée! quelle gifle pour les 400 000 musulmans suisses, dont, d'ailleurs, la plupart est aussi peu religieuse comme la plupart des chrétiens et juifs en Suisse… quelle islamophobie! quel racisme aussi, quelle peur! et ce qui est vraiment frustrant, ce sont les acclamations des lepénistes, des leganordistes etc.… bon, passons.
j'ai fait ce dessin aujourd'hui, qui s'appelle: SARAJEVO 15 ans plus tard. le gros des musulmans suisses vient des Balkans: d'une part la génération de travailleurs de l'ancienne Yougoslavie et d'autre part des réfugié(e)s de la guerre des années 90 et je crois que la position des années 90 envers cette guerre, une position dite neutre, mais en vérité peureuse et de façon: «les Balkans étaient toujours des agressifs», verdrängend (je ne connais pas ce mot freudien en français [= refoulant]) qu'il s'agissait d'un génocide a beaucoup à faire avec les résultats de ce vote.
les derniers 10 jours j'ai beaucoup pensé naturellement plus que d'habitude à cause de ce vote à mon travail de cette époque qui s'appelle dans son ensemble SARAJEVO. je me réjouis beaucoup de notre plan de faire un show avec quelques travaux SARAJEVO! la prochaine fois que je serai à Bâle, j'essayerai de chercher TOUT ce que j'ai fait pendant cette guerre…
je vous embrasse miriam
(pour une raison que je ne comprends pas je ne puis pas envoyer l'image – alors plus tard!)

From: Miriam Cahn
To: Eva-Maria Schön
Subject: Bregaglia beautiful **8 august 2009**

dear Eva-Maria,[151]
now I've been in Bregaglia for some ten days – as always wonderful despite the tourist traffic … but my poor car gave up the ghost on the drive here – red lamp flashing, and by the time I had decided to drive to the side the engine was ruined. it was an ages-old water pipe that had burst. now: touring towing service, very nice garage owner from Zillis, his garage right next-door to the magnificently beautiful small church with the famous cassette roof from the deepest middle ages, a kind of comic strip of christ's life that spreads across the entire ceiling. car therefore a complete write-off, got a rental car + drove on. next week I have to go quickly to basle anyway because of St Moritz transport and tai-chi course, + my nice basle garage-owner probably has a younger model of the same renault espace. PHEW!
then, very slowly and gradually, I have come to see that I want to shift the centre of gravity of my life into Bregaglia, no longer this system of half here, half there, which for a good long time was super for working. I see such things immediately in my work. recently, the most gripping things in basle were my wood workshop + nature in Eptingen, while the giessliweg is simply "too full" somehow, too much my capital, my history everywhere just too much.
which is a good thing in itself, very good even, but for working – now that I have re-painted all the works that are to be re-painted – suddenly a hindrance. it really is a little like the library in Canetti's Blendung, which at the end of the book slays the protagonist.
so I had a meeting with my young landlords in Bregaglia. they think it's great that I want to spend an increasing amount of time here, and since the place in Palü has only one room and I would need some more space, they are going to build a small extension – traditional inasmuch as it is simply a prolongation of the roof at the rear towards the road + and underneath an insulated 3 × 6m room. so super! in the course of the year they'll put in the plan for building permission, and if things work out, building will probably start in the middle of next year.
I've often been thinking of you + your garden, especially because the first thing I had to do was to weed for a whole day – incredible how much grows in two months! I'm looking forward to pottering around on my patch of grass too when I spend my time predominantly here. perhaps it will also be possible to keep cats … but there's no hurry at all about all of this. it is, however, an existential decision against my living in a city.
I won't be giving up the giessliweg: I've still got this huge store of works on paper heaped up there, which I can then sort out more effectively and which is certainly better stored in the city than in the country, even if only because of the mice. but I will be transferring a large part of the oil paintings + new drawings – which are, after all, small-scale – to here. the main office, the filing system etc. and, if it's possible, I'll change canton – here in the valley they'd be keen on that, since I'm a good earner, and tax-wise it would be a great advantage for me – Basle is terribly high-tax (municipal demi-canton with a uni etc.), whereas here they have rurally low taxes. But that's not necessarily the reason: rather that I

always think that where I mainly live I should also be registered – that's how it was in Berlin, with all bits and bobs.
and if I get the mountain+valley heebie-jeebies, then I can always go off to Basle, or even better to Berlin and Milan etc. at least then I don't have the feeling that I have to work with the full programme (oils etc.), but can then do either "nowt" or this interesting, routine-interrupting "literary" form of sitting at some table or other – in hotels or other people's apartments.
there's not so very much for me in Basle anymore: no parents any longer, practically no friends either since my separation from STAMPA, I don't go either to the cinema or to the theatre. I think that after all these false steps (buying a house here that's too small, renting a studio in Berlin for large paintings etc.) this is now the right thing to do: I want to work and live primarily in Nature – that's what has turned out from my work, which, after all, determines my life.
so, that's how it is.
and you? has the wedding taken place actually?
kiss + greetings + kiss too for Hannes,
miriam

From: Miriam Cahn
To: Jochen Meyer
Subject: hands up! **14 december 2009**
dear Thomas + Jochen,
how did things go for you in Miami?
here in Bregaglia it is abominably cold and fantastically beautiful …+ here is another picture painted under the shameful impact of our disgraceful minaret vote!
warmest greetings,
miriam
attached picture: hände hoch! ["hands up!"]

From: Jochen Meyer
To: Miriam Cahn
Subject: hands up! **16 December 2009**
Dear Miriam,
What a fantastic picture! Many thanks for sending it: it's really super.
We've been back from Miami since last week and I am glad that this year is slowly coming to an end … For us the fair was mixed – neither particularly good nor particularly bad. But as far as I can see we covered our costs. We had your wonderful "Tiermensch" ["Animal human"] on display, but despite a great deal of interest couldn't unfortunately find a buyer for it, although on several occasions we thought that a sale was on. That's a pity, but not so bad and I hope you're not too disappointed. It was nevertheless super for us to have your work on our stand.
All in all, one gets the feeling that the market is slowly recovering again, but we are still far from being back at the level of two years ago – and who knows whether we will ever get back there again. On the other hand, everything is now a bit more normal and people are again reflecting more before they spend their money …
Today we have begun to prepare our application for Art Unlimited – the deadline is admittedly only next month, but we want to send it off before Christmas, then we've got it off our minds.
What are you doing over the coming days and weeks? Are you staying in Bregaglia? Up to Christmas we're in Karlsruhe and then in Basle. On 2 January we then go for a week's holiday in Lenk. As an experienced alpinist you no doubt know the area – for me it's the first trip there and another new discovery.
If you're in Basle again in the Old Year, get in touch with me and we can arrange something. Otherwise I wish you all the best for the Festive Season and hope to be in contact soon.
Warm Regards,
Jochen

From: Miriam Cahn
To: Jochen Meyer
Subject: hands up! **17 december 2009**
dear Jochen,
the art hysteria is bound to repeat itself some time or other in a

different form – seems to do so again and again + and as far as I'm concerned doesn't have to be like that at all. What interests me most now is this Art Unlimited thing: very exciting! please get in touch as soon as you get to know something.
and otherwise I'll be staying in Bregaglia; at present it is abominably, freezingly cold. I don't know the Lenk region, only the advertising jingle "länkch – dänkch" with a strong 'ch' at the end, but it is a comprehensive skiing area and of course super in the current snow.
so, all the best + and a fine festive season to one and all!
Miriam
(+ snow pictures for practice)

Federal Office of Culture, Dept. of Art
andreas münch[152] + art commision basle, 19 october 2005
dear andreas münch, dear federal art commission,
following our telephone conversation, I am sending you here a good example of a form of ceremonial act suitable for an awards presentation.
(thuner kulturpreis 2005). The very title: "THUN PREIST DIE KUNST" ["THUN PRIZES ART"] is an excellent one.
what the federal office of culture, section art and design, dept of art has in mind is not an awards presentation[153] but an information session. I see us award-winners sitting there in a row, waiting as at school for our names to be called by the teacher so that we can be asked questions. as a prize-winner I am to be questioned in public like a schoolgirl on the theoretical foundations of my work.
quite apart from the fact that there is no such absurdity as a 'theoretical foundation' to my work, I reject this form of award presentation. if there is to be a state prize awarded in the name of the magnificent artist meret oppenheim, then I request an appropriate form of award presentation in which I can express my gratitude for it. after all, I have won this splendid award not for any non-existent theoretical background but for my work.
for the same reasons, I will neither find the person who should question me for the publication, nor let myself be interviewed. as a counter-proposal I send you my catalogue ARCHITEKTURTRAUM [ARCHITECTURAL DREAM].[154] plunder it as you will, or have it plundered and elucidated by a person of your choice. you are entirely free to choose and I will under no circumstances interfere.
warm regards, your miriam cahn

From: Andreas Muench
To: Miriam Cahn
Subject: Meret Oppenheim Prize
14 November 2005

Dear Ms Cahn,
Many thanks for your letter and for the catalogue. Of course, I think it a pity that you cannot find anything positive in our proposal. It is true, I grant you, that our publication and our public event have a somewhat different objective than that of the Thuner Kulturpreis. But even within the framework we have in mind, a wide range of options would have been available. At any rate, however, there is, of course, no point in troubling you with a project to which you have an innate aversion. I will gladly come back to your suggestion of taking a text from your catalogue should the occasion arise. I would, of course, show you the chosen extract, so that you are fully in the picture and can express your opinion on the matter.
With all good wishes for your work and
with kind regards,
Andreas Münch

From: Miriam Cahn
To: Andreas Muench
Subject: Oppenheim Award Ceremony 11 february 2006
dear andreas münch,
since I've got quite a lot on my plate over the coming months – which is a good thing, after all – I would very much like to know

when the presentation ceremony for the meret oppenheim awards is to take place.
warm regards your miriam cahn

From: Andreas Muench
To: Miriam Cahn
Subject: Meret Oppenheim Prize 11 February 2006

Dear Ms Cahn,
As I have already set out, it is less an award ceremony than a public event. There will be a few words of greeting; thereafter Philip Ursprung will conduct in turn conversations with Gianni Motti, Fickert & Knapkiewicz, Vaclav Pozarek and Michel Ritter concerning their work. Finally, there will be drinks and refreshments.
All this takes place on 2 March from 18 hrs on in the Kunsthalle Bern. Of course, you are warmly invited, even if you do not take part.
With kind regards,
Andreas Münch

From: Miriam Cahn
To: Jochen Meyer
Subject: list for ART 2009 **4 april 2009**

dear Jochen + Thomas,
here is the list of works – it was good to meet you! so was the meal together in the venerable Kunsthalle…but one remark Thomas made has stuck in my mind, namely that chalk drawings would sell better if they were framed.
to frame or not to frame: for all of my works there is an absolute ban on framing, and especially if they are put on display/presented/exhibited. this holds for institutions and for any other public, and hence also for you. of course, there are exceptions that can be justified for technical reasons, but exclusively only after the works have been sold: private persons who cannot hang the works unprotected at home because of children, lack of space etc., restaurants or such like – each case has to be discussed. with museums and institutions, I have fought through this ban on framing by means of fits of rage and discussions.
I am so strict about this because the "raw" quality is central to my work: the raw as material, as method, as biography, but also in the philosophical sense of e.g. Lévi-Strauss ("the raw and the cooked"). even "refined" (cooked) oil paintings are "raw", and in addition, through the methods I use, the provisional quality absolutely must be visible, despite the refinement. with oil paintings I totally forbid framing – there is, after all, no technical reason for it.
of course, I have no way of checking up on this and I know clients who have even framed oil paintings – hatred! so, it is of absolute importance for me that you, as my gallerists, fundamentally understand this "rawness and provisionality" and can communicate it to your customers, and that means, among other things, no frames!
so, if you have any further questions on this to-frame-or-not-to-frame issue, which is highly interesting in itself – questions on raw, provisional, cooked, framed, and on the trite and ingrained viewpoints in the art business and the art world in general – I am always at your disposal!
warmest regards, miriam
<Meyer Riegger ARTbasel 2009.doc>

From: Jochen Meyer
To: Miriam Cahn
Betreff: list for ART 2009 **4 April 2009**

Dear Miriam,
It was really, really good to meet you again in Basle. Afterwards, we did, after all, make the detour to the "Alpenblick" on the way home, and as you can imagine, it got rather late. The following day, I was in correspondingly bad shape for the Schaulager opening. At the meal, however, I had the good luck to be sitting between Adam Szymczyk and Christine Binswanger, so that it still turned into a good evening.
We are very happy with the fine works that we picked out in your studio and are certain that we can make a very good presentation with them at the Art. And have no worries: we are quite clear in our minds about the ban on framing. But it's good to know that it does not only apply to our own presentations (that we were clear

about anyway), but also to any and every other presentation in public. For that reason, it's a good thing that you have again made it so clear – and the reasoning behind it, stemming from your work, is convincing and fully understandable. So, have no worries: there will never be any frames with us, and we will also communicate this with reference to your approach to any relevant collection.
Warmest regards and looking forward to meeting you again before long,
Jochen

From: Miriam Cahn
To: Jochen Meyer
Subject: joy of painting, exhibition delectation and frustration + news **16 april 2009**

dear Jochen, Thomas and others,
currently I'm experiencing the joy of painting. am painting giant-size pictures; for the time being, it looks as if it is a room-size work – but I'll decide on that later. here is a studio impression. yesterday, speedy Jocelyn dashed by + saw part of it – liked it!
then I've seen a magnificent exhibition: Tracey Emin in Bern. you must go and see it: an absolutely top-quality exhibition. I even – sitting bent double on the kiddies' chair and doing my back no good – took in the entire moving conversation with her mum: awesome. I think the last time that I was so impressed by something contemporary was the Trockel exhibition years ago in Düsseldorf.[155] clearly no coincidence that both artists are women; and on the journey home read the fine interview with Lassnig[156] in the Süddeutsche – not a bad day!
but the worst thing I've seen for a long time was the exhibition in the Schaulager – I ran out of it in a real rage and went on foot into town walking through the Dreispitz in order to abreact. such a lousy exhibition! craptastic! these non-spaces in the Schaulager + the unchanging neon lighting completely unsuitable, but above all the hanging so damn non-committal + intellectually nonsensical. and what was really the final straw for me was the big wall: I suppose those were simply the works that were left over and hotchpotched together, in allegedly cahn-like style and with some highfalutin theory or other. and that's just what it looks like – a disgrace for my favourite pictures such as 'Tierschicksale',[157] 'Windsbraut'[158] and Holbein's portraits of Erasmus v. Rotterdam etc. terrible.
then dr Ulrike Thimme, who obviously comes regularly to your Karlsruhe gallery, wrote me an enthusiastic letter and sent me a book[159] that deals with the life + death of her son Johannes, who was an RAF sympathiser in the 70s and 80s, and which she wrote herself – on the one hand striking, but on the other hand somehow unpleasant, but I of course read it all in one go because this biography of a son bears strong similarities to that of my sister, especially this RAF jargon in the letters from prison. the father too was an archaeologist and for a long time director of your archaeological museum.
ok. that's it + I'll paint + carve around a bit here, but soon it's off to Bregaglia to forget again the results of the joy of painting …
warmest regards + i hope that all is well with you, miriam
<viell.grosse serie 2009 008.jpg><viell.grosse serie 2009 002.jpg><viell.grosse serie 2009 005.jpg><viell.grosse serie 2009

006.jpg>

From: Jochen Meyer
To: Miriam Cahn
Subject: joy of painting, exhibition delectation and frustration + news **17 April 2009**

Dear Miriam,
That really is the sheer joy of painting. Many thanks for the pictures from your studio. The new works are very impressive – we think they're really super. We greatly look forward to seeing everything in original form when we next come to your studio. It's terrific that you keep us up to date – in this way we can share your enjoyment and we are once again struck by your energy and your urge to continually further develop your work.
I can well imagine that you liked the Tracey Emin exhibition. I've repeatedly read letters of hers in various exhibitions – pretty striking and intense. A short time ago, an autobiography by her appeared under the title "Strangeland", in which she writes about her horror-trip adolescent years in the British provinces, her search for her Turkish father on Cyprus, and then later describes what it is for her to be a woman and an artist. I have only read about the book so far, but I want to get a copy soon – bound to be very worth reading.
Yes, and then the Schaulager: really an appallingly awful exhibition. Soulless, of no consequence at all, and badly curated. A shame for some fantastic works which are just swamped by this mass whateverism. That the large wall then attempts to imitate a Cahn-style hanging is a pretty helpless gesture. Neither do the works shown develop any narrative, nor is any connection established. A wasted, meaningless exhibition.
What you write about Ulrike Thimme is really interesting. I didn't know that her son was a member of the RAF – perhaps you could lend me the book? I'd like to read it.
Great to hear from you! Many greetings from all of us, especially from Thomas, who is currently in Berlin, and I'm at this moment sitting in the train on the way back to Karlsruhe.
Wishing you a good time in Bregaglia and hoping to see you soon, warmest regards,
Jochen

15 December 2011
Many regards from Panchito. My mother asked me to send you these pictures.
All the best!

15 december 2011
dear Vivian,
please, no MBs – I can't open them …
warm regards,
miriam

16 December 2011
Dear Miriam,
What is an MB? How should I send you the photos? I'm not sending the ones from Rut, since you're bound to have received them too. Sorry, I'm not so good at this PC stuff.
Nevertheless, all fond wishes, Vivian

16 december 2011
dear Vivian,
I too am quite certainly not the most skilful in this will-always-be-an-eternal-mystery-to-me-computer-stuff, but have now been able to open everything, pure chance. nevertheless, MB means "megabytes" and means that the pictures are "heavy", and depending on the system the sending + receiving take longer. all picture material in KB = kilobytes works super and is completely sufficient in quality … Panchito is bound to be able to explain this better. sending pictures is great in itself. have you seen these pictures? they are ages-old b/w photos probably the 6 of us back then in the Kunsthalle – at first, I didn't recognize myself at all, photos of myself are not my thing anyway. but your photos of hanging the huge boat are fantastic, I think– thanks!
here it's snowing like crazy at present: everything white, grey, black – marvellous, and totally silent. of course, I've already had to shovel snow – digging free the path and the car. and as long as I can do that, I'm not "old" either … so thanks again and warm greetings, also to your mother,
miriam

10 January 2012
Dear Miriam,
Sometimes I write to you in my mind. Tomorrow, I'm travelling to Mexico, have an appointment there. Adam got me the address.
Magnolia de la Garza – am pretty keyed up about it. Our house has been wobbling a lot – Panchito had a lot of parties. Wishing you all the best for 2012, all fond greetings too, Vivian

11 February 2012
Dear Miriam,
My mother has reached her 90th birthday. We had lunch in Santa Caterina, Panchito and the two of us. Everything peaceful. I hope you are well with all this cold weather you are having. In Mexico things were sobering, but good. They looked at my somewhat disorganized doc. They'll be getting in touch. Then visited a gallery they told me about. Now I'm sending Pancho with the folder, let's see what happens. Am already a bit down, but life goes on.

All fond wishes, Miriam,
Vivian

12 february 2012

dear Vivian,
what a coincidence! just this morning, I was wondering what you were up to and thinking that it was really time for me to send you a mail again. it's beastly cold here, especially last week when I had to travel to Basle. I stood at my bus-stop for just ten minutes. It was -15° + this beastly northern foehn wind. it was Siberian and I was frozen into an ice block. and when I came back the fuse had blown on my pipe heating and so naturally all the water pipes were iced up, no water… but here, of course, everything works and so the plumber repaired everything perfectly the following morning.
in Basle I prepared the exhibition with my Berlin gallery, was enjoyable, and I'm looking forward to "my" Berlin, will be staying there with my friend Eva-Maria, she too an artist with a son, and she too sometimes has her problems with the galleries + the art world + is therefore "down" as you so nicely put it in your mail. but things are not looking so bad for you now in Mexico, are they? hang on in there – I fingercross you, as my favourite butcher here, who's also around 80 years old, always says. but of course: there are no guarantees, the main thing is that we keep on working; if things don't go well, I too feel down. was so in December after the K-H[160] exhibition, found it difficult to get back into the groove and actually don't like meeting anyone in Basle apart from my one age-long woman friend. but now everything is full of excitement again!
so, here's wishing you all the very best!
miriam
your mother 90! fond greetings.

31 May 2012

Dear Miriam,
How are things with you? After feeling really down and having recovered, being at work and thinking they can all kiss my… an invitation from Adam[161] to take part in an exhibition in Mexico City.[162] I'm so excited. I won't be coming to the Art.
Many fond greetings, Vivian

1 june 2012

dear Vivian,
working is the best thing for everything… Adam makes a great job of things! super with Mexico City!
this year too I'll be in Basle during the ART. not that I like this hysterical business, on the contrary, but everything is always there in condensed form: my able and diligent gallerists organize visits from collectors etc., and this time the female curator of a museum in Michigan is coming… would of course be great to have an exhibition there. the plan is that I exhibit at the re-opening of the new building designed by Zaha Hadid – which I'd find super, but I won't believe it until it actually happens… so here in my Val Bregaglia I already can't sleep for excitement. and at the same time, I'm already tired in advance: for approx. 5 days I'll be only meeting people etc., which for a lone wolf like me is an admittedly exciting job, but a hard one.
so, give me a report from Mexico!
I wish you plenty of work and not much "down"…
miriam

10 June 2012

Dear Miriam,

Again, there's such exciting news. The exhibition in the Museo Tamayo goes under the name/theme OLINKA, and it sounds very gripping. I, of course, also hope that it comes true that I can be there. I have an idea for a modest installation there and hope it will come through. Adam says he is coming to pay me a visit – that is sooo fantastic, because so few people have the courage to do so. I hope he really comes and can look at my work as I conceive it and that it is not much different from what he has in mind. So far, however, I have never been able to make myself understood on account of the transportation possibilities and have not had much understanding for where I am and was.

All fond wishes and much stamina, Vivian

19 june 2012

dear Vivian,

when I landed back in my stable after 1 week, the plants in my garden were at least 20 cm higher…

so I'm still absolutely tired. the Michigan thing will come off, although not to coincide with the opening of Zaha Hadid's building, would have been too tight timewise… but the young woman curator is a Jewish chatterbox from Brooklyn and we immediately hit it off together. I'm already looking forward to it: it'll be the end of next year or spring 2014. and since Hadid's building cannot simply be understood/reconstructed via plans and photos at home, I'll probably go there and take a good look at this building. I find Hadid fantastic, a grade up from "our" super-architects Herzog & de Meuron – and in addition the only top woman architect – otherwise all men… great!

And apart from this, as always during the ART, a horde of people in my studio, women and men collectors sent along by my galleries, mostly interesting people, and also enthusiastic people, and that is good for the soul, because I too tend to have doubts when I am working away all alone on my own (and yet wouldn't want it any other way at all) and, moreover, Nature is a strong competitor if one is living in a valley in the southern alps. but you, of course, know all about that.

I saw Adam from far off in the vast scrum at the opening of ARTunlimited, waved, and I get panicky anyway among so many people and left the area in a great hurry – whew! – they'd all been previously at the documenta, which this time seems to be good. dogs lead visitors through the Karlsaue; a monastery which was a torture prison during the Nazi period and in the post-war years of peace a home for wayward girls, now occupied by art documenta-style and so on and so forth – I like very much the woman documenta director's line of thinking, her kind of "equal-value" philosophy.

on TV I saw a guided tour through the Karlsaue conducted by a blind man with a guide dog, a tour which is offered during the documenta explicitly for dog-owners…so you see the blind man with the guide dog, which seems to "know" the works of art; the blind man tells what he cannot see and the dog people with their dogs trot along, while their dogs communicate among one another – and never will we know about what, perhaps about how strange

they again consider the behaviour of their owners to be. reminds one a bit of your dog, who sang along with you. would have fitted! so, tell me about OLINKA! I really hope it works out for you – would be super if it came through! And also that Adam comes by …
all the best! and I'm fingercrossing!
miriam

2 July 2012

Dear Miriam,
Am going to Mexico next week. Adam is coming here from 18 to 26 August and other artists too. As always, I'm soo on edge. I hope everything is going ok with you. As for the photos I'm sending, have no fears – won't do so any more. Just wanted to show you my Sofi – she too can sing, but not as superbly as Anatol.
Fond greetings, Vivian

22 july 2012

dear Vivian,
am in the throes of preparation stress for the exhibition in the Karlsruher Kunstverein: it'll be called LACHEN BEI GEFAHR [LAUGHING IN THE FACE OF DANGER] … but of course you can send photos – just "light-weight" ones. your Sofi is a very good-looking dog, as is the photo next to it … how were things in Mexico? tell me, if and when you have time …
here again a few photos of my garden, which here makes a bit of a splash, and my new studio "for giant pictures". (had to pile up the sculptures for reasons of space, doesn't look bad either)
kiss,
miriam

25 July 2012

Dear Miriam,
Such beautiful flowers and the studio incredible for the big pictures you'll be doing? And altogether, I now have a bit of a feeling about where you are, since I once saw a television broadcast about you – quite by chance, so super. Here it is now canicula, the sunshine period in the rainy season, and it is wonderful.
What I can tell you about Mexico does not have much to do with museums or galleries concerning myself. I made the trip for my son, and so covered needs I myself and my mother have. Had the door that was destroyed in the near-burglary repaired. Many other things too, and also met his friends, whom I've known for quite some time and whom I really like and who are also struggling to get by and who also create good work, as does Panchito – as everyone says of him. a rap concert and so on – all okay, although Panchito was heart-broken and precisely not so great. But I also saw 1 exhibition in Bellas Artes – Impressionism from Germany and Vienna. I like the building so much and they put on good exhibitions. I wasn't in touch with the Tamayo, since I wouldn't want to be pushy, yet when I got back I had a mail from them – I hadn't bothered with mails while I was there. Accordingly, I haven't anything exciting to tell at all; but we did make an excursion – there's so much to see around Mexico City. I'm already so excited that Adam and Magnolia – she's the woman

from the Tamayo – are coming, and who knows who else, and yet I do have a strange life-style, also with my mother and so on. I'm really curious about your exhibition in the Kunstverein and think the title is very suggestive. Thanks again for the photos. I'm glad you like Sofi and the picture too, All fond wishes, Vivian

1 August 2012

Dear Miriam,

I hope everything is okay with you. All the best for your exhibition in the Kunstverein. Actually, I can't really imagine what it might be like, but I also have recollections of the place. But how exactly is the title to be understood? Intriguing, what you're going to do.
All find wishes, big hug, Vivian

2 august 2012

dear Vivian,

precisely today, I have spent fully 5 hours making photos + list of the works for Karlsruhe – it's always above all this office work that makes staging an exhibition so strenuous, I'm exhausted from sitting … the woman curator is coming up here in ten days' time to have a look at it all – but it's all already been chosen by me and so on; in this new part, she can actually only say yes, yes or fly into a rage. she will too. and this apart, I have to go back and forth between Bregaglia and Basle a few times – the major part of the list + photos has to be done in Basle, after all, that's how it is. and then I'll spend 10 days in the Kunstverein apartment in Karlsruhe and set things up – there are around 10 rooms after all, and I'm really looking forward to that!

and I'm keen to know what you have to tell about the Adam-Magnolia visit! no worries about life-style! Adam, after all, is not exactly a paragon of so-called normality either …

so, I'll be in touch again thereafter! and here are pictures of precisely these new works – just ignore the numbers.

kiss,

miriam

3380 was done after I had seen the film "Avatar" on TV.

7 September 2012

Dear Miriam,

Things went very well in Mexico: the space where I bring and hang and position the works is really suitable. I missed an evening meal because of the distance and my tiredness after so much excitement – I'm just not so used to it. Wouldn't have anything against getting used. Am really keen to hear about your exhibition. The flower was also stressed out because the new annexe to the Museum is being inaugurated. A super work she has curated: "Nueva matematica", Michael Stevenson. There was a lot of other interesting things. Now I am making my final choice. Hope Adam will help me via photos. Then I am supposed to be writing something – not easy for me. Also, still got quite a cold – otherwise I'd have written to you earlier. All fond wishes, Vivian

12 september 2012

dear Vivian,

sounds so interesting with Mexico, the room-spaces and the people!

today the transport company came here to Bregaglia to load up all the works for Karlsruhe in the pouring rain (really terrible, hate it) – I'm still really tired as a result … and this apart, I'm in this interim waiting state: everything is planned, the invitations and poster printed, but they still have to take down the previous exhibition and put in the modifications needed for my exhibition, only then – next Tuesday – off to Karlsruhe. up to then, therefore, I'm prowling around a bit and doing a lot in the garden: among other things I've mowed everything that needs to be mowed with the scythe – something I like doing very much.
and here is the last picture painted for the exhibition (bad Cahn photo with number); but it's pretty large, approx. 300 × 220 cm, and painted in my new, very high studio already.
so, I wish you all the very best in making your choice – Adam the Remarkable is really worth his weight in gold – and above all with the writing. I also find this very difficult. do you then write in German actually? or in Spanish? or in your best English?
fond greetings, miriam

12 October 2012

Dear Miriam,
I can't possibly tell you how difficult it is for me to decide on which pictures. I am really up the creek and up a gum tree, and can't find any way out, but now I must – ultimatum.
All fond wishes, am thinking about how you are getting on after this huge demand.
Full of admiration, really super, Vivian

12 october 2012

dear Vivian,
just back in Bregaglia again at last after pretty exciting 3 1/2 weeks – phew!
so, about your pictures, in basic terms: probably you've already looked at them far too long.
at any rate, my method is then not to look at them any more at all, to put everything away and to dig it out again shortly before the deadline, and then, very quickly, and acting ONLY on feeling, to make one's decision. this is then the decision taken on the day and it must be defended like a lioness. there are no criteria apart from one's own! if you act on the assumption that all your works are equal, and also equally good, i.e. your work = your thinking your feeling your acting your painting, then precisely no criteria apart from these self-same ones for your work.
fuck quality! judging art to be better or worse is not half as neutral and objective as those who use these words think. here too, it is the form on the day/personality/function/position of power/history etc. that rules.
when we 2 were right at the beginning, you in that studio in the vicinity of the spalenberg and me in somewhereorother, you once said: the great thing, if one lived where one worked, was getting up – immediately taking a look – judging, perhaps immediately setting to work etc. perhaps talking a bit with the dog okay. made a big impression on me at the time …
and it's still right today.
of course, there's also the throw-of-the-dice principle or random principle, based loosely on John Cage, not bad either.
if I had such a nice dog as you, I would perhaps let it choose. at this

year's documenta, dogs had equal rights in artistic matters like everybody else …
so, take care and be courageous!
warm regards, miriam

16 October 2012
Dear Miriam,
Thanks, it was a help, am soo happy. I embrace you,
Vivian

21 october 2012
dear Vivian,
for a long time, I've been wanting to send you a few photos of setting up and exhibiting in Karlsruhe …and hope that all is well with you!
warmest wishes, miriam
the last two are from the FAMILIENRAUM [FAMILY ROOM] my mother and my father …

26 October 2012
Dear Miriam,
I am now looking at all your wonderful things again; I really have no words to describe them – I feel everything strongly. I would like to tell you that it is wonderful and I thank you for the photos. I hope that I can then send you something – photos from the exhibition. There are 5 pictures, then one placed above another, and a hanging affair of nine pictures, which one cannot see, but everything has to do with Stan and Agatha, all of it with a lower mud-painting, which was then rubbed away but is still visible. I am very excited, very, and I have to take stress-things, since I am almost unbearable, yet everything natural, and it's all okay. Yet in Mexico I will be alone, since Pachito, my son, who lives there, has a concert in Guatemala at just that time. But that's the way it is, and my mother, of course, cannot come since she's in a wheelchair. Adam, however, has given her an invitation for her collages, and that's so wonderful. He is just, as you say, worth his weight in gold and good deal more besides. I am looking forward to sending you the photos. I don't want to do so at the present moment, and I hope I'm not disappointing you. You have helped me a great deal with your advice, really. Now I am a lioness, and I will defend it.
All fond wishes and my greatest respect – no other phrase comes to my mind, but that's what I mean.
All fond wishes and all the best, Vivian

26 october 2012
dear Vivian – wishing you all good luck and plenty of excitement in Mexico! and I look forward to your photos …
kiss, miriam

4 december 2012
dear Vivian,
how are you? and how did things go eventually in Mexico City?
my exhibition in Karlsruhe, at any rate, is now over and it was really top-rate, more people than ever, and the woman director thus highly satisfied – and pregnant, her baby bump is now visible. that was stressful before the exhibition: she thought she had a back problem and then it turned out she was pregnant.

and during the show I gave a kind of talk, not the usual artist's woffle, however, but my SLOTMACHINE, which goes like this: I have about 500 images – of all types, my own, old and new, other stuff, photos, sculptures, landscapes all higgledy-piggledy, b/w and in colour – and show them one after the other, every two seconds another one. if they have a question about a picture, the spectators have to shout "stop" – just like with a one-armed bandit, a slot machine, and I then answer the question. it's very, very amusing, because the people really have to pay attention, as in a game, and I just react, and so have in that sense nothing to do, and the duration of the whole event is dictated by the questions. without any stops it would be about twenty minutes; in more reticent, self-conscious societies, as for example in CH, it takes between one hour and one-and-a-half, and with the lively Germans it took over 2 hrs! by the end I was really knackered and hoarse. – and then off to the pub! was really good.
and now I'm here in the shadows of my Bregaglia – a time I really love, because there are no tourists, only sheep bleating around with their young and a few nanny goats as well, nothing else. on the road to Soglio, the animals make themselves at home, look at my car and then occasionally get up with right royal nonchalance to trot off to one side. that's how little traffic there is …
and tomorrow my French gallerist is actually coming here with his Maghrebian assistant, and are actually driving through tomorrow's snowstorms via Geneva, Aarau, up the Julier Pass and down the Maloja – he's got some winter tyres specially for this, but at this time of year I don't believe it until the people are standing here on the doorstep. but it's nice. and I'm looking forward to the 2 of them.
and of course, almost superfluous to mention, I am really annoyed that in CH – apart from the unspeakable SVP Baslerzeitung – not a single a medium has so much as mentioned my exhibition. not even the kunstbulletin. the swine! on the other hand, I am very moved by the fact that the Süddeutsche has published a super review: the woman was genuinely enthusiastic, which is rare among journos. I walked out of an SWF radio interview, because the journo began talking about "pussies and tits" and about women as victims – he clearly hadn't got all his marbles. an old 68er, by the way, with long grey hair … grr + yucky type.
so, send me a report, and a super fond kiss/greeting from
miriam

15 December 2012
[Vivian sends pictures]

17 december 2012
dear Vivian,
what did you want to send me? it's all very blurred here – also attractive, but I assume not necessarily intended …
warm regards from snowed-under Bregaglia!
miriam

17 December 2012
Dear Miriam,
Yes, it is blurred, yet I think it's as beautiful as a picture, and it is a picture that is in the exhibition, on the way there. It was so annoying and so nerve-racking with the customs here: the pictures had still not arrived, still in customs, when I flew. I was at the customs office personally and was sent from pillar to post, from one

corner to the other, talking with so many people and waiting. Then, before leaving, as an alternative I rolled up a roll at night, by torch-light, and went into town to dhl and customs – and finally everything arrived, the parcel from the customs and then that from dhl after many discussions since the roll had a spider's cocoon and was thus contaminated. But then Adam interceded on my behalf and Magnolia filed a request and I was able to exhibit everything – one picture above another and the stand filled. I am very satisfied; yet I have to get used to things, and it is a super-fantastic exhibition – such nice, awesome, interesting artists, such wonderful meals and kind invitations from gallerists, simply magnificent, above all Adam, who, as you say, is worth his weight in gold and much more besides – such a wonderful person. And the assembling of us artists simply super, above all in retrospect. And my mother – 2 tables, turned out so superbly. Bought material with Nairi – such a super artist – then Tea helped with the collages, and then Paolina gave the finishing touches. Superb! I am still so tired and excited and sad and incredibly grateful that I was able to do this. I'll try to send you something, separately. All fond wishes and the newspaper report so super and all in all a really great exhibition. We are in the thick of things – you, of course, anyway – but me too a little, that's lovely. Vivian

19 december 2012

dear Vivian,

that's a superb report! must have been exciting and really great, also the various meals etc. … ah, it is so wonderful when one can exhibit one's works, and can work together with people on the project, and in Mexico probably that bit more amusing again!

there is always stress with the customs, which is a mystery to me, but seems to be a rule, especially if the works come from Switzerland – mine also have also got stuck in customs for completely superfluous reasons, because a few photos were missing – which, however, is hardly doable with my quantities. so my assistant, the super Kathrin, simply sent any old photos, and alley-oop! everything okay! I, however, with my nerves in shatters. wouldn't be able to cope at all without Kathrin.

so, you wanted to send me some pictures – but none have arrived – and as regards the density: in the bottom right there is a little field with "large. medium. small" in it – simply click on "small". didn't learn this myself until half a year ago.

warmest wishes,

miriam

8 january 2013

dear Vivian,

these are the pictures from the exhibition, I assume? not by Mussorgsky but by you – so wonderful! especially the strange hanging showcase, but also the other, fine "rags" hung on that pebble wall …something totally new, exciting!

all best ongoing wishes, pleased – and tired, because it's so wretchedly warm here in mid-winter (12°).

kiss, miriam

19 January 2013

Dear Miriam,
I had a difficult time with my son, who was here, and many friends from Mexico and from here, and we didn't part on good terms. I think that in human terms I'm a failure again and again. It's good that you find it fascinating and don't give up on me. I must look up the artist you mention. Is he already dead? Things have not been easy for me, and yet I am certain that it was good the way it was and I stand by it 100 per cent, and, above all, everything was very instructive: I mean it was a great learning curve and I'm continuing on my path, although I know that not many people like it. Gilli hasn't replied at all; actually, I don't want to do an exhibition there, but she is a friend, after all and I wanted to know a bit more. What of it; I've written today [and asked] why she doesn't say anything. We had a gallerist from Mexico, he's super-nice, and we were all invited to his place. He also thinks my mother's things are great – them perhaps more so than mine – whatever. I'm pleased and hope that he comes, but many people say something and then it turns out differently – he, however, has written often. Here it's windy and you have snow.
All fond wishes, Vivian

19 january 2013

dear Vivian,
ha! I'm always pleased when others fail in family and human terms as I do – so I'm not the only one, and really: someone like Gilli, Madame Niminy-Piminy, is not exactly a paragon of decent human behaviour! if she doesn't reply, that means quite simply "no interest". all friendship aside. take the man from Mexico!
there's a pop-song from the 60s, I think West Coast USA: "if you can't be with the one you love, love the one you're with" – goes for gallerists too.
another happy coincidence: I've just been in Basle, and by chance, from the tram on the way from the train station to Kleinhüningen, I see that it is opening night in the Kunsthalle – off I go, and meet Adam there, who was pleased and, when I asked him, explained your fine works in the Mexico exhibition and told me how wonderful those 14 days were and that he will be making an art trip there with the members of the K-H. super.
and Mussorgsky is the very intense and avant-garde Russian composer – nineteenth-century, I think – who composed "Pictures at an Exhibition" – you'll probably recognize it if you listen to it.
so, keep up the good work or bad work in human terms, but at any event keep things lively and always working away.
your miriam

27 January 2013

Dear Miriam,
I just want to tell you that Gilli has written, after I was a bit depressed, and she found it interesting. The man from Mex has written that they are coming to visit, have already got the tickets and are looking forward to it – me too. I hope life is treating you well, that you are enjoying all the snow and can get some good work done.
All fond wishes from Panajachel, Vivian

6 february 2013

dear Vivian – things are looking good with you!
here I'm longing for the first rays of sun on my house, as always at this time of year – everybody has already got sunshine, I'm the last. till mid-february.
and this apart, things are all normal – at present I'm fighting a running battle with the woman curator who wants to make a solo exhibition in her brand-new, Zaha Hadid-designed museum in the USA, super! a nice, quick-witted American "tough cookie", but in sheer communicative terms we have yet to get the knack of things – she is young and perpetually online, I am older and check my mails only once or twice per day. on the other hand, she is incapable of just phoning, although she definitely wants to: first she has to announce via mail when she's going to phone, then we fix a date, which she then postpones seemingly a hundred times over – until in an e-mail fit of rage I suggest that she just phones through ...etc. gets on the NERVES. tomorrow she has sworn blind that she will phone in the evening – we'll see! that's how it is these days ...
all the best
from Bergell
to Panajachel
(it even rhymes),
miriam the older

12 February 2013

Dear Miriam,
Today the people from Mexico arrive in Guatemala City, then they'll be arriving here on Friday. I am so excited – it's the first time that someone comes from a gallery abroad. Since it is Mexico, they'll perhaps have more understanding for all the things they'll be exposing themselves to, and I am very nervous, since I'm a very private person, as you too, I assume. Yes, Bergell-Panajachel, it rhymes wonderfully. All fond wishes,
Vivian

13 february 2013

dear Vivian,
I wish you super-much good luck and the courage of a lioness and, as the wife of my favourite butcher likes to say: I fingercross you! (she is Belgian).
I'll be in touch when there's more time! and, too late, my congratulations to your mother on her 91st ...
miriam

21 February 2013

Dear Miriam,
Our visitors from Mexico were here. They looked at a lot of works and I could have been a better host-cum-caterer – but that's something I can't do, i.e. two things at the same time. The studio could have been cleaner and tidier and painted whiter, and the other studio up the hill too, such a mess, which I, however, feel at home in – or perhaps not, since I work more outside. Now I'm improving things, not too late, I hope. He said he wants to take us to the art fair in Buenos Aires – that would be great. And apart from this, I wrote to him asking why he doesn't take anything to the trade fair in Mexico, to which he replied that he plans that long in advance and

that we should remain in contact and I should keep on sending him photos. And that he would like to come to know my work better. He is on the list in Basle. What pleases me is that he likes things that others do not like at all: I think that's not a bad thing, but does he like them enough? ... Dear Miriam, the postcard arrived yesterday. Many thanks, I find it very optimistic, and that helps. I've put it in a very special place and take great pleasure in it. All the best to you for this year.
Un abrazo grande desde Panajachel, Vivian

23 february 2013

dear Vivian,
again, what you report sounds interesting! being represented at art fairs is without question important nowadays, even if I have come to find art fairs unbearable. at the stands of my otherwise kind and normal gallerists, I recognize neither my own work nor the gallerists themselves, who have this absolutely weird yikes-this-could-be-a-buyer-look about them – like animals in the jungle (which it also is).
at your description of your "not so clean and tidy" studio, I had to think of the shock I got a few years ago at the Francis Bacon exhibition in the Fondation Beyeler museum: on display there were also photos of his studio – a total rubbish heap, unbelievable, up to knee-height only rubbish, cigarette ends, beer cans, encrusted paint, rags and I just don't want to know what else. I was all the more shocked as I had always tended to assume from his clear and pure, gleaming colours that his studio would be "clean and tidy". so that means nothing! Francis Bacon stood with his feet in garbage up to his knees, and above everything was clear. what a contrast, so I believe at least, like to imagine so. could also be that he didn't see his garbage at all.
I myself have a very tidy studio: there is not a single work to be seen, there is nothing hanging or standing around, because I myself do not want to be forever looking at my work. because I work from the memory of it, not from the seeing.
so, when people come to look at art (ok, if it really is art, let's assume so), I bring it out. in this way, I also have something to do and do not just stand idly around looking at the people looking at art. in addition, everybody has to decide relatively quickly what they find interesting. I absolutely hate this long staring at art, and so make everybody nervous.
an exception is my Norwegian gallerist, who is extremely slow by nature. He speaks slowly, and also eats really slowly (crazy: he always needs 3× as long as me). with him, we do it like this: I pull out relatively quickly the pictures which I think will interest him: he has to say "Yes" or "No"; and all the "Yesses" I line up along the wall. then I give him approx. 3 hours to make his choice, during which time I go shopping, do office work etc., and am at any event not in the same room. this works very well! and he then sets up the exhibition in Oslo, and since we both hate opening nights, I don't even have to go ...
unfortunately, the man is ill, and I don't know whether he'll be continuing.
on the other hand, the curator of the Broad Art Museum, Michigan State University, has phoned at last, and the exhibition will take place in May or June 2014 – I'm really pleased!

so, keep up the good work!
kiss, miriam

22 March 2013

Dear Miriam,
Perhaps I'll see him this time. I haven't written for such a long time, but I have been thinking of you, and I'm so very pleased to hear that your exhibition is making progress. It's bound to be sensational, as also the entire event there and you in that building. I am very pleased. I haven't got a lot to report. But on the 8th I am flying to Mexico and will be seeing the Olinka exhibition again, also Adam and co. and Panchito, my son, who will be there then – I hope that our relationship has improved in the meantime. I am also taking pictures with me for the art in Buenos Aires, which is pretty exciting for me. Otherwise, things are quiet here, which is good – I hope it stays this way. Sometimes it begins to rain, and that is a good thing, since it is extremely dry and the plants are thirsting for it. I hope that spring arrives in your valley and the sun.
I send you all fond wishes, my greetings and a hug,
Vivian

1 april 2013

dear Vivian – this is what it looked like here a few days ago at night!
2 days later, everything gone again.
and, that apart, I don't have much to report, except that from tomorrow onwards the small annexe (it's only 2.00 × 6.00) to my place is at last being built – it will be a proper, insulated room where I can then store my pictures. previously, it was a provisional structure I had built myself, but which withstood all the weather, and the locals thought I was growing tomatoes in it…
and thanks to my Parisian gallerist my 14 giant wood sculptures are going to Paris; so that I at last have more space! so super, because he can now show them to people, instead of them lying around here in my place, being hard to move, getting on my nerves and taking up a lot of room.
but the 4 saws are staying here!
so, I wish you all the best for Mexico!
miriam

27 April 2013

Dear Miriam,
I've been wanting to write to you for some time, but I am still too firmly under the impact of the Mexico experience. It is always so great to meet Adam, he is simply unbelievable – broad knowledge and a super person, worth his weight in gold, as you say. It was a lot, really a lot for me, the Mexico gallery to which I took the pictures for Buenos Aires – at present not a word about that. Then all these important people in the art world, so many curators from all over the place, a whole nestful. And gallerists, and the celebration with candelabra in the wood in front of the Museum, and again coming to know and meeting again some artists from the exhibition, and so kind and wonderful; and yet then again this gallery – enthusiastic, then when we met again almost no reaction at all, then later an e-mail

saying she wants to visit the studio in Basle. Then precisely the business with Argentina that is pretty close to my heart and then not a word, and then I think: it was like this once before and then I backed out, now it'll be similar, and the questions what and how and so on tend to occupy my thoughts. Yet now I'm much older and perhaps I have to do more to keep up the excitement… I'm sure you can well imagine. A woman artist whom I very much liked and who also took part in the exhibition but couldn't come to the opening was there, and I find her really fascinating: Susan Hiller – she lives in London. Now I am really wondering about whether I should come to the ART, since I also have an appointment and so on – I have difficulty actually making the booking. I send you all fond wishes and hope that your preparations for your big exhibition are making good headway.
All fond wishes,
Vivian

28 april 2013

dear Vivian,
sounds really super-interesting, this Mexico! rather different from here.
and Susan Hiller I have also met, donkey's years ago: super artist, super person, I agree.
and if you already have an appointment during the ART in BS, I would go at all costs. I would also straightaway give an invitation to the enthusiastic gallery to come during ART, because you are there anyway, and also let the people in Argentina know that you are in BS at that time … it is a total privilege to have a studio in Basle at this time, because quite simply at precisely that time EVERY art big shot in the world wants to go to ART and – so practical! – could also pay you a visit. in addition, at the same time is the opening of the Venice Biennale, which attracts even more people. you just have to exploit this!
I also always do so, because, of course, only very few come to Bregaglia. however, all of them, without any exception, go crazy, act hysterically – you don't even recognize your own gallerists, because they go boggle-eyed on the look-out for sales – and I always find this super-stressful and feel tired in advance on the journey there. but at the same time, it is a very good and exciting thing in this environment to attract and have people in your studio, because they are all not only hysterical but also motivated and super-committed – the opposite of the artistic inertness and slackness typical of Basle.
Zaha Hadid's crooked walls and spaces are very intriguing for my exhibition. for the first time in my life I have had to make a model precisely because of this inclining wall business. the model looks as if it was made by a child, with Sellotape and cardboard – but it's completely sufficient.
so, keep up the good work! and here it's been pouring and chucking it down for days now: everywhere the most delicate leaves on the trees and in between, as always in springtime in Bregaglia, the lovely white blossoms of the wild, or no longer cultivated, cherry trees. and I'm living beside a building site: at last my little annexe has been authorized and is now being built, by super Italian

muratori, who can still make dry-stone walls. when it's finished, I'll send you a photo.
warmest greetings, also to your mother!
miriam

18 May 2013
Dear Miriam,
I've been back to Mexico, on account of the transportation of a picture – somewhat complex, so I had to do it myself. Now I'm arriving in Basle on the 4th. I don't have your phone number. I hope we can meet then. All fond wishes, the photos are so beautiful, so much snow. All fond wishes, Vivian

21 may 2013
dear Vivian,
yes, that would be wonderful! my mobile no.: ***. at present it looks as if I will be there from 10.06. …
all the best,
miriam

24 May 2013
Dear Miriam
It's really a great leap from over here. Am already a bit nervous. Looking forward to seeing you. All fond wishes and all the very best, Vivian

25 may 2013
dear Vivian,
of course! I'm already a bit tense too – even if the geographical distance is not as huge as yours. already my entire ART week is full + perpetual visits – super! but strenuous for me too … it would be wonderful to meet you, absolutely – do you have a phone number already? I am definitely in BS until 17.06.
Miriam

24 June 2013
Dear Miriam,
I've not fully arrived yet – it takes time. I saw you, but you did not see me. I now imagine you as I saw you. Strange how one reacts in unexpected ways. I'll write more soon. All fond wishes from the rainy season, Vivian

29 june 2013
dear Vivian,
I too am slowly coming back to myself – thanks to the garden and my new annexe …
more later
warmest wishes from a rain-swept Bregaglia,
miriam

31 July 2013
Dear Miriam,
I've been writing to you in my mind for some time now. How are things with you and with your preparations and with the garden and everything? Here we've got canicula again, this time in the rainy season with no or little rain. Just now, admittedly, it's starting to rain again – something that could be foreseen, because the clouds were hanging rather low and somewhat heavy. I was so busy with a bio, also of my mother, and photos for a journal, friends of Adam. My mother now has an exhibition with others in Costa Rica – strange, isn't it, I

have to get used to this too. I think it's great, but it means that she too has her ups and downs due to these matters. Yet it doesn't come any better, getting old like this. Today, I have freighted 2 pictures, which have been sold, to Mexico: that does one good and so I can – or better: I must – help out my son with the rent and food. But that's the way it is. This apart, I'm groping my way forward. I've heard nothing more from that gallery in L.A. who came into my studio. As a precaution, I've not yet written to the other one in N.Y., and am waiting for the article in the journal. The picture with STAMPA at the ART was not sold, and I'm thinking that perhaps this Basle is not the right thing for me, although the Stampas were very kind and greeted me in friendly fashion. One dog has died – Snoopy, now there are 2, Sofi and Flor. We are thinking of a puppy, also because of their work as watchdogs. I also wanted to say that you looked very nice when I saw you – fully in action and like earlier, so super, Miriam, I liked the hair-style too. It was only a wave with the eyes. I am glad that I now have time for things. Yet all this excitement was an elixir. A firm hug, Vivian

2 august 2013

dear Vivian,

here too it's ferragosto – fine weather for weeks and unbrokenly hot, which is unusual up here – absolutely wonderful.

things are going excellently for you! Mexico better than Basle! there is nothing lovelier than the selling of pictures – apart from the money it is, after all, THE endorsement of the work: the people want to own it, to live with it. the publication in the journal is also super, and this apart even the gentlemen and ladies of the galleries have a holiday break… and thanks for the "wave with the eyes" – next time, please don't hesitate to give me a prod!

I myself had a crazy amount to do during ART: every day interesting visitors. take pictures out, put them away again, take pictures out, put them away again etc.: by the end, I felt I was like Chaplin in the film "Modern Times". but it was great, especially the woman from Broad Michigan (the Zaha Hadid building) for the exhibition next year, who came with my New York gallerist: the 2 women worked at some pace! and such a really great way of choosing, talking and looking! and they just love art totally above anything else, and show it too. and they are practically-minded people, working together on such a project.

also great was the visit of Philipp Kaiser, whom I hadn't seen for years, because he was curator in the Museum of Modern Art in L.A., and has now just been appointed head of the Museum Ludwig in Cologne. For a few years, Philipp was for me something like Adam is for you: gold! as head of the Museum für Gegenwartskunst BS, he rescued me from incipient neglect, first for a group show and then for a solo. back then, he simply came into my studio and said something like: "oh, you've got such beautiful nuclear bombs? could we perhaps show them? and photos of your motorway drawings? we could make a wallpaper of them" (it not having been clear whether they were originals or repros, so a wallpaper…). and on we went and made our choices, briskly, merrily and jauntily. the solo exhibition in a large space was a short-term stand-in for an

exhibition that had to be cancelled – no catalogue, an improvised poster, no real first-night opening (which suits me fine) and a magnificently merry form of choosing with Philipp. the exhibition was super and a success. and from then on, I knew: my work is much better than this lame and limping "Basle scene" wants me to believe.
Philipp recently did the same thing with Gerhard Richter in the Museum Ludwig, and the world celebrity was so enthusiastic that he himself leapt into a taxi during the setting-up phase to fetch new and fitting works from his studio … that's Philipp, who is worth his weight in gold for me.
and this time he was standing at my door with the woman head of the Santa Monica Museum in L.A.: the lanky, always elegantly dressed Philipp with his heavy Bernese Swiss German alongside a hippie girl of my age wearing walla walla clothing, matching sandals and various fabrics somehow wound around her head … and Philipp wants to curate an exhibition there with me, some time around 2015 – super! for me, that was the best bit of ART.
and my gallerists were also highly active and able and sold some works even before the actual opening …
at any event, I travelled back to Bregaglia completely shattered and with a strong urge to be back in my stable, and had the feeling that things are now really beginning on the exhibition front.
tell me: how many dogs have you got actually? definitely get a puppy – it's so sweet and good if the "adults" take care of it. and your mother? it's really fantastic that she is now exhibiting.
and here are some photos of the remarkable flowers in my garden – the one is a salad plant and will now be eaten!
here's wishing you all the very best, and greetings to your mother,
miriam

13 August 2013
Dear Miriam,
I'm not afraid – but suddenly he was standing at my door.
Again, all fond wishes, Vivian

13 august 2013
dear Vivian – who was standing at your door?
All fond wishes,
miriam

17. August 2013
Dear Miriam,
I'm thinking of you and hoping that things are well with you. Here we are cutting a Bejuco – this is a creeper that previously never came. I kept on watering it and it became as big as a house. Unfortunately, it had climbed up a tree that we had to chop down because of our neighbour, since his wall had been cracked by the tree on which this plant was – and then everything toppled down, and yet I love this plant, since it blocks the view of the neighbours. It's nothing, nothing worth mentioning, yet for me it's a major affair which brings me back to reality from all the other things that do not exist. All fond wishes, I'm thinking of you and of all your wonderful work. I'd like to have a photo of your annexe. All fond wishes, keep your spirits up – here, far away, I am thinking of you, Vivian

18 august 2013
dear Vivian,
where you are, things sure grow rampantly, like crazy!
cutting down trees I always find strange. in spring, they cut down 4 here that were leaning threateningly towards my house, and promptly one of them fell awkwardly and tore off a few stones from the stone roof + gutter – it made quite a bang.
I'll be sending you a picture of the annexe … and here I'm assembling things for the room at the Frieze, can't get my head around it at all.
kisses,
miriam

18 august 2013
here a few photos … warm regards, miriam

6 September 2013
Dear Miriam,
Yesterday I sent a photo – that's my studio, lower down among the banana trees, there I also store the pictures and look at them. Up on the hill I paint: up there, there's a smaller studio, and I mostly work outside. I hope things are well with you. My son is back in Mexico – it was as feared, but it seems I have to take it. It hurts and you can't just shrug it off. I hope I've learned something at last. Now the rainy season is here right and proper. And I must also confess that I haven't followed your advice – we've got an Oso, and he is still very young and inquisitive, sharp little teeth and, as they tend to be, such a sweetie. We took the decision so as to give us something different to think about. I hope you're making good progress with all your projects.
All fond wishes from damp Panajachel, Vivian

6 september 2013
dear Vivian,
yes, thanks for your photos of dog + studio! both very lovely, a nice dog and a huge studio with bananas? beneath banana trees? or in the studio also bananas with the pictures? or bananas in the pictures? (ok, I'll stop going on about the bananas …)
here in Val Bregaglia we have wonderful late summer weather: even I am sometimes working outdoors – but only "dusty" drawings (chalk, charcoal, crayon); it's practical if the dust can simply dust away into Nature. but working outside is also something very special, I like it a lot.
sorry for not having written for such a long time – time flies, because there is so much going on, even here: first, my Paris gallerist came all of a sudden, was very nice, even stayed overnight in the dilapidated old grand hôtel; then we also went to visit my brother, who has a house up above Lake Sils, fantastic. I love my brother, but he gets absolutely on my nerves, talks only of himself, without stopping, and I absolutely cannot stand his wife, and his child, born late in life, has already turned into a totally spoilt little princess … as you see, family is simply not my thing, and nevertheless I'm caught up in it.
then my German gallerist came too, and we put things together for the solo show at the Frieze in London – was really super. the space will be called SITUATION ROOM, there will be 3 huge pictures involved and also some very small stuff, as for example a crayon

drawing of a tulip, naturally from my garden. am greatly looking forward to going to London again.
drawing in coloured crayon is something I have adopted straight from my mother: up to her death, she drew fine, very dense circles and lines, in rich colour – this was her own thing, her calm anchor.
what is an Oso actually? not a puppy?
from dry Bregaglia I wish you all the best in damp climes!
warm regards, miriam
but the tulip, that was in spring …

11 september 2013
dear Vivian,
thanks for the bananas and oso – he's really sweet!
and here, spring in a sketchbook – the view from my only window …
warm wishes, miriam

14 September 2013
Dear Miriam
Thanks for your mail – kind letters, good photos of wonderfully attractive works. Now a woman has written concerning a project in Costa Rica: a nice e-mail and much info on the project – but I don't know anyone there and she wants to sell and especially have photos of works very fast, which she can sell to a client. That's good, excellent, since there is nothing else on the horizon and some horizons have even been blown away … Yet, my reticence – should I give my latest works, for what and to whom? Should I wait with my eternal illusions and calm, or abandon myself to what is? These are my musings and pipe-dreams – ask the Stampas what is happening with the gallery in N.Y. – but I haven't written, not least because I'm waiting for an article from a Greek – really strange – periodical, and Adam wanted the text – then stress, and we (our/my mother and I biography) – but too emotive for sure and anyway – yet that's the way it is – nothing will come of it for sure – yet it brought about other actions – hope, direction-driven activity, and certainly not in vain. So I've written to N.Y., to the Bortolami Gallery, who buttonholed me in Mexico and were then in my studio in Basle, but I have not heard anything from them. I must just wait and take a look at this Costa Rica thing – after all, I am a Central American artist, having lived here for almost 30 years. The man from Mexico has already sold several things, really super to good addresses, yet he has no space any more, and who knows whether he really wants to represent me … I am always so eager to know how things are with you and what you are doing. All fond wishes and a firm hug, Vivian

15 september 2013
dear Vivian,
oh, your horizon is not so bad! above all, do NOT ask the weirdo Stampas, who have not a clue about the situation in Southern and Central America and humiliate you by their never-exhibiting of your work.
if you think this Costa Rica project is a good one – get involved, why not? and ask your new contacts, for example the one from Mexico,

about it. is then a good opportunity to sound out how he wishes to continue . . . and I would also ask the woman in N.Y. about Costa Rica + sounding things out a little, and also Adam – it's a good lead-in, after all. take this Costa Rica project as an opportunity to approach self-confidently all the people YOU are interested in – something like this: hallo? I've got this offer here, what do you think, should I follow it up? Is it a good thing? What photos should I send them? etc. nowadays this can be done so fast and effectively by e-mail. in this way, you at least get a bit away from this very unpleasant period of waiting, which assails one's spirits and above all gnaws away daily at one's self-confidence, as I know only too well. THAT is emotive.
after all, you define yourself as a Central American artist after this long time spent living and working there. as far as I have gathered from my gallerists and others, Central + South America are burgeoning, coming areas in art terms and are very exciting – even my N.Y. gallery sent 2 very young gallerists from Brazil to my studio, and they were interesting and in gallery terms highly improvising intellectuals, who had studied philosophy at the Sorbonne in Paris – great! not so stalely "reticent" as with us in old Europe. Whether it will lead to anything, I don't know either . . .
so, now I've almost got a bad conscience for having given you such advice, which may be wrong for you, but I feel sorry for you, because you so lack self-confidence in these dealings with gallerists etc., although you know full well how good your work is.
wishing you all the very, very best!
miriam

29 September 2013
Dear Miriam,
Thanks for the horizon, from the no longer so rainy Panajachel,
Vivian
Bonzo is growing very fast and looks as if he is thinking, contemplating.

1 october 2013
dear Vivian,
do you know this fine aphorism by Gertrude Stein: – "I am I because my little dog knows me" – ? she also always had dogs like you. I tend to go for my garden: now, it is turning autumn so swiftly that every morning, when looking out of the window, everything is different from the day before – sudden yellow, where still green yesterday, sudden brown, yesterday still red, and my sunflowers suddenly bow their heads, bow down to the ground with all of their approx. 3m.
in 2 weeks' time I won't have any sunshine any longer, only in 4 months' time again, and then everything begins all over again – it is so full of life here! also a little uncanny, my plants, the nature here and, in any case, the weather – fantastic.
yesterday, the transport company came to fetch my works for London – more space again!
and at the end of next week I'm flying to London, then Paris, then Basle, phew! and then here for a short time, then – phewphew! – to New York for a week, and I'm not getting any younger in the process. but naturally it's stimulating and fantastic. moreover, at the end of the week my N.Y. gallerist is coming here to Bregaglia – I'm all agog . . .

and apart from this, nothing new – am always pleased when you write!
warmest greetings,
miriam
and this little old dog hasn't been with us for a long time now. belonged to an old couple near Maloja, and whenever you were waiting for the bus it came to say "hello" and sniff around you.

4 October 2013

Dear Miriam,
We are celebrating the festival of the town's saint, San Francisco – is my favourite saint on account of the animals. There are festival crackers that explode on the church square, giving you a start and making you flinch every time. Now it will rain properly – actually, this is also my favourite time, although it also always puts the fear into you. Like you with the no-longer-any-sun-time. Many thanks for your wonderful letter. I am so pleased and I was also so excited because of all your deeds and doings. I am with you in my thoughts and I wish you all the very best. Be courageous and strong – that's something you've told me before. All fond wishes, a big hug, un abrazo grande y un beso from Panajachel.
I'll keep on my guard, Vivian
Good-looking dog, really shaggy. Sunflowers 3m high – incredible, a joke? All fond wishes

10 october 2013

dear Vivian,
now I'm off, hitting the art road: first to London, then Paris, then Basle, to collect the wonderful prize …and back to my Bregaglia, where it's snowing just at the moment!
all the best!
miriam
The Basler Kunstpreis, initiated by the Kunstkredit Basel-Stadt and worth CHF 25'000.-, is to be awarded for the first time. The first recipient of the prize is Miriam Cahn (b. 1949 in Basle), whose artistic output has met with international success and acclaim since the 1970s.
We warmly invite you and your friends to the Award Ceremony, which will be followed by a wine reception.
Monday, 21 October 2013, 18.30 hrs
Kunsthalle Basel, Steinenberg 7, 4051 Basle
Welcoming address: Dr Guy Morin, Regierungspräsident, Kanton Basel-Stadt
Laudatio: Adam Szymczyk, Director, Kunsthalle Basel
Response: the prize-winner, Miriam Cahn
Isang Yung, Sonatina for Two Violins (1983)
Mirka Scepanovic and Friedemann Treiber

27 October 2013

dear Vivian,
thanks for your weird photos! and here this one from N.Y. totally shattered by the journey …
kiss, miriam

8 November 2013

Dear Miriam,
I can almost say that I miss you – you're certain to be in the Museum now, to take a look at everything. I hope

that the opening was really brilliant, and your time in N.Y., and that you are satisfied with everything. The photo of the exhibition is excellent. Have a good time and a good flight back home to your stable, Vivian

10 november 2013

dear Vivian,

back in the stable and in my sombre and gloomy favourite month of November – so beautiful! grey, golden-yellow, brown and no tourists, only animals – sheep and nanny goats which roam freely and from time to time camp in the last sunshine on the little road to Soglio and get up with regal, stately slowness if one needs to pass through in one's car …

N.Y. was fabulous – great people, great opening night. and I walked around an incredible amount – I'm always through with the hanging at breakneck speed – and N.Y. has become an attractive city with interesting new buildings and cycle and pedestrian paths along the Hudson. with all my walking around and about, I managed only to get to the Hayward to look at the Robert Indiana exhibition – really fantastic.

the best thing of all was that my gallerist[163] took me into THE typical N.Y. restaurant – very local, no tourists, and I knew from literature and films that such restaurants do exist, but you can't get in "just like that": they're all called "Oyster and Lobster". and that's precisely what you get there, and in addition magnificent seafood, which is anyway my favourite meal. Dee also took me to one of the largest, "The Oyster and Lobster Bar" in the glorious Grand Central Station building, which was rescued by New York citizens – a gigantic restaurant with a bar, table seating and other options, where there is simply just seafood on the menu – a noisy, huge establishment, some 50 possibilities of eating oysters, and above all lobster, which you choose yourself at a lobster tank after a seeming 1 km walk through this grandiose restaurant. unbelievably good. and the man behind our bar was absolutely the zippy, nimble-fingered, slick-talking N.Y. barman in person! he had every sleight of hand down to perfection.

awesome!

so, here are a few photos

and the warmest greetings,

miriam

(Dee also took me around Harlem, where she has just started to live …)

and a very fine outgoing flight

19 November 2013

Dear Miriam

I hope things are fine with you. Just wanted to say that I don't have to see any photos of the exhibitions. I am satisfied already with the description of the rail-station restaurant. I was there myself many years ago and then outside it has arches where, if you whisper something from one end, another person can hear it at the other end of the arch. I send you all fond wishes, have a good week, enjoy being at home, Vivian

19 november 2013

dear Vivian,

of course, I'll send you some photos – thought I had done so already …

kiss, miriam

29 november 2013

dear Vivian,
well, what do you know! “our” Adam is to be the next director of the documenta!
just wanted to pass on the news to you quickly …
kiss, miriam

6 December 2013

Dear Miriam,
I hope everything is fine with you. Have you got snow outside your stable? Here everything is okay, a bit depressed, but otherwise ok. Just wanted to send you a kiss – till later, I’ll write more then, although there’s really nothing to write about, but I’m thinking of you, all fond wishes, Vivian

6 december 2013

dear Vivian,
I was recently in Basle to assemble the exhibition for Meyer Riegger in Karlsruhe – all “historic” works, also interesting for a change. and then I went to the offices of my sister-in-law, who is a lawyer, to settle and disentangle our inheritance. about 5 years ago, when my mother died, my brother and I inherited half shares of two houses and some collections, and apart from this a whole stack of valuable individual objects from my father’s huge collection. my brother and his wife organized everything and took the collections into their care, which I found absolutely fantastic – I would have been completely at a loss as to what to do – and we casually agreed that we would go shares when things were sold.
My brother, however, is just as much an out-and-out collector as my father, and consequently it breaks his heart to sell anything. and I hate possessing things that have nothing to do with me, like half houses etc.
so we have now agreed that over the next five years my brother will pay me for the two half houses and for the collection of Goethe first editions in toto. then everything is done and dusted, and he can do what he likes with the many other things, collections etc. everybody is satisfied with this, we have a very straightforward contract. and it takes a weight off my mind – when I’m old, I do not want to be dependent on my brother …
travelled home in blithe spirits, the Engadine was a blaze of colour, and Bregaglia all the more so. here are a few photos taken from the bus, which reproduce only a little of this radiance.
we have had some snow, now melted, the weather is mild.
kiss and all the best!
miriam

From: Miriam Cahn
To: Eva-Maria Schön
Subject: snow **8 february 2009**

dear Eva-Maria,
that was something! from last Wednesday on it has snowed continuously – at my house down here always wonderful in the morning, then very quickly becoming damp and subsiding, the sound a kind of squelching. the white landscape squelches. I was already thinking that I probably couldn't drive home by the usual route at all – Malojapass–Julierpass, since I knew from my time in Maloja that the way is blocked up there – the pass and then the road to Sils because of the danger of avalanches. and that's how it then turned out: on Saturday morning at least 70 cm of snow at my place down here total silence, no traffic at all, which up in Maloja means at east 1 m or more = totally blocked road, and probably closed too on Sunday. then on the radio: Maloja closed, Julier closed, the Rhaetian railway operating only as far as Bergün, 5 hrs waiting time at the car loading terminal etc. and so forth, and at that moment I knew: danger! come what may, leave now and take the low road, meaning in this case via Chiavenna-Lugano-Gotthard Tunnel etc. and so I travelled yesterday in pouring rain.
one drives along these escarpments by Lake Como, actually a wonderful area, Stendhal's landscape from "La chartreuse de Parme". but it was eerie, dripping palm trees, grey villages, everything very gloomy due to the mist and extreme rain, which I don't find so great on escarpments in the Alps. then the motorway in very impressive and gloomy evening light, snow from Lugano on, the Gotthard Tunnel, 17km long with oncoming traffic, luckily not much, but this tunnel too I take only when it is absolutely unavoidable, I have to keep pulling myself together so as not to imagine the Gotthard massif up above. then, relatively quickly, one gets to Basle. I got here in the evening after 6 hours, then in the late-night news heard that the Gotthard motorway was closed because a few giant rocks had fallen onto it. it is still closed. I had gone through a few hours earlier! YIKES! was absolutely knackered. the stupid thing was that I absolutely had to be here on Monday, and consequently had to assess hour by hour how I could get out of my valley. at first I thought: on Sunday things will be alright again. on seeing the heaps of snow, however, I knew: get out immediately. normally, of course, I'd have simply stayed in my valley until the situation had normalized. these nature situations, where it is entirely clear who rules, I find impressive and wonderful – after all, they force me to think about who I am and what a human being is up to here. and immediately such an "appointment" somehow becomes literally stupid. but I preferred the idea, had the Gotthard been closed, of staying over for a night in Bellinzona for example and if need be to travel on Sunday by train or something or just drop the whole thing, but not to be compelled to travel through a danger zone.
when there is too much snow, the Maloja, the road to Sils and the Julier are avalanche zones – on the Julier seven have come down at one and the same time, and it was pure chance that nobody was underneath. will never forget the deathly pale avalanche officer on TV. because it is the beginning of the holidays/a weekend and 10,000 people are travelling to the Engadine, there is a great danger that the pass is opened too soon. these trials of strength

between the logic of tourism and the perils of Nature!
that's how it was, once again hazardous…
kiss, miriam

From: Miriam Cahn
To: Evamaria Schön
Subject: snow + shame **2 december 2009**

dear Eva-Maria,
that was really something, once again! on Friday I went by train to Basle in very warm weather – everything snowless and attractively yellowish brown – to meet a collector with my Parisian gallerist – and we sold a picture, it was all pleasant and amusing (with Stampas it was so vile that I soon broke things off), and I then went for a meal with Jocelyn and discovered that he is highly educated – studied Philosophy… and then very early on Monday morning I had to be there for workers from the Basle City water authority, who had set up a huge drain-box in my entrance.
and then off to Bregaglia – so I thought. already in Zurich snow, around Chur snow, and the more the narrow-gauge railway push-pushed its way upwards, more and more snow, on arrival in St Moritz vast amounts of snow, got in the bus and then it was finally all over: Sils closed, Maloja closed, so back to St Moritz and stayed overnight with friends, waited the following day in this silly place etc. towards evening at last on with the postbus, a huge line of traffic from St Moritz to Sils, in Sils the bus waited on that side of the little bridge until these huge snow blowers had cleared the bridge and then, however, we were the very first for two days on this black, cleared road. in Maloja a huge line of traffic came from the other direction, but we sped all alone down the Maloja – the driver was thrilled and wanted to be on time in Chiavenna. so it had taken me two days to get from Basle to Stampa, and today I spent the entire day shovelling snow, digging free the path, the car, the completely frozen snow, like it is down here in contrast to the Engadine. it is more like chiselling out, almost sculptural – I enjoy it, just as I like such situations anyway.
what I like less, what I consider a crying shame is this vote on banning minarets in Switzerland: by our standards accepted by a devastatingly high margin. the 400,000 Muslims in CH must feel as if they're just dirt. logically the areas with many foreigners, like the City of Zurich, Basle City, Geneva etc. rejected the initiative + and where there are fewer "foreign strangers", as in all rural areas etc., it was accepted. it's a disgrace, it's racist. the praise coming from LePenfrance, Haideraustria, Leganorditaly + co. shows which way the wind is blowing, and "our" corresponding beasts can be seen and heard ceaselessly on TV – so horrid!
i also see a certain pictorial affinity (iconography?) with anti-semitism: the dark, hook-nosed men with long beards + garments, suppressing their women with veiled heads etc. in style as if freely copied from the "stürmer": the initiators' poster was precisely in that semiotic language – only whereas in the "stürmer's" day practically no women were depicted, only the "money-grubbing" Jew, today women, veiled, are used as icons. these appalling SVP men set themselves up as protectors of women's rights, seconded by, of all people, self-righteous feminists – not my feminism! I would straightaway box such a man's ears – he should kindly take a good look at himself in the mirror and at the reality of CH today, where, although the equality of man and woman is rooted in our

constitution, in reality women are paid at least 20% less for the same work, for example. ... but no: a ban on building minarets allegedly protects women – against what, against whom, in what way? and now, after this nauseating triumph, these same nasty pieces of work are preparing an initiative to ban the burqa, which, by the way, is the wrong word: the burqa – I believe – exists only in certain Afghani regions, so here too cliché and prejudice reign without any differentiation.
perhaps in the CH there are 20 women who veil their entire bodies, ok perhaps 30? And so the remaining 399,970 Muslims have to listen to how hostile to women their religion is.
because of our ballot result I have just listened to part of a discussion on the ZDF. the only Muslim there tried to explain things in a more differentiated way; all the men – of course – interrupted him shouting in a most ill-mannered way and not listening to what he had to say – and yet he was actually trying to explain the simple fact that the majority of Muslims – like the majority of Christians + Jews after all – are not orthodox at all, and that, therefore, this full body veiling thing concerns a tiny minority, who, however, are being portrayed by the media etc. in simplified terms as a threat to the west. this lack of differentiation is a disaster. this broad-brush, simplistic thinking nullifies any separation between church and state, an achievement that is at the very heart of our democracies and allows believers and atheists to live side by side and, within the various religions, very pious members to exist alongside all shades of belief up to non-believers. and it remains my opinion that wearing the veil and its interpretation are the Muslims' affair.
if women are beaten, suppressed and forcibly married, our legislation is quite sufficient: it needs only to be used.
if full body veiling is banned, then that also affects nuns, or what? basically, my general view is that the state stops 1 m away from my body, i.e.: it is nobody else's business what I am wearing and what I have on my head.
that holds without any reservations for all people living in my country, and the argument that we have to veil ourselves in Muslim countries doesn't hold water because in the normal case these are governmental forms in which there is a separation of church + state.
etc. etc. I could go on getting worked up about this ballot result for ever and a day, and when one is in the act of writing more things keep occurring to one's mind anyway. we, the CH, are now one of those little xenophobic European countries like Holland + Belgium + Austria, which the big European states are so fond of admiring – not a bit of it!
so, that's the way things are – I'll send you a few snow pictures and a big kiss, miriam

From: Eva-Maria Schön
To: Miriam Cahn
Subject: without snow **8 December 2009**

Dear Miriam,
On reading your mail I was really agitated – the snow sensationally immense, above all when seen from inside the train compartment, like a grey ghost – I'd love to paint like that!! Grey always gets me really agitated again and again, when it speaks of a wealth of colour that cannot, however, be seen – and then your rage

about the towers – I had to think about you all the time and was really wondering about your reaction – I think as you do but cannot rage like you at all – don't feel so close to the issue – although in a city like Berlin I certainly must be, day in day out. I think I don't have the staying power for severe rage – can't endure the anger – but I do feel it! Today I have been packing because tomorrow I'm off to Amsterdam by train, am looking forward to having plenty of time on the journey – then the arrival at the new station, immediately a whole lot of black people there with their children – i.e. the augmented Dutch, who, like the Swiss ...? It's the modernity that astonishes me, the architecture with no basement area – I'll ride Toine's old bicycle again, into the wind – here Hannah Hurzig[164] (Vienna) again made a guest appearance with her Discussions with Experts – fascinating, in the Hebbeltheater I sat on the old revolving stage and listened in audio to what they were discussing – somehow always a good thing! One snoops in. Earlier on the same evening at Karin Sander's,[165] who had invited 500 artists!!, one could hear – also via AUDIO – what they described in 2 minutes – I had the number 477 ... everybody wearing headphones – afterwards I was completely wacko – heard direct or on tape – but witty – Fritz Rahmann[166] was among the speakers, long since dead, but so alive with his voice – Tomas Schmid[167] too, a super text from him, 2 minutes, like a ghost. The most boring things were descriptions of the person's own works – there I immediately switched to the next – the Temporäre Kunsthalle full, the walls empty. In a week's time I'll be back from the Flatlands, don't let yourself get snowed in, incredible stuff ...
Your shivering Eva-Maria

From: Miriam Cahn
To: Stefan Kunz
Subject: work **7 november 2016**

Dear Stefan,[168]
now I have seen your fine museum – and in the exhibition I very much liked above all the Kirchner space and also his carpet designs.
I don't find collective thematic exhibitions interesting actually – here a work, there a work, all individual pieces from individual artists grouped together under one "theme"...
what I find absolutely frustrating is that you didn't ask me how my work is to be hung – I'm still alive! I can be asked! what is possible for the Schaulager Basel, my gallerist in Tokyo and all the others – to inquire via photo and mail if they are not certain how a work is to be hung – should be possible also for the Kunstmuseum Chur. but no: there my work is high-handedly installed with kitschy little paper clips and is thus falsified for the entire duration of the exhibition.
a big vote of thanks!
and many greetings,
miriam

From: Miriam Cahn
To: Madeleine Schuppli
Subject: podium discussion **14 march 2015**

dear Madeleine + Katrin,[169]
an interesting topic completely down the drain!
that podium[170] discussion was quite deplorable! which again confirms my view that what you put into something is what you get out of it. in this case the audience was influenced by your guided tour, Madeleine, which was quite certainly not intellectual or emotionally stimulating. and the topic, which was quite evidently unwelcome both with you yourselves and with the really poor podium moderator, was naturally not covered during this one hour. always just Cahn and her conceivable states of mind and sensitivities! how sad! and how misogynistic too, in the sense that women are in any case not taken “seriously”, no matter what they say! it’s no help that you women run the Kunsthaus – that makes it even worse, this supposedly gender-determined “soft” management style, because it quite simply conceals laziness.
and Galler, who hid away behind the language issue and behind the fact that it was, after all, “my” exhibition, actually told me face-to-face during the evening meal that Swiss Germans couldn’t express themselves so well in High German. Aha! that simply leaves nothing more to be said on this identity guff.
all of which ties in with the fact that my work had been given only half the ground floor, which the media, without any prompting on my part, considered at the very least disconcerting. and having to pass first through the Stäbli[171] room! although you, Madeleine, had originally planned a kind of first-stop information room on Stäbli-Cahn – was probably too much work for you, something like that. a very great number of people object to this meaning-less having-to-see-Stäbli while really wanting-to-see-Cahn. yes! there actually are people who don’t want to see Stäbli but only Cahn – as no doubt also vice versa. seems to me in this case like the sweets and chocolate by the checkout in Migros/Coop – kids nag and parents buy, just to have peace and quiet. and the food chains profit …
and while I’m about it, to claim that my exhibition was created in co-operation with the CCS is simply a lie: you took it over when everything was done and dusted, and then shared certain costs – that’s all, and very cushy it is, means far less work than one’s own, independent Cahn exhibition.
in my life to date, I have had a very large number of exhibitions and I distinguish in a rough and ready way between two experiences: the good ones, where I have received fitting co-operation, as e.g. in an excellent way with Jean-Paul + Olivier;[172] and the bad ones, the most extreme example of which was the Haus am Waldsee, Berlin, where the curator, for goodness-knows-what reason, was so frustrated that he never came out of his office during the entire setting-up stage. I am fully capable of carrying through a super exhibition totally without the curators.
and my exhibition in the Kunsthaus Aarau is now below the latter level.
greetings,
miriam

we were old we we were elderly old elderly and old and very old elderly. we were older than earlier old we were older we are. some of us are over 90 over 80 over 70. of those over 90 over 80 over 70 we are the youngest we are the young we are elderly old elderly yet yet the young among us us the over 90 over 80 over 70 years old ones old ones older ones. we were old we were elderly old and were in the third final segment of life we we looked back to the first two thirds of our lives we looked back look back see ourselves as children adolescents grown-ups grown-ups in their so-called prime becoming older as being we. we older than earlier we. we becoming old being we elderly being becoming old being were being becoming we were old we were elderly. when getting up we were old and after the training moving loosening shaking of our bones sinews muscles no longer old but older than earlier in the so-called prime years now not earlier now we were older old.
we were older old and had nothing more to lose old we were and impolite for reasons of shrinking time for reasons short in dealings with everyday matters short + precise for reasons of shrinking time the shrinking short-shift thinking + acting we. we had this freedom of impolitely short thinking shrinking time-shortening acting + thinking of work of working efficient time-foreshortening acting + doing. we were older + better in acting we. we were old + much better in doing we. we worked fundamentally better we worked foreshortened synoptically for reasons of time shortage yet yet for no reason passion for time because short still in the last third of our lives with luck maybe without luck – then end. we end. we were old + closer to the possibility of ending we old in the final third possible no time more with luck more so we all know. can be today tomorrow we old know nothing more we. we were elderly and old we. when working acting we knew that time was limited short or no more at all we were. we knew this. we were older in acting + doing + thinking + working we were yet yet we had always forever for our entire lifetimes been the same people we were the same children adolescents adults in their so-called prime elderly + old we were always the same people the forever identical the same people in feeling. feeling the same thing we were the same people the same thing we. we were older and always feeling the same thing. we feeling beings were older we were old and the same people we. inwardly ever ever eternally the same people ever we ever older the same people ever. older we i. i was old. old we.
we are old we look at the young younger young we see the young who watch us we are older and watch the young younger look at see watch us. we old see ourselves as younger young observing watching the older. we old saw ourselves as younger young back then earlier observing watching looking at the older old us we them us. we were older old they the young younger young watching us we older old watching them the young younger.

we were old. our bodies were decaying our bodies functioned worked or not our bodies bodily above all bodily we were old older the body above all we we watched our bodies our decaying bodies we looked at observed keenly our bodies were old older old our bodies in the final third of their existence we we were older old.

we observed ourselves we old older watched observed saw observed. we saw ourselves and the others we saw our bodies we observed kept an eye on the others watching our bodies we the old older kept an eye on ourselves we observed kept an eye on ourselves and our bodies. bodily we were we were old we were bodily more frail frail fragile even we were old the fragile watched us the not yet fragile but already decaying older not yet old we were older and not yet fragile feeble. we were only older yet yet as viewed by the old over 80 we were young full of vigour vigorous. as viewed by the young 20 30 years old we were old very old, as viewed keenly observed very close-to by those in their so-called prime only older. yet we were old this was our final third of life we were old.

we were old and elderly and old and old two thirds of our lives were delineated marked on our bodies two thirds of our lives we remembered bodily psychologically intellectually strata geological archaeological strata memory strata delineated marked embossed engraved hewn in our bodies and minds marked. old elderly meant marked. old elderly = MARKED old elderly meant embossed marked and when we were in landscapes we always saw the other landscapes that we knew. we were old and saw the altiplano in the engadine lake titicaca in lake sils the andes in bregaglia and in the alps the alaskan ranges. it was the same not the same but adding a stratum to the landscapes that we knew in strata so seeing was twofold threefold manifold stratified seeing, history's strata, marked. marked by our lives marked by our age we were old when seeing feeling thinking we older ones incessantly sedulously ceaselessly stratified what we had experienced had seen what had left its emboss heaped storeys on top of one another over one another into one another muddled among one another we were old. we had to wanted to ought to we were old we had to act quickly quickly act in the final third of our lives already almost panic quick panic when watching our decay quick just in time in the nick of time act quickly and economically. economical in our movements so as to act even quicker economically not routine-like but swiftly thought out thoughtfully economical. we wanted to show record open dig show draw as much as possible we were old little time any more panic at being forgotten panic quick just in time want to can do must do ought to. hence we have acquired an economical technique of clipping, clipping away every needless thing, cutting away everything needless, cutting it off economically. no needless movements, no needless friends, no needless objects none no loss of time nothing could incense us more enraged than loss of time nothing was worse.

we were old we elderly saw the engadine lake necklace and the altiplano and lake titicaca simultaneously we saw everything together and ourselves standing young by the shores of lake titicaca today standing elderly by the shores of lake sils elderly we no time to lose.

we were old our energy strength had to be harnessed focussed economically so as to deliberately have even more strength we old ones harnessed dense strength densify mark marked harnessed economically. proliferating inwards. young as young 30 years proliferating from inside outwards. elderly old proliferating inwards. strength economically used as engine of acting and doing.

we were old we no longer had to go up into the val da cam imagining the val da cam was enough it was enough for us to imagine ourselves hiking through the val da cam to imagine while we were rambling along the bed of the bregaglia valley from vico to stampa rambling in the valley bed we looked towards the mountain range and behind it forming part of it the never seen val da cam and saw ourselves rambling from vico to stampa hiking through the val da cam, in high alpine terrain. we could imagine the val da cam on account of hiking maps wonderful military maps obsessed with detail on account of these images we could imagine the val da cam, in detail as we could imagine ourselves could see ourselves hiking around the foot of the badile at the foot of this climbing wall which we could see from the bed of the valley from the viewpoint of the valley bed imagining hiking along the foot of the badile was enough we were old. we had these huge immense possibilities of imagination our brains our bodies were huge immense gigantic storehouses of already done acting doing seeing a huge stored world of images not only of the landscapes we had seen and hiked through but also of the images of possible landscapes of possibilities possible composite images of landscapes and movements of our elderly bodies possibilities of imaginings of possibilities activities such as climbing walking hiking which we did not have could not should not did not want to have we were old. the imagining was doing acting doing the imagining noting drawing painting carving sawing doing. the imagining image and movement. the imagining.

we were elderly, we still functioned, our bodies still functioned, trainable to perform everyday functions still. we were elderly we could still travel we wanted to travel did not want to withdraw to a definitive final house really old animal-like retreat into the final cave not yet we were still not really old but elderly still wanted the world we still were able to wanted to see do everything act we were still able to function even if travelling even if we travelled purposefully didn't travel just anywhere but purposefully + if possible travelled comfortably we were elderly + privileged could travel comfortably better more expensively privileged we were old + privileged in a privileged rich country privileged so privileged we were able to wanted to had to watch the world at all costs. our privilege was that we were able to had to travel observe commentate on the world it was our duty our privilege watchfully observing our surroundings near and far ceaselessly to observe describe record commentate on our privilege our work our binding rich privilege. we were old and did not want to have to withdraw ought not to were able not to did not want to withdraw into our final houses into the final and only house always living there with animals in the final building with cats for example we were elderly and still wanted to be cats ourselves we wanted to be cats not keep cats but be a cat live cat-like now here now there on the move be at home in caves houses but not definitively only 1 house cat-like at home yet yet here and there and elsewhere we wanted to be cats.

yet yet yet we were old our bodies were not cats no longer cats our bodies were human beings human being elderly human being man woman elderly human being old. we were able to be wanted to be a cat yet yet were no longer able to be a cat wanted to be a cat cat-like bodily feline supple swift soundless be a cat now here now there never be really there away and here there be a cat be a woman artist cat yet yet.
we were old elderly physically elderly almost old elderly older than before we were afterwards. and before + before and afterwards at the same time cat human being elderly at the same time elderly old physically a human being at the same time cat do something.
we were old elderly do something.
we were old our bodies elderly bodies could not be did not want to be cats our minds however however cat minds strayed around stray often went astray stray intellectually psychologically strayed strayed between animal human cat woman woman artist human straying straying hither and thither malentendu hither and thither erred errors erring the cat human here and there and nowhere having to be able to be wanting to be image of artist image of cat womanartistcat yet yet yet.

we were impatient we were elderly + old + impatient we. we did not want to were not able to lose any more time unforbearing me not we to lose time sitting in cinema auuditoriaa + theatre auuditoriaa + concert auuditoriaa watching mediocre theatre watching bad films watching mediocrity no time any more for the middling humdrum that which we had chosen for ourselves we ourselves not me as essential as what absolutely had to be viewed absolutely be there must ought we there all view experience see must ought absolutely be part of it must ought in being there we. not me. all simultaneously viewing something in a room being at one viewing one thing viewing something viewing a mediocre something viewing a cultural event now become mediocre at one viewing to the front. a unified bored moderately interested polite being part of it looking to the front. we you not me.

we were older and impatient so impatient unforbearing with our with our our our kind with our fellow human beings all around us unforbearing. we me not we. i got up and left unforbearingly impatiently when all my kind when we all I got up and left ran fled from cinemas theatres concerts exhibition openings fled me not we me if mediocrity if and when. all you we old ones we were elderly old sat there. not in flight you. we being part of it sitting standing in these cultural spaces not fleeing not fleeing leaving the mediocre we not me we you we just about still having to be ought to be part of it narrate it. the narrative of the event the communal the lubricant of being involved just about still definitive we elderly old still being there despite loss of time through culture consumption timepoisoning brainwearandtear you we not me sitting there standing there – me, in flight, running away, already after a few minutes of this cosy worship me, me off and away, the poisoning of my ageing brain, destruction by timepoisoning destruction by mediocrity have to ought to want to escape, me, fleeing, wildly.

in our habitats we settled down.

to our habitations we returned.

in our beds lay we lay lie and rest and lay we lying resting laagering lairing.

in and on our chairs we sit.

at our tables in our rooms our caves habitats habitations we house ourselves.

2009

13 january 2016

dear Elizabeth,
I am thinking about our future, about how we should act in the coming years. my main problem: you don't sell. 2015: nothing. 2014: absolutely nothing. with no question, I like you a lot, but I think that things aren't working out. I can't have a gallery which doesn't sell, as I live ONLY on sales of my works.
we have had several discussions on the "co-operation" between shows in institutions – or participation in shows in institutions – and sales. your tactic of making the prices higher so that collectors would take my work more seriously works very well for my other galleries but, strangely enough, obviously not for you, who had this idea. and until now there has not been much possibility of a show – group or even better solo – in an American institution.
to me, you seem very much interested in gallery politics, like inventing "independent" and so on. this is intelligent and interesting, but in our case it isn't working in the sense of selling and looking for other external cahn shows.
so, I am thinking of leaving you.
I will decide about this for good at the end of March after having installed and opened my show at the "kunsthalle zu Kiel" and having in mid-March moved the content of my whole studio from Basle to Bregaglia.
all my very best wishes to you!
miriam

18 January 2016

Dear Miriam,

19 january 2016

dear Elizabeth,

after having read your analyses more carefully – and I hope I have understood more or less even with my English – I felt I have to answer at least some points now and immediately, and I will try to do so one after the other as in your text and thoughts.

first and generally speaking: ok, you say I am not established on the US market. but I don't think the art market is very different from country to country. I think gallerists are different as individuals and therefore in their strategy. and I as their artist look at the results, which means mostly 2 things: shows in institutions and sales. and all prices on my lists of the works I give are the same for every gallery. and there is 50% of these prices for me in CHF Swiss francs. how and what the several gallerists do within the speciality of their countries in terms of taxes and so on – I really don't want to know and it is the business of my gallerists how they manage all these specific gallery problems and national specifics.

1. existing strategy:

my large paintings are large paintings (= a rose is a rose is a rose). in my work they have the same function as any piece – a small drawing, a room installation, a photo and so on. that's why I think it is wrong to focus a cahn strategy only and mostly on these large ones. sure, it's nice to have enough space to INTEGRATE the large paintings, if and when I install myself.

if you install, you are free to show only large paintings. but then you have to come and choose them in my studio. I won't make propositions by photos. and it's then YOUR comment on my work, not mine. this can be ok. I accept this, but I am not coming to the opening and so on. this even can work: it did with John Doblough in Norway, and I think my gallery in Tokyo, Kiyoshi Wako, works the same way. it works because these gallerists choose and exhibit works they somehow know they will sell and do sell. even room installations, such as Kiyoshi did. he did it this way: he bought the room installation and then owned it and then sold it. that's ok by me. as long as there are sales and I have money.

2. the current market

I think what you write about benchmarks is right. but your thoughts are too one-dimensional and too linear: you have the same and equal access to my works as all of my galleries – but you haven't made use of it, and that is a capital mistake of yours and of nobody else. last time you came to Bregaglia to look at my new works, I was quite astonished that you chose only 4 paintings. and you didn't even look at my drawings and series and photos. but then I thought: ok! she knows why. it's her style of running her gallery … and now you think it has to do with my EU galleries? no way. and this leads to the main point:

3. key concerns

no gallery has access to my work without coming and choosing in "reality".

I never give my inventory, I never make propositions by internet photos, unless they are very specific as I already wrote to you for Rubell: YOU have to decide to choose in my studio, it is you who makes the proposition to Rubell. this is the work of my gallerists, not my work. my gallerists have to choose; then they have the works and then they do as they think is ok and as they wish. this has to do with my doing all my business work more or less by myself – so it has to stay simple.

in the case of my inventory, you are completely wrong: my inventory is not only an inventory of new work: it tries to be everything and never-ending. and never all is really super-right … and it has/it is nearly 4,000 pieces. so there is no way of using it unspecifically – and I am, along with Kathrin, the only person who uses it as a whole (= deutungshoheit [sovereignty of interpretation]).

also very wrong: you compare yourself with my EU galleries and say they have much more than you: yes, they have much more, and

this is because M-R and Wolff choose directly in my studio in Basle and here in Bregaglia periodically, about, let's say, not more than 2 times a year, and periodically also give me works back. it's your decision if you also want to do so or not.
in my case, your linear thinking is very wrong: for me, each gallery has its style, its strategy, and it's not thinking-by-numbers like you do and it's not enforced working together. you say there are tensions between Wolff and M-R. of course there are tensions, so what! but until now they have managed to work together on certain things concerning cahn. it's their affair, not mine. if it works: very good. if not: also ok, as long as they do their work at managing shows in institutions and selling well.
what you call "global strategy" M-R and Wolff already do in part without the "full inventory from my studio", but with the works they have chosen and have at their gallery or somewhere else in their stocks – not my concern. these works are NOT in my studio. in my studio I work and there are the works which I use for shows. up to now I have managed more or less not to do shows with lendings – which very much simplifies the concepts of my shows. and for me very important: this simple thinking leads to the core of my shows, because I see every work in reality (= analogue whatever!).
what you call democratic is not so to my mind. you plan everything by numbering, controlling and so on. democracy for me is speaking together from case to case and finding a consensus/agreement that is ok for everybody and changes every time and according to content. in my eyes, Wolff and M-R are working together in this way, and therefore it works sometimes, and sometimes not – with or without tensions. it's NOT a cahn inventory problem ... if you want to work together with M-R and Wolff – do so, or don't do so, but not via me. the raising of the prices of my works made sense because I had had the same prices for about more than 15 years. it was high time. and that's all.
now for the sales: there is a German proverb "kleinvieh macht auch mist", which means "many a mickle makes a muckle".
I don't agree with you about focussing mostly, maybe only, on big collectors/collections and so on. it's ok to sell to them, but it's also ok to sell to "everyone" interested. this was always my strategy to sell "everything to everybody" – it's how I see my work: a small drawing has the same importance as a big painting or even as a room installation. and to have galleries which have somehow the same way of thinking and working.
there your analysis of my EU dealers is completely wrong: they also sell to big museums and super-big global collectors. and also to totally unknown persons ...
this is why I have lived for 40 years and more on my sales – BECAUSE of this large range of selling. now, what you call the "power market": you may be right, but I am quite sure the "power market" is possible only for the big ones, the big "power" galleries like Wirth and so on with a lot of money in the background and a big infrastructure.
ok! I hope I could make myself clear, even with my quite poor English.
and I am sending this also to Wolff and M-R – for the sake of transparency I think that they have to know what's going on and how you see them.
anyhow, it's I alone who decide what I do, but, as I wrote to you, I will

do so after my show and the move of my studio to Bregaglia.
all the very best!
miriam

26 January 2016

Dear Miriam,

28 january 2016

dear Elizabeth,

my impression on reading the first part of your mail was: ok, let's do so. but when I read the second part, where you try to describe my life and work before and after my accident, I thought: what? how does she dare?

I had this accident and about 1 year of convalescence. during this time, I did the show at the CCS, Paris – the curators had chosen here in Bregaglia (I still had the rack-thing on my head). and the same for the show at the Kunsthaus Aarau, where the curator had also chosen in Basle during this year of convalescence.

and: we spoke together last year during ART Basel, remember? so, if you were interested, you could have come and chosen in my studio in Basle, no problem – you didn't. that's your choice, not my problem.

mailing is only and simply written language. my impression concerning your use of my accident remains bad: in doing so, you lack style. also, how you wrongly described my "EU" gallerists in your last mail lacked style, and it was highly unnecessary to try to show me a non-existent competitive behaviour – do you think I am naïve?

also, I really have had enough of being told like a beginner how the market is: I know it more or less, I grew up in an art-dealer's house. at least I know enough to say, ok the US market is important, but the others are also, and everything is accidental, coincidence. therefore, to give these exact figures, as you do, is absurd.

and who says I am "absolutely out" of the US market if I don't stay with your gallery? simply nobody knows … and threatening me revolts me.

you maintain that doing a show in your new and very beautiful space would be finally and at last the opportunity to show big works. this never was a problem in your old gallery space (you had the biggest of my galleries). the main problem was that you wouldn't consider me using your whole space with my performative manner of installing my work – "free-style" as the curator of CCS, Jean-Paul, called it – and this is very much my mistake: not to have insisted in our second show on doing so and installing all by myself – there would have been plenty of space for it.

so it's not a question of space, but a question of attitude, and my feeling is that under these circumstances we won't come together. and therefore, I prefer not to stay in your gallery.

all the best.

miriam

From: Galerie Michael Werner[173]
To: Miriam Cahn **13 May 2014**
Dear Ms Cahn,

From: Miriam Cahn
To: Galerie Michael Werner
Subject: gals and guys **13 may 2014**
dear Michael Werner,
I am glad that you have seen my latest works from recent years. your inquiry pleases and yet surprises me at one and the same time: I am most pleased to welcome anyone to my studios in Basle and Bregaglia; your inquiry surprises me, however, because I see from your programme that you do not represent any woman artist at all. I will not be in Basle during the ART, but am represented by my two galleries, Jocelyn Wolff, Paris, and Meyer Riegger, Berlin/Karlsruhe. They will be showing some of my latest works.
If you wish, you can visit me in my studio in Bregaglia and so step out into what is for you new territory…
kind regards,
miriam cahn

From: Galerie Michael Werner
To: Miriam Cahn **26 May 2014**
Dear Ms Cahn,

From: Miriam Cahn
To: Galerie Michael Werner
Subject: gals and guys **26 may 2014**

dear Mr Werner,
many thanks for your answer – of course, I would be pleased to see you in the beautiful Bregaglia of Jolanta! whenever you wish and are able to come. I live here, after all, and can well understand what you write about "thinned out" planning …
warm regards,
miriam cahn

From: Miriam Cahn
An: Jochen Meyer
Subject: gals and guys **26 may 2014**

dear Jochen,
Michael Werner[173] has a sense of humour and a witty use of language, which says something for him – he will perhaps drop by your stand during the ART – and today Sandrine[174] is coming, to which I look forward!
warm regards, miriam

From: Miriam Cahn
To: wolff jocelyn, djerouet sandrine, meyer jochen, riegger thomas
Subject: Michael Werner the king **4 march 2015**

dear gallerists of mine,
Michael Werner was here in my stalla after having seen the show in Aarau. he likes very much the single paintings, but this guy thought my whole installation would be leading the public too much, a "big illusion" and my hanging all alone pretentious …eh???
of course, when I knew the old warhorse would be coming here, I knew also he wanted something from me – he wouldn't come without reason.
and, of course, he wanted to do a real shitty show at Knoells in Basel during ART. me and his Japanese girlfriend, who is "also a painter"!!!
discussing with him what art might be was like discussing this with a charming and intelligent man who is stuck in his history of post-1950 Germany. he + Baselitz + Lüpertz in Berlin … oh my! painters and their works have to be and think like these 2, in my eyes, very bad artists.
he was very surprised to find in me a person who is not so-called "naïve" like how he saw my work (which is wrong) – and talking so much, as you all know …
he hasn't changed either since the 1970s, when he very loudly and in public found the whole performances, videos and so on total shit.
after 2 hours, even he realized I was really not interested, but of

course King Werner asked whether he could buy some works here. I told him in a friendly way to go to you and buy there, and anyhow it would be the same prices. then he was sincerely astonished! and he went away, having seen nothing and not having got what he thought he could have. but, as he is a charming old chap, laughing, was interesting!
all the best + amitiés,
miriam

GRANDMOTHER
28.1.1897 born in Paris, IVème
–1910 taught by mother, who has a teacher's licence. does lace-work at home. father, originally a sailor, works as accounting clerk; in evenings, he draws and paints watercolours.
1910 école communale, top of class
c. 1913 on advice of drawing teacher sits entrance exam for école des arts décoratifs. Best of 400. her parents forbid her to attend the school for moral reasons and place her in the same firm as her father as a shorthand typist.
1914–18 world war. soldiers camp in the firm's yard during retreat and have to move on, their washed shirts still wet.
1919 meets her husband, a Swiss engineer.
1920 marriage. stops work.
1921 birth of daughter
1922 birth of a son
1925 birth of a daughter
1939–45 world war. when the Germans invade France, the government flees. panic in Paris. sends her children on a "children's train" to southern France and flees on last "Swiss train" to Switzerland. for two months no news of the children. later they join her.
1946 return to Paris, to old apartment.
1970 death of husband.
1971 winds up apartment, comes to Basle, and takes an apartment close to one of her daughters.
1976 suicide of granddaughter.

MOTHER
3.7.1921 born in Vanves, Paris
–1936 primary school. the new laws of the Popular Front allow her free grammar school education, cheap music lessons. her mother teaches her drawing, guiding her hand.
1938 passes Conservatoire piano exam brilliantly. Parents suggest she does Matura first.
1939 world war. Matura. Intends to become German teacher, to be able later to attend the école des arts décoratifs. Topic of entrance exam for Sorbonne: the literature of the Weimar Republic and Mein Kampf.
1940 German invasion of France. panic in Paris. exam postponed. mother cuts off the two sisters' long hair and puts them on the "children's train" to southern France. shock at separation. bombing of refugee trains. they take three days. she takes care of her sister and is made female leader for young boys in children's camp. exam in Toulouse. later she is taken to an uncle in the "free zone". teacher in a private school, where she teaches above all refugee children. first offer of marriage rejected.
1941 uncle sends her to Switzerland. her parents get her a post as secretary. brother goes to university. with her first wages she buys skis. she takes evening courses at the commercial school and comes to know an artist. on sight of his erect penis she faints.
1943 steady boyfriend. marriage plans. changes job, entering an art trading firm. love relationship with her boss and later husband.
1945 end of war. stay in England.
1946 beginning of studies at the école des beaux-arts in Paris. lives with her parents.
return to basle and to same job. own apartment. evening courses at the commercial school.
1949 marriage. birth of a daughter.

–1956 breaks off evening classes. wish for larger family. infertility. operation on uterus tilt. several miscarriages. takes piano lessons. teacher recommends her to turn professional.
1956 birth of a daughter. husband goes to America for two months. move to a large house. husband increasingly on business trips. miscarriages.
1961 birth of a son. operation for a myoma. partial removal of uterus.
1963 operation for prolapsed bladder. beginning of depressions.
1964 journey of husband to America. girlfriend. severe depressions. referral to a clinic on account of "exhaustion depression". son put in a home. sleeping cure, electric shocks. she becomes friendly with a nurse, who advises psychotherapy and prevent further electric shocks. back at home, her husband takes her with him to America. she often looks down from skyscrapers. decision to become sculptress. at home, refusal and collapse. referral to clinic. anti-depressants. she becomes fat.
– c. 1966 treated in clinic.
1966–68 a woman doctor encourages her to undergo psychoanalysis. slow return home, first for hours, then days, then longer. son returns home.
1968–75 difficulties with her daughters: the elder one beats her, the younger leaves home, takes drugs. on her sister's advice, she does an art course. she makes the smallest room in the house into her studio. discovery of orgasm, ability to orgasm. end of analysis, further psychoanalytical counselling. The painting course is made up of women, friendships with women develop.
1976 suicide of daughter.

DAUGHTER
21.7.1949 born in basle. father numismatist/art dealer. mother housewife.
–1968 primary school, diverse schools, difficulties at school. Her mother teaches her drawing, by illustrating concurrently illustrating the stories told.
1968–73 leaves home. Kunstgewerbeschule basle, special class in graphic arts, boyfriend, journey to South America.
1973–1976 work as drawing teacher and academic draughtswoman. separation from boyfriend, group therapy, beginning of activities in women's movement.
1976 suicide of sister.
1977 journey to South America, delegate of women's movement at peace congress in Warsaw, dreams of falls/crashes, involvement in the kulturinitiative, a series of events organised by figures from cultural life in the Basle Holzhalle. Exhibition in STAMPA, basle.
1978/79 City of Basle artist's studio in Paris
1979 involvement in feminist art international in Holland. Group exhibition in an old storehouse in Paris. affaire d'hommes? affaire de femmes, group exhibition in Goethe-Institut, Paris.
1980 mein frausein ist mein öffentlicher teil, drawings on the Nordtangente in Basle (part of motorway). Sirenengesang, studio exchange project with a friend, basle-düsseldorf, art 80, room at STAMPA, exhibition at STAMPA.
1981 6 künstler aus basel, Kunsthalle Basel.
1982 WACH RAUM 1, konrad fischer, Zurich. WACH RAUM 2, documenta kassel (taken down before opening). WACH RAUM 3, Kunsthaus Zürich.
1983 szene schweiz, Kunstverein Köln. das klassische lieben, Kunsthalle Basel. STAMPA, Basle.
1984 förderpreis baden-württemberg. re-opening of the museum of modern art, New York. DAS WILDE LIEBEN, musée la chaux-de-fonds: STAMPA, basle. Frauen, frauenräume, état de guerre, DAS WILDE LIEBEN, venice biennale. DAS WILDE LIEBEN, serpentine gallery, London.

1985 daad berlin. strategische orte, Kunsthalle Baden-Baden and Museum Bonn; elisabeth kaufmann, Zurich; schelma, Düsseldorf; STAMPA, basle.
1986 biennale Sydney, Australia. strategische orte, daad-galerie, Berlin; STAMPA, basle.
1987 states of the art, England. stiller nachmittag, Kunsthaus Zürich. LESEN IN STAUB – strategische orte, schelma, Düsseldorf; STAMPA, basle.
1988 award of Hypobank, Geneva. the impossible self, Canada. Elisabeth kaufmann, Zurich. van de loo, Munich. LESEN IN STAUB, gemeentemuseum, Arnhem, Holland; haus am waldsee, Berlin. LESEN IN STAUB – weibliche monate, Kunstverein Hannover.
1989 das verhältnis der geschlechter, Bonner Kunstverein.
1990 verwandschaften, STAMPA, Basle + art frankfurt; cornerhouse, Manchester. am anfang war das bild, van de loo/villa stuck, Munich. zur sache selbst, künstlerinnen des 20. Jahrhunderts, museum wiesbaden. vollbild aids, Switzerland. idea and joint organization of: wissenschaft, künste und alles andere, symposium in Basle with women invited from around the world.
1991 verwandschaften, galerie espace, Amsterdam. a swiss dialectic, the renaissance society, Chicago.
1992 STAMPA, Basle. Szenenwechsel, MMK, Frankfurt am Main.
1993 sarajevo, STAMPA, Basle; raum für aktuelle kunst, Vienna. über leben, Kunstverein Bonn.
1994 STAMPA, Basle. centre contemporain, Geneva. beyond the pale, Dublin.
1995 körperlich, room, MMK, Frankfurt am Main; art 95, STAMPA, Basle. WAS MICH ANSCHAUT (körperlich), obala art centar, Sarajevo.

dear mum,
I am sending you here a digital recording of the letter that you drew/wrote for me after our telephone row in march – a quarrel like the renowned straw that broke the camel's back.
I had to think a lot about this letter in Maloja. when recalling it I always had the impression that there is something essential concealed in it. now that I'm back here I have studied it again with distanced and fresh eyes and have seen that it contains a completely unachievable piece of information. for this reason, I have now photographed it with my pixel camera, so that you too can consider it at a distance and in peace and quiet.
your letter contained two "folders": the one with the circle, the other with the square. in the circle part you are lividly angry: quite rightly, you feel unfairly treated, brutally trampled over etc. the drastic quality of your drawings reveals a red alert.
in the square part, you draw a door that is at first closed; then a happy mum opens the door, and your house is always open for your daughter.
sent in one and the same letter, the two folders say to me: my daughter has treated me unfairly and brutally, but since she is my daughter, my house is always open for her, so that she can again treat me unfairly and brutally.
that is – well, goodness knows what it is – but it is something to be avoided at all costs.
the main misunderstanding on your part is this house that is always open. I can't stand it when somebody does not explicitly invite me into his or her house – into my house too come only guests whom I have invited. over the last years in the Rütimeyerstrasse, I had a key on account of your age. but I always rang the bell and waited and only then "invaded" – which is what it is for me: I'm coming from outside and would like to give the people inside time to get adjusted to the coming visit. even family members I do not want to see in a situation that is not intended for visitors (when on the loo, when picking their nose or whatever else, when naked etc.) – such things are far too intimate for me: for decades now I haven't had anything to do with either of your day-to-day lives, or now with your daily life, and I won't have anything to do with it in future. please understand this as a form of behaviour, and not as a withdrawal of love. please understand me at last as a reticent person. understand me as a person who has no interest in "family as a place where one can let oneself go and let it all hang out", and as a person who has little interest in family anyway.
so when sometimes, talking to you, I have "unfair" fits of rage, it means that you have invaded my house without my inviting you. and since I can only react to this with rage – just as you only can in other matters – I would like, logically, to avoid these moments as far as possible. above all, however, I am absolutely terrified by being asked as in your two "folders" to repeat an ugly and nasty form of communication – it is like in Bruce Naumann's work "feed me – beat me"…
I love you, but I have difficulties in dealing with you, and, if you're honest with yourself, you're not so good at dealing with me. but we have one super asset: pictures, art, working at art, a form of communication which not many mothers have with their daughters. let us act in a ladylike way – like the ladies and divas we are! in

Maloja, I've hung all your things on the wall. every time I see them I think of you and am happy: I can see you in your lovely work-room, calmly working away, and that consoles me. why shouldn't we continue this pictorial path here? it makes no difference whether I am here or in Maloja or anywhere else: my life-style is in any case one of absence, in the positive sense.
miriam

From: Miriam Cahn
To: Jean-David Cahn AG
Subject: we children **23 november 2005**

dear david,[175]
I'm very reluctant to phone you at your business premises on family matters… how about e-mailing?
here we go: I wanted to give you a summary of my personal impressions concerning Mum. even if I know that patience is called for and that she really is making progress and I too think that everything must be done to get her back into her apartment – I am not quite as optimistic as I was to the doctor and have to be in this reluctantly accepted Felix-Platter-Spital situation. for this, there is a simple reason. already during the winter/spring I had the feeling that she doesn't really want to go on any longer (and this has nothing at all to do with her usual depressive talk). she has gradually changed her behaviour towards me, to something more tender, with relapses of course, but nevertheless. on the phone and elsewhere she called me mon bébé, as if her life were gradually coming full circle, in a natural and lovely way. when we were together – certainly not more than once a week – she was very kind to me and really spoke in a very level-headed, down-to-earth way, which I always describe as lucid. she knows the score regarding herself. what was new for me was the forgiving manner in which she talked about this family, but also about herself, and still does so. in springtime, I had the very strong feeling of a natural leave-taking. and I must confess to you that when travelling over the Julier at the beginning of October I wished intensely that she could die. I would have granted it to her. she is old. but of course, I now accept that things are as they are, just as I always – even if it doesn't seem like it – accept everything just as it comes. precisely, however, because I am rather passive towards what is generally called life, because I observe passively what goes on, I am also less optimistic regarding Mum. "optimistic" is the wrong word. rather that, in my way, I have already taken leave of her, just as she probably also has of me. one small sign: when I told her that I was going to Maloja at the end of the week, she was glad. yes, she was glad! up to now it was always more a matter of wailing and gnashing of teeth, and nastiness. now, in her really not so super situation, in this stupid, execrable café, which at least meant not lying in that horrid 4-bed room, she was glad, in a quite natural, dispassionate way.
I also had such experiences with Dad, also approx. 1 year before his death there were sort of tender farewell gestures, farewell situations, farewell rituals that said to me actually that his death was probably no longer so far off, in line with nature and the end of being.
naturally, it is very hard to die nowadays. nobody wants to die. everybody, contorted by pain, will say: I want to live. if one has such agony, one wants above all for it to go away. I profoundly think that it is as simple as that. in pain, one can only think one thing: away with the pain. and today, after all, doctors can operate in such a way that even old people survive. I think it's terrible that gradually everything is becoming possible. I find it a harrowing prospect that in 20 years, when I am old, a good deal more will be possible. by this I don't want to say that you acted "wrongly", but that you acted as you do. I mean that seriously: the person who is there takes the decision. probably, however, we have totally different views of what

is called life. if by any chance I am "there", I will act more reticently. the example of your friend who operates on his own mother and she then lives to be over 100, is for me really and quite existentially an abomination. not only that I consider it fundamentally wrong, lacking in respect and megalomaniacal for doctors to treat their own relatives – it is this crazed belief in doability that repulses me – and, in a wholly egoistic way, the prospect of never emerging from the status of daughter or child, even when I myself am old.
so, just as I accept your action, I would like you to take my thinking and action seriously: I am in favour of us carrying through this ploy with chrischona[176] and then perhaps the apartment – but please not à tout prix. please don't see it as a failure if it doesn't work out, because she does make strange confusions and have strange absences, which, if they do not go away will be a problem and were in part problematic even before her operation. David, man! it is not a failure if our mother can no longer live independently – neither a failure of our mother, nor of her children. it is not even a failure of the state. it is simply an end of life as it takes shape in our society. and sure, it's beastly, terrible, unpleasantly revealing.
actually, I don't know whether and what you think about life and death. why, for example, did you not react when I sent you my advance healthcare directive? after all, that's something existential. I listed you as my no. 1 contact person …don't you want that? can't you do that? don't you want to think about such things? (and please don't come along with the I-haven't-got-time-right-now sledgehammer …).
we could start up a kind of really slow brother-sister dialogue by e-mail. I think that might perhaps be the right form for us, perhaps better than telephone, which in your case I think is good only for a swift and necessary exchange of information – for that, sure. how about it?
in Maloja, I have my mobile on only when I am away for several days or in Bregaglia, where the Maloja telephone is re-directed to the mobile. otherwise please on the answering machine – I'll call back. and, sure, if there's an emergency I'll come down, but only in a real emergency.
so, KISS, miriam

From: Jean-David Cahn AG
To: Miriam Cahn
Subject: we children **24 November 2005**

dear Miriam,
Thanks for your mail. Lengthy! I haven't forgotten your advance healthcare directive. It moved me a lot. It is only that recently there has been a great deal of illness and death happening around me. I therefore noted your directive and filed it in my already jam-packed archive i.e. brain under "matters pending". Seriously, I thank you for your trust.
I am still a novice with mails because I regularly struggle with my Mac.
Concerning Mum: I share your observations in part. But in the hospital on Monday with embolism but without morphine she said to me in all lucidity that it was too early for her to go. I acted accordingly, in full awareness that it will bring enormous complications and difficult situations in its wake. At the moment, my concern is that

she should become healthy enough to live in an apartment. If that is no longer possible, then, okay, in a care situation. I am in favour of more patience and am firmly convinced that she will make it, although very slowly.
Today, Danica brought the laundry – I hope, the right stuff. I am now off to visit Mum.
Till later, by mail
Kiss,
David

---

dear David,
just for a start I'm sending you the name + address for tai chi:
Kathrin Rutishauser
tai chi chuan info@taichi-*** tel.: 061 ***
Kathrin was at the same table as you during the meal after my exhibition opening in Aarau …
she is a master pupil, which means that she continually takes further training in tai chi from a master by the name of Chu. as I said, this a bit like learning an instrument as a lay person – good music teachers, after all, also go regularly for further training to "masters", and we lay persons can learn from them and the system works – but, as with e.g. the violin, only if one practises regularly and really abandons any intention of ever being "masterly". "regularly" can also be not so much. every day I do about ½ hr; at the beginning I did that about only every other day, and that worked well. what is much more important is to find "one's own" time. mine is in the morning after waking up – late, as you know – other people do it at midday or in the evenings before going to bed, or at a different time, or more intensively 2× per week. it sorts itself out and establishes itself and is totally different from one individual to the next.
I hesitated a little before sending you this info because after our conversation I had a bit the impression that you are somehow "at the limit" and "transparently" fragile and that in a panic reaction you now simply want to do "the best" "as much as possible". understandable, but again also stressful, because then one "never manages" it …
and when walking home I had a really bad feeling when I thought of your account of the marriage counselling: 3 hours! without the therapist, whom you probably overestimate, recognizing that the longer it lasted the worse you felt? but then with her so-called magic-working ability was able to give you renewed energy? and so made you even more dependent on her and on the "marriage counselling" situation she had created?
that makes me absolutely uneasy and above all – I have, after all, some experience on the therapy front – because in this case I think that an agonizing and agonized process is going on here, a process which you yourself cannot halt – e.g. by leaving because you find it unbearable – or any other reaction, whatever, which concerns only you and your nature/existence as a human being.
and in that regard, I consider this woman unprofessional, indeed dangerous for you – because, putting it cheekily, you always find all women you have to deal with so mega-fantastic that you can't put up any resistance, especially when they employ the so-called feminine weapons ("witch", weeping, the "I'm so hurt because you thenandthere suchandsuch" line etc.). it would be your admission that they are perhaps not quite so fantastic, and that you are to

blame for everything, to whatever extent. of course, every psychotherapy has its super-agonizing phases, can last weeks, months. one hates the therapist for putting one into this situation – but that is clearly something different from what you described. and what I consider absolutely the pits in your account (it is your account) are these 3 hours (unless you had arranged it like that beforehand). what I always found strange/incomprehensible and, depending on the situation, an aggravation of my hatred/rage, and yet at the same time always a good thing was that, in whatever the situation during the therapy at some point the therapist said, "okay, now the therapy hour is over, we'll meet again next week." there's a coolness about it, but it dismisses one – out of a very special, very intimate situation back into everyday life – and so shows the "cool empathy" which is the mark of really meaningful professionalism. this cool empathy really does help and I can sense this attitude in your accounts of your therapist.
oh dear! and I hope so much that you'll be finally moving out – after all, it's a nasty situation and Johanna is 200% right! it's simply nonsense for 2 people to have to get up at 5 a.m. because of the one child! really! one can take turns, rotate – and then the still very little 8-year-old girl does not, first thing – before going to school! – have the dubious and in the long-term harmful pleasure of squabbling parents! but has either the father OR the mother first thing in the morning – she loves you both, after all, but you, out of sheer thinking-of-your-own-misery (which perhaps isn't misery at all but a life opportunity), are in the process of not doing the simplest thing, namely listening to Johanna and acting accordingly. of course, for you she's the most intelligent and super kid in the world. but she is also still very little and totally exposed to you.
well, now I've got it all off my chest …
kiss,
miriam

dear David,
now April has come, and I have again received simply no information from you concerning the payment of my inheritance.
and you know what? I am simply sick and tired of always having to ask you to at least inform me about what is going on. do you treat your customers like this, actually? probably not, but when it comes to family one can do what one likes.
you are living like a lord – that's your business. but as long as you have not paid out my full share, you are also living in luxury at my expense.
we both know that my inheritance demands are extremely modest. that is how I wanted it, so that the payment takes place relatively quickly, and alas also because over the years I have come to recognize that you would never voluntarily sell our joint collections and objects, despite my offer that you could have 2/3 of the price to cover the work involved.
I don't want to hear now: oh, deary me! the banks! yikes! just at the moment is not a favourable time to sell e.g. the Feininger.[177] etc. it's always the others or the circumstances that ostensibly justify your failure to act. but, you know, and just in case you have still not grasped this fact: I am an extremely successful artist, in other words, a businesswoman, and hence I find these excuses extraordinarily laughable.
and so from now on I wish to be treated in the matter of inheritance

payment on the same footing as a customer, and not as a sister, whom you, "poor David" – in a highly charming manner, of course – can twist around your little finger.
My proposal: by the end of April you set up a legally binding plan of payment, i.e. here, just as an example:
2016 CHF 150'000.-
2017 CHF 150'000.-
2018 CHF the remainder
and, in addition, the payment modalities, i.e. for example: 2016 in 50'000.- instalments, 1st instalment June, 2nd instalment September, 3rd instalment November.
you can arrange the manner of payment as you see fit. these are only examples. but how you arrange it must simply be stated in legally binding terms in this new contract, even if you decide to pay me everything this year.
but no two ways about it: this contract must be here, on my desk, by the end of April.
I am therefore sending a copy also to Antje on the assumption that she will make a legally binding contract – no matter how your relationship is at the moment. what I, for sure, will no longer do is to "ask" you.
I have a specialist lawyer for my own inheritance issues, but would like if at all possible to avoid involving him.
that, however, now depends on you.
warm greetings,
miriam

From: Anette Hüsch
To: Miriam Cahn **25 February 2016**
Dear Miriam,
In Bregaglia, we talked about the naked and nakedness – unfortunately, without making a recording. Could you give me again a few key points?
All the bodies you show are naked – even the veiled figures tend to be denuded, left without any protection through the semi-transparency of the materials that cover them.
Naked figures in all age groups – could you say something on the topic of veiling and denuding?
What is the meaning of a taboo (for example, the ageing female body) or precisely the question of the culturally connotated clothing, which you after all address – again through signs and hints?
Warm greetings,
Anette[178]

From: Miriam Cahn
To: Anette Hüsch **25 february 2016**
Dear Anette,
I'll try to give you an answer – but you have already described my "naked/denuded" pretty well, with the exception of the taboo.
I consider the portrayal of the body – no matter whether man or woman – to be a central point in working on the contemporary world, or in capturing the now, the present moment. and in the case of the female body, all types of interesting things are shown, veiled or not, from the classical ideal up to today's representation in the pictorial media – consider selfies.
I try to capture this when drawing/painting. my body is then the instrument, the tool of working. this is very visible in the room "DAS WILDE LIEBEN" ["WILD LOVING"]: the size of the – in this case – only female figures is identical to my own or that of others, and the room is very clearly eye-to-eye = at eye-level.
in these intensive + very swiftly drawn body-works of the 80s I could not possibly add clothing – it didn't interest me at the time either. and it should not be forgotten that at the same time as these "primitive creatures", these sexual or pornographic representations of love-making, thousands of drawings were created that are all always called "das klassische lieben" ["classic loving"]. this was also a redaction of the feminist claim that women are repulsed by pornography – oh, yes, the man as a visually-oriented being! which, however, is nonsense. what interested me was that part of pornography that makes people horny – namely, the classic portrayal of the body with the sexual equipment also clearly visible and the well-trained, muscular body, clearly drawn in classical style, but without the gaze, without specifically directed eyes ... or something like that ...
in contrast to my "wild" primitive creatures (as I call them today), where the sexual parts are unequivocally drawn (mostly), but precisely not in classical style, but "primitively", while the gaze, the looking, becomes central.
when people, for whatever reason, look at us, we therefore look back. in contrast to the famous "Le milieu du monde" / "L'origine du monde".
ok. and in my painting today, this entire naked-veiled-covered issue

is more complex. when it comes to taboo, you are on the wrong track: it is not a question of old/not old, but rather of what does one look at? why is so much fuss being made nowadays about the veiling of "Muslims", why so much fuss made anyway about women and the female body? or about the relationship between the sexes (see Cologne). what I find gripping here above all is the question how far I can go in my portrayals, how far I can go (see above) in terms of classical/primitive/realistic etc., without going beyond my own shame threshold. here precisely, the large pictures with the tiny figures are interesting because here I have often operated a self-censorship in the form of a black bar painted over the actions of the figures. what is taking place underneath is left for the beholder to imagine.
and today the "veiled" figures have this function – that the perverse thing about this entire burqa-ban thing is precisely that: the imagining of what could be under these veils and the current assertion that "our freedom" has to do with the fact that we are allowed to show as much as possible of our bodies. in the process, no consideration is given to what women actually want, whether the woman as individual chooses, for religious or other reasons, to be veiled, or whether the woman wishes to dress in today's "western" (= so-called free) manner.
all of this is the code of contemporary society – see Foucault.
wearing as little clothing as possible is not freer than going veiled: it is only the interpretation that turns it into a custom – and it is precisely here that I find it super-interesting to work, because here again the questions arise as to realism, naturalism, the primitive etc. and as to myself as the instrument of working. some of my presentations actually do get people horny – why not? – I can see this from their purchasing behaviour.
taboos are always something sexual: can I show masturbating women? men? If "le milieu du monde"/"l'origine du monde" shows a head with eyes looking back at the beholder, what happens then? can I show that committing torture or inflicting beating turn the torturer on – as a good few soldiers report from war or torture situations? the best film here and one that at the same time was thereby unbearable was Pasolini's SALO – a prototype model for me. "folterbilder im mai" ["torture pictures in may"] is, among others things, about this issue of torturing, of beholding – hence, at the end, the blind and their imagination.
I see that it is very hard to answer this question of nakedness and denudement.
so, warm regards from Bregaglia – where, not so long ago, there were women who went veiled …
miriam

From: Miriam Cahn
To: Anette Hüsch
Subject: to Geneva **16 september 2016**

dear Anette,
yes, I wasn't so thrilled either at that invitation – nobody had asked me whether I considered it suitable; I just found the invitation in my letter-box. and then I thought: at least the journey there should be attractive! so I took the palm express from Stampa to Lugano, then on to Locarno into a fine hotel, as you can see. the following day on the narrow-gauge railway through the Centovalli to Domodossola, then the Rhône valley and Geneva – magnificent! the narrow-

gauge train wheezes at approx. 20 kph up the steepest valley – at first it is tropical (I felt I was in Peru in the valley leading to Macchu Picchu), then alpine, then a high plateau, and then down again into Italy. from time to time, the train emitted an asthmatic pffrouoooooouugh, other than this there was nothing else, just vertical walls totally covered in forest.
and in Geneva:[179] what a mess they'd made of the installation! I'd feared as much. the series of drawings were all without exception hung with practically no distance between sheets, i.e. approx. 6 mm irrespective of size and material and naturellement a super straight line above or below – somebody had decided on this sitting at his desk ... so, despite my frustration, changed everything, it then looked sensible to a degree, even if it was simply Blondeau's choice without any sense, just "attractive".
the pictures in the windowless basement room also with no real sense, just attractive and museum-like. really bad, however, was that the dinner then took place in the midst of the pictures, seemingly because those invited then look at the pictures in a "different" way ... and iartist and artdealersdaughtersister had to sit next to this conceited and for me thoroughly dislikeable Blondeau and listen to his well-worn acts of art-dealer's heroism – it was terrible, all of it, and what I said to him went in one ear and out the other. at the same table, elderly female collectors, most of them with face-lifts ...
PHEW!
through a stroke of good luck Sandrine and Jochen were also there and the three of us all had to go and recover – in the super summer temperatures – over a sundowner in a street-corner bar. and because this was the total clichériddenartdealerbehaviour from beginning to end, Blondeau is bound to be a good salesman – this is money I have really earned! yuck, ugh! was all upside down and inside out ...
so much for that. scarcely am I back in my stable than it's all forgotten and I'll try to avoid such things in future.
and apart from all that I've today again sent you something from Chiesa's our valley butcher: an air-seasoned hunk of venison – really fine. at present it's the hunting season and I'm eating chamois in all variations – cutlet, fillet etc. ah, fantastically good! in october comes ibex.
kiss,
miriam

1 september 2016
dear Bogo,[180]
this is my next escapade – although without any doing of mine. M. Blondeau made his selection here in Bregaglia and at Meyer Riegger and also installed it himself, which naturellement is something completely different. in such cases, my own works become alien to me… so I am going to the classic dinner with important people and then off back to Bregaglia, and so won't be standing around at the opening.
in old age I am becoming more radical! is it like that for you too sometimes? one just no longer has so much life-time to squander on stupid stuff, I reckon.
and how are things with you? and with Ingrid and co.?
Eva-Maria and Hannes are now grandparents three times over…
kiss!
miriam

27 September 2016
Dear Miriam,
There's been a bit of a delay in my replying because only now can I type with my hands.
We had a relatively dangerous accident driving my ATV on a country road, but had an incredible amount of luck in the process.
In a collision with a car we were hurled about 6m through the air and luckily landed on an embankment where bushes and grass cushioned the impact somewhat. No tree, no stones, no lamp-post, otherwise things would have looked nasty.
Ingrid had, and still has, severe contusions to her legs, and is still not allowed to walk. With me, it's massive contusions to the chest and a shattered right brachial joint. After an operation, I now have a metal plate that holds everything together.
But things are slowly on the mend and because being frail and infirm is gradually getting on our nerves we are already making jokes about ourselves.
So much for the medical bulletin.
In the meantime, I've already had to set up medium-sized works in the museum and it went okay to some extent – I had nice people helping me.
But I find it difficult to just stand to one side and do nothing. I guess I'm a person who prefers to do everything alone, and always has the megalomaniac idea that he can manage things best himself (which, however, is true in most cases). Since July, I have ceased working at the University of Art, which pleases me greatly – so, viewed from that perspective, the hell-bent ride with the ATV, with which I have hitherto really enjoyed spinning through woodlands, across meadows and down country lanes, was a dramatic start into a new stretch of life. From now on, a bit more careful.
Apart from this I regard myself as a lucky person, am amazed by the crazy, mad-hat art business, enjoy all and any beautiful art, and am absolutely not prepared any longer to follow conventions. Just as you describe in your mail.

I have now turned 66 and time is finite, so why should one concern oneself with senseless crap.
Since in my present handicapped state I can't work much, I am shifting my papers and paperwork, the mountains of material, into a somewhat more manageable shape.
In the process, found the photos and a few small jottings of yours. From back then, our studio-exchange project. Siren song. Was really pleased to see the photos again, which you, of course, also had in your glass-case in Kiel.
Some time ago, Jovan separated from his girlfriend of nine years and is now going solo, lives in Stuttgart and has a good job as a construction engineer in the most famous offices in Germany. But he's now totally into adventure, alpine climbing, surfing, discovering the Balkans, most of all farthest and loneliest Albania, where there are only old grandpas and goats. How and where should he find a wife like that? Ain't going to be any grandparents or kids there for the time being.
And Leonard lives with his girl-friend in Frankfurt, continues his studies in Sociology and would like to go to Paris, to the Sorbonne. Ain't going to be any kids there either.
So we wait.
Tomorrow evening, I'm simply going to spare myself the hassle of the opening in Brussels, with thousands of speakers and a dinner, under the pretext of pain in my hand and ribs.
Dear Miriam, when one has survived something like this accident more or less okay, one becomes humble. And one takes pleasure in all the friends one has and in whose company one loves to be. In that spirit, a firm embrace and a fond kiss to you!!!!!!! We should meet up again soon.
Bogo
...here's what it looks like when one is hung up by one's fingers with 15 kg weight on one's lower arm, so as to move the bones apart again.

27 september 2016

dear Bogo,
yikes and horror! your hand looks like a totally exaggerated peace sign ... but happily it can now type. what a bit of luck that precisely that piece of Nature was there. and sure, it sets one thinking if one has just escaped death like that – or, what is even worse in my eyes, being totally dependent on care. I'm glad that everything is turning out okay with the two of you!
recommendation from me as an accident veteran tried-and-tested: be the good patient in physio and re-train your hand and everything – that really does the trick! after my outside-of-myself experience I had a really strong sense of re-conquering my own body in these prescribed movement sequences.
physical strength and suppleness – okay, diminishing with every year! – is important for your work, after all, and important too and really much more interesting is doing it all by yourself, setting things up by yourself! these are the only real moments in this

predominantly unpleasant art scene with all its kerfuffle and brouhaha … luckily, we old specimens can then say: sorry, my back, my arm, my neck, hand, ribs, can't come. Louise Bourgeois, in advanced old age, once said: you've got my works, you don't need me in person.
only I don't know, for example, how I'm supposed to manage: in the actual working at art, physical work is always possible. after all, it can be small-trembly-hesitant, it's still one's own body. but setting up an exhibition may, sooner or later, be something one doesn't do any more. since the accident, for example, I've been really unhappy about travelling. By train, it's okay, but these hour-long procedures involved in flying = unbearable.
sometimes, I think, by skype? then I could remain cooped up in my valley and order the technicians around by skype? well, hmm …
a short time ago, I was in Geneva. there through the mediation of my gallery, Meyer Riegger, a "renowned" art dealer by the name of Blondeau ran a Cahn exhibition. he had been here in Bregaglia, had made his choice of works, had chosen old works at Meyer Riegger, and had set everything up in his really super 3-storey building with huge library – an old watch factory – in the heart of the Pâquis district. But: asked no questions, neither concerning the invitation (classily printed sales prospectus), nor concerning the hanging – already I had a sense of foreboding, dreading the worst etc., etc.: all, really all the series were wrongly hung, had to do everything again, and even worse, the dinner with important people took place in the midst of my pictures, with I myself seated beside the vain, elderly gentleman Blondeau, who, although he had been in Kiel, had understood zilch, or rather finds everything so wonderful and simply deliberately snaps all his ears tightly shut whenever I so much as say something. seemingly listens only to himself; in the end, I could no longer stand it and to relieve my feelings slanged him as old school – see ears … at these round tables, as in an American film, many, very many elderly ladies with face-lifts, horrific.
as a form of solace, I had to think intensely of Louise.
but here in Bregaglia it's super and my new magazzino/studio gets more magnificent with every day that passes: really love this building. now, together with the architect, I'm planning the garden as well, and when it is done next year, I'll move out of my stable to here, still keeping the stable for a while, however, as a "cave to retreat to". after all, I really love it too.
today I have just re-organized, and all my oil painting work is now coming into the magazzino. even while I was unpacking everything there, a quite new feeling came over me, because in point of fact for 20 years I have had 2 work spaces – and now, all the oils are together. an exciting prospect! and moreover, I'm collecting and copying out all that I have written, with the intention of making a pure text-book – in print and in digital form.
In part, it's very amusing to copy the letters today, e.g. my correspondence with "my" authority in Basle concerning the non-existent scholarship system during my stay in the cité des arts in Paris …
the letters themselves have something highly historical about them, even the very materials themselves: carbon paper, Hermes baby typewriter. the 80s a kind of watershed in time, and the 90s a real watershed!

so, all, really all the best and a good recovery, also to Ingrid!
kisses,
miriam

write i must so that my mind empties so that my mind becomes empty so that there is roomspace in my mind for other things things other than these oppressive ever-returning circling thoughts earlymorningthinking in the early hours in the morning only everything always the same thinking about my rump family.
preferably forget! so that this wretched family rump may not assume this spatial importance in my mind, this lost blighting blighted space. preferably forget my family!

my brother little brother is separating from his wife mother of their only child daughter niece. this wife of my little brother girlfriend first then wife then mother now motherspouse i always found unpleasant liking cannot be summoned up by words want to have to ought to because suddenly family has to ought to be. idaughter of my mother my father solely big sister of my little brother certainly not aunt, i always wanted to be have to be no aunt. never be aunt, inonaunt, solelysister.

if i am isolelysister nonaunt my little brother's suffering is the language possibility of language with him with sympathy sympathizingsympathy. this way i can talk with him this way he is my brother i his sister on the same level, from the same family, this way my brother is this human being with imagination + joie de vivre + joie de penser, who is going through hard times.

yet yet yet his suffering is also part of his inflated view of himself he himself as man battered by fate he himself innocent and as someone portraying himself as someone to be pitied he himself at the same time completely inflated responsible for everything to be pitied, which is difficult for me sister then being obliged being compelled being able to pity to talk. for my little brother his wifespousemotherofdaughter super-intelligent the most intelligent woman in the world. his new girlfriend is the most super-sensitive andsoforthabsolutelyfabulous. both women now are suffering underbecauseofhim because he believes hethecentre.

yet yet the money. because i am in the throes of having my inheritance paid out, which is being carried through by my brother's spouse lawyer. were it not for the money i could simply let go of what i don't want to know and only my psychefeelingi could should wanted to ought to concern itself with these rump family things as older sister solelysister of my little brother solelybrother.

alas alas alas yet yet the money.
alas alas my brother's wife in charge of this, who, like all wives husbandmirror mother of the only daughter spouse believe to have been living a life that now lies in ruins because the husband no longer wants can would like or whatever or howsoever this narrow maritallifeform.
alas alas yet yet now revenge is being wrought through the money, now my brother's spouse the mother of his daughter will make the sister of the brother feel that she comes from the same stable.

sisteri tries to gain information on the telephone about the missing money transfer. on the telephone the brother's wife weeps sobs the spouse of my little brother is deeply deeply hurt because of mesisteraunt who never wanted to see all the family united together but only my brother alone. she the wife sobbed at me thinking so to impress me, womanlywomanlike, she sobbed at me without recognizing how much she was producing an exclusively self-targeted intimacy which had never existed between us. she sobbed at me because i too exist only mirrored mirror of herself with her life-plan family, aunt, sister of the husband. me nonaunt and solelysister of my brother she is incapable of perceiving.

stupid of the wife of my little brother to assume through this womanly technique of sufferingsobbing that i a much older woman sister of my brother might show sympathizingunderstanding for her being because of the separation not in the psychological state to make progress with paying out the inheritance. businesswomani consider that to be
unprofessional unreliable stupid.
my brother little brother too plays the big illtakecareofitman over the phone.

and i getintoapanic i. i dontknowhowmuchi shouldoughtoshalli believe him?
howoverthephoneanyway?
igetintoapanic
musthavemoney now
toogoodnaturedi
toolongwaited
inheritancefrommyfather verylong after his death.

this family of mine was never understandably reliable. interesting individual beings eachandeveryone. yet yet yet in terms of feeling among one another utterly malfunctional.

2014

From: Miriam Cahn
To: Hannes Böhringer
Subject: super book! **31 july 2010**

dear Hannes,[181]
many thanks for your fine book![182] I read a piece from it every now and then – I haven't yet got into "Bauen" ["Building"], but I really liked "immer kommt etwas dazwischen" ["something always intervenes or interrupts"]: that's the way it is ... and I really liked this starting again and again from scratch lying in bed at the beginning of the texts. I find it musical, a passacaglia[183] of every not entirely identical awakening, the days, the years, passing by. It's super in your language. and it reminded me of one of my texts, of course only in form: "folterbilder im mai 2004",[184] in the book "überdachte fluchtwege"[185] in the middle, the flesh-coloured leporello. I'm not so keen on leporellos otherwise, but at that time this text was part and parcel of exhibitions and was hung as a strip at eye-level on an equal footing with drawings and paintings, surrounded by "heads", which I installed in such a way that they stared at the people reading.
In the same catalogue, there's also a picture "herumliegen" ["lying around"] – could be related at the 700th remove with your "liegen-gehen-stehen" ["lying-walking-standing"]. it is extraordinarily heavy-going, psychologically, to portray people who are lying down, and something totally different from people standing + walking – provided that it is not a question of a replica figure but of a configuration/configuring.
so, a great book of yours – now I'll be off into the buildings ...
warmest regards, miriam

From: Hannes Böhringer
To: Miriam Cahn
Subject: still life **9 August 2010**

Dear Miriam,
Thanks for your response! My original wish was to publish only "Immer kommt etwas dazwischen", but no publishing house was willing to do that. So, it has now been packaged together with already known pieces. Yes, the "Folterbilder", same principle. I like passacaglias. Hoping we can meet up again soon, warmest regards,
Hannes

24 October 2016

dear Eva-Maria,
here is the famous Maloja "snake", and you know this bridge … and apart from this I'm hard at work. I've discovered another boxful of letters – moving house like this is a real big deal – that had accumulated over the decades. and, of course, I had to look through them, not least because of my planned book: WRITING IN RAGE.
the most extreme part is the huge quantity of letters from my mother – she wrote to me everywhere, almost daily, so to say, always with drawings, altogether detailed scenes from her day-to-day life, which, to be honest, were only of moderate interest to me, which again was a matter of total indifference to her. what sounds great from the outside is not so for me, the daughter: I look at this gigantic heap of her tragedy as a wife, mother, always concerned, anxious woman etc. – incredible the energy that she invested in this thing called "family", which in reality, however, often existed in the way she would have wanted it to be only in her imagination. with me , a bit more distance would certainly have been better, even today this pile of letters gets on my nerves, above all because of the sheer quantity … but I won't throw them away, and won't use them either: I'm not the sort of feminist who finds this kind of extreme female family-energy-consumption interesting.
this apart, I'm hunting out and collecting anything I like as "text", and there are some I had totally forgotten: e.g. the letters from Terry Fox, the cards from Pippilotti Rist. a good number naturellement from you, from Anne,[186] all of them also very fine … they're being bundled and boxed … and I tend to think that I won't be using them, perhaps 1 – 2 "exceptions" or so.
all in all, however, I'm glad that nowadays this communication no longer takes place in paper form but as e-mail.
so, what are you up to?
kiss!
miriam

on towards me came a twice as fat brother! twice as fat as last time! down the little path leading to my workshop! i knew immediately i cant stand it with him for long nonono i will havetowanttooughtto foreshorten this visit even if wanted this siblingstogetherness. i will not be a mirror not his mirror I will not or only briefly beabletowanttohaveto.

hardly was he inside, hardly in my house my workshop my studio than he spoke only of himself scarcely was he in my workshop to pay me a visit after having not visited for a longish time 3 months or so relatively long perhaps longer than he spoke uninterruptedly exclusively perpetually only of himself of his ailments and his professional acts of heroism. the ailments + his turnover of doctors his ever-repeated ever-recurring onlythebest, the bestforme, onlythebest and extraordinary becauseofme, formethebestonly I was just barely scarcely able to block off, ward off ward away from my house. always, always, always the same talk the same language alwaysalways the same procedure if no longer thebestonlyforme this treatment will be will have been broken off again as after all not good asnotoutstanding asbad, because never no one never can come up to his my brother's his lofty demands nor he himself neverever never.

luckily luckily for me i was able to interrupt stop these for me unpleasant since much too intimate inconsiderately intimate descriptions of his organs his ailing organs his everailingbody these ever-recurring always unspeakably transgressive these intimatelydetailed bodyailingdescriptions luckily. to my deliverance i was able to banish from my workshop from my studio this horror of his own corporeal condition of this only brother.

this brother my little brother very much younger almost next generation so much younger littler another generation i hardly know reallytrue. hardly and not from so-called family life. I lived for 3–4 years or so under the collapsing family roof of so-called family life. he was the last child suckled suckling babe babe in arms untouchable untouchable male jewel untouchable protective rampart of my mother he perhaps possibly so-called sickly we 2 sisters we 2 dirty girls were not allowed to touch this infant this brother not play with him and if so then only under the strict dark eyes of my mother. writing today my impression remains that this little male child was absolutely the only one that my mother held and cuddled and carried around and looked upon scrutinized with her dark eyes and her strong arms enclosing this little creature like an ape mother animal mother female ape.

in those years unbearable i an adolescent already fled from this family home luckily for me I ran iaway into the world with gilrfriendsiaway into other houses away into cinematheatreexhibitionsmusicart. ran away to my interested and interesting aunts ran away hadtogetaway wentranaway luckily for me. now as an adolescent I did not compellingly although female not necessarily compellingly + at all events have to take notice of or even love this suckling this male infant in our collapsing family home. I had far more interesting things interest interesting pieces of work to do outside this house.

then my mother broke down sat there crying asked herself asked others as to wherefore as to why why at all in existence whylife made sense had any sense havetowanttooughtto. no sense any more sense in living, no strength any more to get up no life strength any more she sat she lay crying perpetually crying sat could not raise herself up could not move only cry.

so psychiatric hospital Friedmatt hospital hospitalization + my little brother into a children's home my younger sister i dont know was at home no recollection on my part of her staying under the collapsing family roof she was in the house or something somehow put up yet yet yet not present submerging + later submerged.

after some years my little brother came back into this family house when he started school. my mother baronmünchhausen-like had pulled herself up by her own hair by her hair-soul up and out of the hospital with her very strong inner power out of this psychiatric beingillhospital she had moved herself out and moved back into her house and was again mother for her son.

i had left this family house and was sohappy sohappy without any family environment everyday perpetuallyalways. no little brother no younger sister no puzzlemother yet yet a father who supported my going fleeing from this house despite his grief at the loss of his lifegoal idyllicfamily.
i therefore very very happy in my first own room only bed only table only mine only people by invitation to visit only my room only mine away from the family houseaway from direct daily influences and intrusions. free. i myself becoming imyselfi possibly. at last being i i into the future. i my future my life my future life able to decide myself alone. i not having to not having to be under obligation not havingtooughtto love my family family existence being so as a family. no longer havingtooughttolove these family creatures as family creatures, but as individual persons humanbeings fathermothersister individually only possible.

i spent too little time with my little brother had done played held too little nothing cuddled with him not at all as brother little brotherchildsucklingbabe not played not spoken nothing actually really true almost actually nothing at all.

when grown up i tried with this brother when grown up grown away i tried to love this brother as an individual being individual person humanbeing alone human. today i recognize see that it is not possible i am not capable inolonger able to inolonger wanttooughtto. too alien. alien to me this brother to me this man who is supposed to be oughtoshouldbe wants to be my brother. this brother is a hollow shell into which everyone canpourin whattheywant i not want to. he fills his emptiness with possessions, with wantingtooughttohavingtopossess. this brother this male human who does not see observe perceive others not really as others but only as mirrors of hisself as a selfie with background = the others or or or at any event at least refers everythingeverybody to himself + as filling material for the body of his existence and if that is not possible rejects them with fits of rage tears or or or offended sendstothedevil no longer wants to have anything to do with these people insulted or or or.

what is missing is patching things up between brother and sister. that is what i dont want, cant do, dont want, grown-up and having never lived together as brother and sister, nonono! untrue, unreal these ostensibly iron family bonds at all events for all events always rigid as iron these so-called family bonds. not for me, nonono. i dont wish to. i dont want to today elderly old.

so this brother of mine this suddenly fat man here today visiting me in my house in my workshop studio perceiving nothing not seeing no observing seeing nothing apart from himself hecentre talks uninterruptedly perpetually of himselfself hehimself sits there in my new building newly built workshop magazzino here. here in my valley in this for this valley unusual building he sits distended despairing my despairing brother evidently very despairing my brother and sees only himself and zilchelse.

he leaps therefore at a little photo that portrays my father getting a banana from the Guerillagirls. my old father gets this banana because after the Guerillagirls' performance lecture he has asked an intelligent question which the Guerillagirls in this performance reward with bananas. my brother is interested neither in the Guerillagirls nor in their performance in the context of the symposium i had organized but only in the posture of our already old father which this brother interprets defines as "intimidated/hunched". this brother of mine is thereforethereby completely incapable of seeing on this photo, this brotherson oversees here completelyasalways that this old man his father is sitting in the audience below the Guerillagirls' platform + and hence lower.
then this brother sees leaps at a small piece of occasional furniture in my magazzino a small piece of my mother's in the style of classic modernism which he remembers hehimselfhe alone can remember. and then sits again in his chair fat and talks uninterruptedly perpetually always and only about his work and his heroic deeds in his work and his heroic deeds towards the people at work who are either exceptional extraordinary and onlythebest or zilch thepitspants and so on etc or or or.

how many many times really often many toomany many times when my brother this man speaks acts expresses himself like this above all not moving does not move sits there etc. or or or i inwardly and also physically ought to want to have to run away. otherwise passive as mirror for hours on end only mirror cardboard companion to this man somebody else could be sitting there opposite him yet yet yet i believe i know amcompletelycertain only some other female person woman patiently listening female woman patiently listening female inclined agreeing commenting havingtooughtto agree. yet yet yet not me not me myself not me but somehow anybody anywoman exposed for decades to this spate of words spate of always identical reports exposed to always the same person always the same things will not change. nonono!

so i broke this spate of words i interrupted this word avalanche broke off with the assertion still having something to do office he thereupon already alarmed superoversensitive: "dont feel under any obligation".

so he off and this sentence revolving in my head in my brain. sleeping sleepless sleep awake this sentence thought its way into my head into my skull into my brain into my head. sleeplessly sleeping i awoke one morning this morning and thoughtknewfelt: nonono I do not feel under any obligation! i no longer feel under any obligation, i am fundamentally under no obligation, i am not under an obligation i am not obliged to carry to bear to assist in carrying to assist submissively this depressive this depression behaviour this illness of perpetual revolving in the head in the brain in the body or or or. nonono.

towards my mother i was under an obligation felt under an obligation wanted to be under an obligation even if reluctantly i considered i felt iobligation towards her despite a great tendency to flee tofleehavetofeel in face of these eternally identical circularly revolving conversations revolvings refusals and not wanting to being able to see observe what i am was i am under an obligation to my mother to my mother i was under an obligation also because grateful very grateful. all drawing all music all reading all anarchy all fantasy i had inherited or learnt or copied or imitated from her. as a child happy with her with her mother as a child very happy i had great happiness much happiness doing much with her the sporty running drawing story-telling piano-playing anarchist and cinemagoer. much great much happiness happy much more happiness than my littler sister + my tiny brother. much much more happiness + happy.

so for a long time i tried and found a way even if a bumpy way in untrodden terrain yet yet yet idoable always the attempt 1 per week with her to her or at least to phone if iaway when she old and when she became ill in need of care. when she had to spend the end of her life in a state-prescribed home in a room 16m2 small earlier large apartment evenearlier 3-storey house. and now while writing in the flow of writing in the writing-flow my brother is again present I again think of my little brother and why I do not feel under an obligation to him.
i cannot forget. i will never forget not forgive never even if i oughttowanttobeableto and embarrassing to me i can to all eternity not forget his behaviour when our mother became in need of care. he did admittedly see to it illtakecareofit that she was moved from the oldpeoples hospital horrible unspeakable 6-bed room into her a single room in her beloved psychiatric Friedmatt. and then he disappeared. was gone disappeared no mails nothing answered simply gone simply disappeared simply no longer contactable because his mummy no longer functioned mummy-like could no longer cook meals for him + listen to him for hours on end + support + be proud so proud of this one son her product therefore proud of this manson formerly sucklingbabe in arms.
he gone he the always illtakecareofit bigperson man great zampano gone not there in refusal + gone.
iunforgiving unforgotten unforgiven always when seeing my brother unforgiven unabletoforgive.

when my mother into her 16m2 room in the strictly chosen home in the home chosen from 3 identical possibilities all fearfully correct equalright socially just for all identical therefore she into this room made available by the state for everyman everywoman she planned she was planning with drawings and her exceptional feeling for space she planned she drew she was able she without hesitation to select coolly draw from her large 3-storey house her 4-room apartment what came into her 16m2 room. very coolly very unsentimentally together with me choosing the most important things for her for her last room to the end of life. one chair one table one little piece of furniture for her jewellery a few chosen antiques the gleamingly green woman by Niki de St Phalle, the oil painting by Max Bill that she had bought with her own money, her library, clothing. anyway she always had this room exactly in her mind + drew accordingly and so did not take any piece too many into this 16m2 room.

we both knew that she would be mortally unhappy in this home unhappy to death. designing the room together in this way was a rescue the rescuing of her self being able to remainbe at least a little personal her own she herselfshe. the manner the way the production of this room 16m2 united us because we both thought felt were be are identical similar identical.

so we then furnished this room 16m2 we both knew that she would be unhappy here unhappy to death because she did not want to could not possibly adhere to these social sides these consultation times these meal

times this language in any case these normed sides to life impossible not practisable for her alien to herselfself alien with the others the others too close to her much too close another planet this home.
furnishing her room exactly identically large for everyone 16m2 a hopeless future bulwark hopeless because alien for all others for the others in the home. Niki de St Phalle-Bill-antiques-artlibrary-frenchliterature hope for the future memory for my mother and her life-long surroundings mine too. for these reasons i felt under an obligation to visit her 1× per week or to phone sure 1× per week when i was away even if it was difficult for me even if talking this talking with her even if this language perpetually actually always as with my brother nowtoday turned circularly rotated circled incircles thinking and feeling in depression enclosed in depressions thinking and feeling. even if often in panic days in advance i thought nowimustgothere nowimustphone.

my mother and i invented little rituals: i fed her with chocolates – les truffes que j'aime tant – while i myself ate my favourite chocolate-coated almonds. that was our greeting ritual.

then the conversations proceeded as they had always been could be ought to be had to be are.

i felt it my duty to accompany this woman this mother my motherher up to her end. i was thankful to her expressing profoundest thanks for her legacy of gifts i was most profoundly perhaps i loved her perhaps not but i was am thankful at any event most profoundly thankful alwaysalways always.

this being thankful is absent in my feelings for my brother. by nature naturally there are similarities determined by family genetically perhaps certainly in terms of behaviour a sibling similarity has to be ought to be there. yet yet yet this man alien to me my brother remains alien to me this little brother remains alien despite a familyrelationshipsiblings likingsimilarity. gratitude is missing love is missing. and i no longer feel under an obligation to bear to stand nonono and so on etc. or or or this illness depression which has now befallen this poor man my little brother like my mother. this terrible communication illness probably an illness in other societies perhaps not an illness perhaps an essential characteristic perhaps ability perhaps magic of the over-sensitive person perhaps a possibility of the shamanic element in art perhaps part of being human. yet yet yet in my society in this society environment today now life or or or illness.

Palü, 2016

2 december 2016

dear Anette,
i simply had to send you this weather phenomenon in the Engadine! it occurs over still warm water in super-dry air below zero at 1900m above sea level ... was taken by "my" architect Armando Ruinelli,[197] who is also re-designing hotel rooms in the very attractive Waldhaus Sils hotel.
and I am so pissed-off politically! now there are elections in Austria, just next door to me so to say. I look on the black side, because the fascists always have massive success using the same agenda: they promise the people an upturn through racism and xenophobia – and it works, unfortunately!
normally I don't do this – drawing historical comparisons. but if one looks at the "success" Hitler and his Nazis – here in Switzerland often naively "admired", because "things worked" – had with their really excellent use of self-presentation/performance/image and sound material etc. right down to the gathering of young people in the Hitlerjugend and BDM (the "Weisse Rose" were at first BDM and Hitlerjugend), I find the skilful form/presentation/use of the social media at least similar, if not an exact copy.
now the ARD has just reported that the stolen gateway to Auschwitz "Arbeit macht frei" has been recovered. the interesting thing is that the lettering on the gate is a Bauhaus script ...
and there is a similarity also in the helplessness of their opponents: the refusal to see how skilfully these right-wing populists make use of the available media, and the refusal to analyse the history of the 3rd reich in these aspects, so as to have an intelligent and not merely reactive approach to dealing with these neo-fascists.
it's no use at all appealing to "reason". the right content must necessarily be communicated in the new forms. this is the backlash from the tame unadventurousness of the "left" and their refusal to deal with aesthetics ... oh, baby! doesn't go down well at all!
saluti miriam

28 October 2016
Dear Mic,
I wanted to send you the article[187] by e-mail, but it didn't work, I think. It will now come by post – I'll send it later today.
And the award for your magazzino is SUPERB – your joint work in the design, building and realization stages is really top rate!
Warmest regards,
A.

28 October 2016
dear Anne,
yes, it did come through, the text by Alfred Schlienger.[188] the man is right, for sure, but I don't like his style of writing at all – it's so daftly leftist-cum-critical-cum-polemical …
and Tuesday, 8.11 is fine by me! looking forward to it.
kiss,
m

29 October 2016
Dear mic, yes, I think the text is illuminating only on account of the quotations in it. I wouldn't have expected this extreme agglomeration of abominable stuff in the commentaries … and 8 nov. is fine – looking forward,
Bacio, A.

30 october 2016
dear Anne,
yes, that's true. but I don't need to know these facts in soo much detail to evaluate people like Somm[189]/Blocher etc. correctly, because their very style betrays them. and that brings me to this atrocious style of leftist, so-called critical writing: it is simply pure reacting. the texts (and images) "ape" the highly successful SVP style and believe that they are achieving more by doing so. they don't invent anything of their own – and for the same reason as the SVP and similar schoolmasterish people: the stupid "populace" has to receive instruction. This is why I find the WOZ, the Wochenzeitung etc. so unbearable.
after all, it was not for nothing that the nazis – the great model for all our nightmarish right-wingers – called themselves national socialists: very cleverly, they adopted a good number of forms and topics from the socialists and communists and were highly successful because they did so.
and I also recall a formative experience I had in an OFRA plenary session:[190] for fully two hours, the plenary session in the Holzhalle of those days discussed my calendar – and exclusively its form, which, so it seemed to them, was incomprehensible to the woman "of the people" – how should they know? – and therefore this calendar was too élitist . . . whatever that is supposed to mean. today, this example can be carried over and applied excellently to the really poor quality of the way in which the SVP and equivalent movements in other countries are subjected to so-called critical analysis – the style is totally wrong, self-congratulatory, self-affirming etc. no matter whether the facts are right or not, c'est le ton qui fait la musique …
in "sternstunde philosophie" – often very good – I have just seen Pankai Mishra[191] and that is what moved me to write this e-mail: he sees history very differently from here in the west and has good

reasons for why the western democracies are no longer functioning – among other things because, he argues, empathy is missing from politics and is being replaced by feelings, which in contrast to facts (and I think today even to numbers/algorithms) are being exploited by the far right. a typical vacuum, which the fascist pigs are logically using without any qualms.
and that is why I find these left-wing schoolmasterish texts so unbearable – despite having the right facts they have understood zilch, they have never, owing to the left-wing tradition, given thought to forms, because in their eyes these are élitist and bourgeois.
so, looking forward to seeing you in reality!
kiss, m

17 November 2016

Dear Mic,
Thanks for your post! Yes, I too have read this and that, above all on the web (Guardian, NY Times, Le monde, Spiegel online, Zeit online) – some really intelligent interpretations of post-Trump reality, others also very self-opinionated. As far as women are concerned, I had a very nice conversation this morning at the Spalentor bus-stop: I met one of the residents in the neighbouring house to ours on Spalentorweg – a residential house run by the local community for women who have some type of disability and live in assisted accommodation. One of these neighbours has a tortoise which during the summer strayed into the Lenosgarten – so I came to know her a little and we talk a little whenever we meet (she mostly smoking outside her building) or, precisely, at the bus-stop. She tells me that the tortoise is now hibernating, and then, all of a sudden: the fact that this Trump guy has been elected is a scandal – and for us women a slap in the face. That this is possible, she says, upsets her maddeningly. – At that point I recognized how much this media-run election campaign has got under people's skin, and leaves nobody unaffected, I guess, no matter what their political position. Moreover, I read this morning how in certain areas of the USA everyday expressions and acts of hatred are on the increase: previously completely inconspicuous middle-class citizens in Dallas are being molested and verbally abused on account of their appearance – are being told they should damn well go back home, they no longer belong (as said to a Dallas businessman, who has been there for ages with his family, owns a firm and has parents who are university professors). The dismay and fright are enormous, because this election victory has opened the flood gates to racism in public. The Mexican Embassy has set up a hotline and counselling services in various cities for all those who now feel threatened or are afraid of being deported and has obviously, in co-operation with the administration still in power, started "fast lane programmes" for legalization measures between Mexico and the USA, in which the US-born children of illegal Mexican immigrants can still be naturalized…
At present I'm reading the memoirs of Tony Judt (do you

know the book: The Chalet of Memory?) – he was our age, Jewish, an historian, and was professor in N.Y. among other places. He died of an awful disease, which leaves one totally paralysed (ALS), and then lived exclusively from the memories and images in his mind and left these short texts as his legacy. In her review of him and his book, Maike Albath wrote: "Tony Judt embodies the spirit of criticism. Without being defeatist or succumbing to a nostalgic idealization of the past, he names the weaknesses in our society. It is long since overdue that we return to intellectual virtues." For me, he is a discovery.
One simply must stand firm and not allow oneself to be led astray by the nasty creatures in politics and the media.
A warm embrace from
Anne

18 november 2016

dear Anne,
these boyos Trump is bringing into his government are so awful! really absolutely awful racists, at least sympathizers of, perhaps even members of, the Ku Klux Klan, really awful. and of course, not a single woman, and even if one is brought in later: one = none ... we all thought that such things were once and for all a thing of the past – how wrong we were.
I often still think of a remark my father once made: before and after the Nazi seizure of power, he said, it was much more difficult for Germans to think and act correctly than for Jews (his best friend at school was not Jewish and died on the eastern front). well, I think that one shouldn't necessarily reach back into the past and make comparisons, but when reflecting on the emergence of the Third Reich critics tend to forget that the Nazis were avant-garde in the sense that they no only used the totally new media of the day in a decidedly skilful way, but, with e.g. the BDM etc., also invented a new form of togetherness for the young – after all, the young people who formed the Weisse Rose were first of all in the BDM etc. and thought it was super because it was doing one's bit for the "nation" outside the parental home (and they had leadership roles), before they became critically thinking human beings. and, of course, job-creation through war industries involving munitions, autobahns etc.
and of course it was super how Leni Riefenstahl, the first female film-maker, was able to film the Olympic Games with 16 cameras and so be absolutely in the forefront as far as film technique went. and here one can make a comparison – in this super-clever and deliberately used technology of self-portrayal and portrayal of the nation.
It is just as wrong to see the Nazis as backward-looking as it is today to see Trump in that light. precisely the skill at myth-creation through simple images and slogans is similar and this is possible only with drastic and absurdly racist bogeyman stereotypes.
so terrible!
kiss,
m.

20 november 2016

dear Anne,

thanks for the fine article on Trump[192] as bullshitter. it's super and it's true! only the "solution" Pascal Engel suggests is simply absolutely wrong: it is just not enough to give people access to the facts and the truth – and why does a philosopher believe in this simplistic way in THE truth and the so-called really objective facts? without talking about the HOW, the form? Clinton (and also Hollande) seemed untrustworthy not because of the facts – they were good analyses and proposals – but because of the way she campaigned. and her major error was, behind the scenes, to call the people who put their faith in Trump idiots. that's something I or you can think, but certainly not a politician. that is simply not on, comes back to roost, and actually is élitist, above all the belief that reason will win through ... I don't know either what has to be done and how. but the "élite, the intellectuals", i.e. we etc., need to begin to think differently and not always react like Pavlov's dog.
till next time!
kiss,
m
and here it is already, my super iPad pro, magnificent

ALLOW REFUGEES FROM SYRIA INTO SWITZERLAND'S EMPTYING AREAS 2015

on a day-to-day basis, I read/see/hear about the refugee situation in the Middle East. and now even the international aid organizations such as the UNHCR do not have enough money to feed all the people in these gigantic tent camps throughout the winter of 2014/15 – a scandal!

in privileged Switzerland, there are emptying or already emptied rural areas. putting it simply, these are areas such as my place of residence, the mountain valley of Bregaglia, which are gradually losing their populations. "emptying areas" means that in these regions fewer and fewer people want to, or are able to, live – such as families with children and people with professions for which there is no demand here. the consequences are the imminent closure not only of shops but of school classes and kindergartens. residential buildings stand empty, their status remaining unclear since the adoption of the initiative on second homes.

an example from everyday life: I am sitting in the postbus to St Moritz. in the largest village, Vicosoprano, 2 small children are brought personally by the woman kindergarten teacher and passed into the responsibility of the postbus driver, who then passes them on to their mother in Casaccia – every day at the kindergarten brings this little, attractive scene that I witness. at the same time, however, it strikes me that in Casaccia there actually are only 2 children of kindergarten age.

as an artist, I love emptied spaces, be they in towns or, as here in Bregaglia, in rural areas. for freelance professions such as mine, emptied spaces have the great advantage that they are "empty" and can thus be "filled" with all kinds of things – in the ideal sphere and in so-called reality.

so why not use our emptying or emptied areas in Switzerland to house refugees? for example, refugee families from Syria with children? and, accentuating the specific/especial case of Bregaglia, with artists, intellectuals etc.?

given consultation and co-operation with the valley's inhabitants and with the people who would rent out their empty houses (e.g. to a family from Syria) and in close co-operation with the Swiss Refugee Council, I could imagine that there might be an advantage for all concerned: the refugees would receive decent accommodation and hence the opportunity to live normal everyday lives. and the emptying areas would be filled up a little …

30 september 2016

dear Adam and dear Andrea,
recently, I read Hélène Cixous'[193] latest book, about the same time as reading your fine programme for Athens. and the idea came to me that Cixous would fit very nicely into your way of thinking. I have known her texts since the 70s (or thereabouts) and have always found Cixous magnificent, especially in her use of language: she writes a French that is somehow "German" – when, for example, she amalgamates various words into one word. in this "German" form it does not exist in French, which gives her texts a very fine sound. some words she leaves in German. in addition, she invents onomatopoeic words and sentences – probably untranslatable.
her mother, who died a short time ago at almost 100, was a German Jew from Osnabrück. Cixous was born in North Africa and lives in Paris.
anyway, her mother is the subject of the last books of hers that I read. and at about 7 long removes her texts are related to Hannah Arendt's text "Wir Flüchtlinge" in your first SOUTH.
so I thought: perhaps the documenta could extend an invitation to Hélène Cixous?
apart from this, I ask reticently whether and what you would like of mine in Kassel, and what about the spatial question in Athens? I ought to know by the end of the year...
oh, and one more question: can I order the next issue of SOUTH from you?
saluti! and warm greetings from Bregaglia,
miriam

5 October 2016

Dear Miriam,
How good to hear from you – many thanks for your mail. I hope all is well with you in Bregaglia.
We will take your hint to heart.
We are sorry that we couldn't get in touch much earlier: we too don't want to wait until the end of the year to take the decisions concerning the presentation of your works at documenta 14. Since your work also has a literary element, Adam has named "Parnassos" (Greek Literature Society, founded in the nineteenth century) as one of the possible locations that might be of interest for you in Athens. You have visited this site and liked it, haven't you?
Would this be a possible path we could pursue together? I can gladly have a word with Katerina and check the availability. Please let us know what you think of this.
As far as Kassel is concerned, Adam could well imagine a kind of updated copy (repetition) of the Wachraum [WATCH ROOM] – precisely because you withdrew this from documenta 7. Would it be conceivable for you to combine available parts of this work with new pictures and further works?
We look forward to hearing from you what you have to say about these suggestions – let us keep on the ball.
South 2 is on its way to you.
Warm greetings, also from Adam,
Andrea

documenta 14
Andrea Linnenkohl
Assistentin des Künstlerischen Leiters /
Assistant to the Artistic Director /

5 october 2016

dear Andrea,
thank you for the swift reply! and sure, both suggestions are absolutely fine, but both now depend on the technical side – precisely because with me the "technical" aspect is minimal, almost a nothing …
"Parnassos" I consider super: I'm really enthusiastic about this convincing idea, but you would have to clarify whether it is possible also to drill holes – small ones, but holes nevertheless, and also drill them through this fabric covering (if it remains) – in order to hang the pictures. this must be clarified especially in the upper room with its overhead lighting, which would be super, before we think any further. I would find the space interesting because of its "old-fashioned" dark-red fabric covering and these remarkable/ strange wooden framings. without the fabric would also be super, simply white … and of course all the old pictures would have to go and the space be empty.
in addition, it seems that on the floor below there are also possibilities, which, however, I could not view on my visit, because the responsible person did not have the key. since I do now know its style and dimensions, however, it would be good at any event to send me photos, if it could be used – so I could choose between 3 possibilities: overhead light room, room in between, and the small room to the right on the ground floor.
but as mentioned: first of all, clarify the situation – before that there is no sense in making a choice …
the same would hold for the WACH RAUM: it requires in any case as enclosed a space as possible, a minimum of 4m high. before that is settled, it makes no sense to give it any further thought …
i.e. what I mean is that the "technology" must be super-simple, because if I myself carry out the hanging "performance-like", there is no possibility of improvising and "considering another option". I must be able to do the hanging without any complicated planning, just with a very nimble, quick-acting person to help me, with a ladder, with a small drill, with nails, with fine pins etc. in the case of the "latest works" in Athens – and I already have many too many, very many new works and so that will be in any event an interesting choosing process – I'm a few steps ahead of you! but I won't start until this minimal technology is clear and I can choose the space in Parnassos.
as for Kassel/ WACH RAUM I work with a bostitch or fine nails. (Adam knows what I mean: I hanged in this way in his exhibition "künstler aus basel 2 x"). i.e. a mere concrete wall is not possible, apart from that, however, everything should be more or less white and "soft", not hard-as-concrete.
so, and now the ball is in your court, and don't hesitate to ask …
looking forward to this!
saluti dalla Bregaglia
miriam

22 october 2016

dear Andrea,
I will attempt an answer …

so: I have laid out this 6× field in order to measure the height and to see whether this height also fits the fine space in the documenta hall. It is the only "position" that I have laid out from currently 17 positions (= large single sheets, series, fields). apart from this, everything is neatly folded together again and tidied away, which brings me directly to material and transport: they are very light works on architect's paper, folded up, with a variety of dimensions and needing only one flat crate (approx. 100 × 200 cm ×10 cm – I'll send the exact dimensions when transportation takes place) into which they are laid flat. and everything is here in Bregaglia. and from a purely bureaucratic standpoint it will be very laborious to make photographs of every single work... is that necessary from the customs point of view? could we not work on the principle 1 space = 1 work etc.? at some point or other next year, when the time comes, I'll send you a list with all the positions/works and dimensions, but not until then, please.
here I'm sending you the text[194] that goes with the work WACH RAUM, which I've copied out from my book LESEN IN STAUB [READING IN DUST] and which must also be mediated with this typographic layout, and with it a few mobile-phone photos from this book concerning WACH RAUM, which has the most writing about it. if you want reviews, texts etc. from the period of the 3 rooms, or also printable photos, it would be best if you got directly in touch with Kathrin Dunst, who works for me and is a very good internet archaeologist.
WACH RAUM is a self-enclosed room work (1 room = 1 work), which is at the same time fluid inasmuch as its appearance is always dependent on the space in which I install it. the 3 rooms of 1982 – 1. Konrad Fischer Zürich, 2. documenta, 3. Kunsthaus Zürich were a "chance offer": I was able to exhibit in these 3 spaces in this way, because without any specific intention I had just produced a huge amount of material under the heading WACH RAUM. there were always very many more positions than spatial possibilities. the choice made in those days was thus always determined by the time: Zurich tended to be a content-based choice with an emphasis on "wachsaal" [observation room] (the 3 hospital beds) and signs related to the female world, and the Kassel documenta tended to have signs of the male world on account of the political situation at the time with the new, underground missile systems positioned alongside the iron curtain – which on the western side were concentrated above all in the so-called Fulda Gap. when taking the train to Kassel one travelled along this iron curtain.
given, therefore this "fluid" and simultaneously self-enclosed nature of the work, therefore, it makes no sense to reconstruct or quote it today, as e.g. in the "quotation room" in the Kunsthalle Basel (6 künstler aus Basel 2×), where the quotation actually was a tiny current-day oil painting of a house instead of the then huge house on architect's paper. the space back then, however, was also not a "self-enclosed" room...
and for that reason, therefore, I will not do the actual installation of WACH RAUM until I am in Kassel in the space of the documenta hall – and this performance-like nature of my installation is the current, topical element and links it to the work with the latest material in Athens through this "unplanned" + corporeal quality.
what that means in concrete terms is this: I will take all positions to

Kassel and will make my choice only there.
that now sounds all more complicated than it is: you must imagine the spatial work simply as words: house, ship, boat, hospital bed, woman, computer, TV, table, key, missile launching ramp, World Trade Center etc. then I organize these objects/words into a contemporary sound poem and the space is complete …
the most acute example is the World Trade Center: in the 1980s and earlier, the Twin Towers were used (not only by me) as a sign for "US turbo-capitalism". in the meantime, 9/11 has happened and has hence totally changed the content-matter of this sign – the current situation has to do with this event. the Twin Towers will then certainly be involved in your installation of WACH RAUM, just as in all the presentations of WACH RAUM a women's series has to be involved.
that's how history changes – and that is sufficient for me as the "current day" element WACH RAUM.
so, saluti from Bregaglia!
Miriam

30 December 2016, at 15:18 hrs
Dear Miriam,
Alexandra[195] and I are in Champfèr until 7 January and I was thinking we could visit you and your studio. Two artists who are part of documenta 14, Daniel Knorr and Nevin Aladag, are with us (leaving 1 January), and maybe Christine[196] could come too. And my best Polish friends, Andrzej Przywara (Foksal Gallery Foundation) and Joanna Mytkowska (director of Museum of Modern Art Warsaw), are in Maloja, so it could be a group, and we could have lunch or dine together somewhere near your place, if you like. Just let me know if you feel like receiving some guests, and if so, how many.
All the best,
Adam
Adam Szymczyk
Artistic Director
documenta 14

30 december 2016, at 15:44 hrs
Dear Adam,
so nice! and interesting people in Maloja … visits are very welcome and I don't mind how many persons. the best would be later afternoon, and then we could have dinner – maybe here or nearby in Italy.
here is my phone number: +41 ***
all the very best and wishing you and Alexandra a good start to the New Year,
miriam

30 December 2016, at 20:20 hrs
hi Miriam,
I haven't been able to reach you on the phone – to sum up:
1. you are very welcome to join us for dinner, per Christine's invitation – tomorrow evening in our Champfèr house, unless you have made plans – or prefer not to make plans ;-)
2. I could come to your place around 12 noon tomorrow with Nevin, Daniel, Andrzej and Joanna, another artist,

Monika Sosnowska, and her partner Marcin.
3. if tomorrow doesn't work for you, we will be happy to visit you in a different personal configuration on 2 or 3 Jan.
just let me know what you prefer.
all the best,
Adam

30 december 2016, at 20:27 hrs

Dear Adam,
here is my address: strada principale ***, 7605 Stampa – it's the new concrete magazzino building at the end of Stampa after the bus-stop and the val d'arca restaurant on the right.
looking forward to this!
miriam

30 December 2016, at 20:57 hrs

cool, thanks!

1 january 2017, at 12:05 hrs

Dear Adam,
it was great to see all of you including the swwweeeet Emilia at my place!
and now to the documenta in Athens. after thinking about your project and my place in it, I know now how to proceed: it is not possible for me to install my work in person if it is not a closed space without "others", also one big wall doesn't work either. I am simply not able to do it this way – never have been, and never do so in group shows. I am a lone wolf! so I think the best would be – as you are in Champfèr – that you come down here again and choose with me the works that you want and that fit your show and thinking, and, then, of course, it's you and your crew who install the works in Athens.
this works! I did something similar in Kiel: one of the 2 big spaces was installed on the choice of the curator, Anette Hüsch, and she also did it as she wanted. the other space was installed by me – it was a big surprise how different they looked and it was very interesting.
so: if you could manage to come down here again, this would be the solution – even if you by any chance find in Athens the solution of a self-closed room for me. your choice would then ideally influence my choices for the room installation – and then I would come to Athens and install the space my way. I have, however, one request: come alone ... I'm simply not a group person, no way, when it comes to work.
if you can't manage to come down here again, I would choose myself for your proposition, but only oil paintings. and you and your crew install as they want and think right, and I am also sure it would work.
the presentation, however, then becomes so alien to me that my own work seems to me like something done by somebody else ...
so: your choice!
all the very best,
miriam

3 January 2017

Dear Miriam,
Peter Handschin would like to buy this drawing from you.
If you are interested, may I put Peter in contact with you?

All the best,
Adam
P.S. I will answer your email concerning Athens later today.

5 january 2017 at 12:03 hrs
dear Adam,
I got this today – nice photos, bad text – and send it to you and hope to hear from you soon …
all the very best in this terribly cold wind!
miriam
enclosed: January 2017 number of Monopol

5 January 2017 at 13:05 hrs
Thanks, Miriam.
In terms of your presentation in Athens: I am trying to clear the space at the Benaki Museum so that you are not sharing it with anyone, will send you floor plans.
I have a question/idea in this context:
I would like the two presentations (Athens and Kassel) to be different, also in terms of medium, to a degree. And I am really keen on your work with text, your writing in relation to drawing. Could you imagine an installation in Athens that would focus more on drawing and text (your existing and any new texts) and the installation in Kassel focusing on paintings and drawings (and mixed-media works) as seen at your studio? It could be also the other way around — paintings and other new work in Athens, text work and drawings in Kassel. I feel it would be interesting to have an asymmetrical relationship between the two presentations (and also a way of showing the full spectrum of your practice).
I am looking forward to hearing from you.
All the best,
Adam

5 january 2017 at 13:36 hrs
dear Adam,
that would be fantastic and very interesting, to do it "spiegelverkehrt" [the other way around] in the way you suggest. if I have understood, you would want WACH RAUM in Athens, and "the latest" in Kassel? of course for me it would be super to install "the latest" in this fantastic space chosen for "WACH RAUM" in Kassel – and WACH RAUM in Athens?
if it's WACH RAUM, the problem of the closed room is the same and has to have minimum 4.00m height. the big drawings are this high …
if you don't want WACH RAUM, I could install a "free-style" room with several drawings from the 1980s, but this procedure would be some kind of similar to "the latest" … I choose, I install and it depends on the space. but naturally it looks completely different. "WACH RAUM" is not similar, because it has its own regulations, which have to be shown.
ok! I'll try again: even if the order of WACH RAUM is installed by me definitively only on site, this room installation has its own "laws", whereas the "latest" actually has none, except perhaps the possibility of eye-level height – which I can also do without …
doing it the other way around I would find super! because it's not so obvious at all – such a good idea! also because in my case many

people are already talking of a kind of "making amends" – it's unimportant admittedly, but it really gets on one's nerves and it's craptastically wrong.
saluti!
miriam

---

5 January 2017 at 13:51 hrs
Hi Miriam,
I agree it is not at all about Wiedergutmachtung [making amends] and the same people who now sing in the Wiedergutmachtung chorus around you could have been on the side of your opponents in 1980s…
The magazines, the galleries etc. It is the event industry, unwichtig [unimportant].
But I asked you what about TEXT WORK, your texts? Can you imagine including these alongside the drawings in Athens, if we go for freestyle selection and not strictly WACH RAUM? And show new work in the cabinet in Kassel? Ich faende es super [To my mind, it would be super.]…
In any case, I will check the height of the space at the Benaki.
All the best
Adam

---

5 january at 15:38 hrs
dear Adam – perfect!
the space at the Benaki works very well for "freestyle" with "old" drawings – but of course I should know the height… and yes, I am interested in including texts – or even all texts you saw hanging in my stalla. but of course I don't know how at the moment – we'll find a solution. but then we have to leave out WACH RAUM with its strict regulations also in terms of its only one text. which is very okay to me, because your proposition is more open and therefore more exciting to plan and to install for me. spannend! [gripping] super! and also for me much greater to choose "the latest" in all possible techniques for this super-nice space in Kassel. so I hope maybe the public in Kassel think a little of Athens and MARE NOSTRUM …
all the best,
miriam

2 december 2016

dear Eva-Maria,
Armando[197] sent me these wonderful pictures – a typical Maloja weather phenomenon: the water is still above zero = warm, and the very dry air well below zero, and then the rays of sunlight…
so, and apart from this I have now got my Foundation "maggazino cahn" all done and dusted, with the help of a young Rhaeto-Romanic lawyer from St Moritz: when I am dead, the maggazino and its contents, which are today worth millions, will become a foundation for young artists, who can work and live here with the help of a scholarship. my gallerists, Armando and my landlady, the art historian Patrizia Guggenheim (yes! a relative of the famous Peggy Guggenheim – they were originally Swiss Jews) form a board of trustees, which then decides who receives this scholarship. the whole thing is financed at first from my ready cash and from the sale of my works, which my gallerists deal with under the same conditions as during my lifetime – they, therefore, also earn their share and my work is made accessible to a wider public …
so, sure thing: an ideal case that works in the here and now – who knows what things will be like in a few years' time. but I am totally relieved. I am no supporter of artists who bequeath their "oeuvre" to museums – the latter cannot deal with it financially, nor do they want it from a content point-of-view, and rightly so: a gift horse etc. …
in Switzerland, setting up a foundation is happily not bureaucratic at all.
i am very relieved. ever since I've been the owner of a building, I've felt that I owe something to the community at large.
so, that's the way it is … and I think it's super.
baci!
saluti
miriam